Titles, Conflict, and Land Use

Economics, Cognition, and Society

This series provides a forum for theoretical and empirical investigations of social phenomena. It promotes works that focus on the interactions among cognitive processes, individual behavior, and social outcomes. It is especially open to interdisciplinary books that are genuinely integrative.

Editor:	Timur Kuran
Editorial Board:	Tyler Cowen
	Diego Gambetta
	Avner Greif
	Viktor Vanberg
Advisory Board:	James M. Buchanan
	Albert O. Hirschman
	Thomas C. Schelling

Titles in the Series

Titles, Conflict, and Land Use

The Development of
Property Rights and Land Reform on
the Brazilian Amazon Frontier

Lee J. Alston
Gary D. Libecap
Bernardo Mueller

Ann Arbor

THE UNIVERSITY OF MICHIGAN PRESS

2002   2001   2000   1999   4   3   2   1

A CIP catalog record for this book is available from the British Library.

Library of Congress Cataloging-in-Publication Data

Alston, Lee J., 1951–
    Titles, conflict, and land use : the development of property
rights and land reform on the Brazilian Amazon frontier / Lee J.
Alston, Gary D. Libecap, and Bernardo Mueller.
        p.   cm. — (Economics, cognition, and society)
    Includes bibliographical references and index.
    ISBN 0-472-11006-3 (acid-free paper)
    1. Land reform—Brazil—Parana (State)   2. Land
reform—Brazil—Para (State)   3. Land reform—Government
policy—Brazil—Parana (State)   4. Land reform—Government
policy—Brazil—Para (State)   5. Right of property—Brazil—Parana
(State)   6. Right of property—Brazil—Para (State)   I. Libecap, Gary
D.   II. Mueller, Bernardo, 1963–   III. Title.   IV. Series.
HD1333   B62   P373   1999
333.3'1811—dc21   98-58060
                                                        CIP

We dedicate this volume
to those closest to us

Mary, Greg, and Eric
Ann, Cap, and Sarah
Suely, Charles, and Suzana

Acknowledgments

We began this research project in 1991 and have benefited from the encouragement, insights, and support of many people and organizations. We want to thank the World Bank, the National Science Foundation (grants SBR-9213603 and SBR-9512107), and the Earhart Foundation for financial support. Robert Schneider and Ricardo Tarifa were centrally involved in the conceptualization and design of early stages of the project and the associated surveys. James Dalen and Jeffrey Fuller provided careful and innovative econometric assistance. Pablo Spiller, the University of Michigan Press reviewers, and participants at various conferences and workshops also gave us valuable suggestions. For all of this, we are grateful.

Contents

Figures

Tables

CHAPTER 1

Settlement, Government Policy, and Property Rights in the Brazilian Amazon: Introduction and Implications for Frontiers Elsewhere in the World

> What I have done is to show the importance for the working of the economic system of what may be termed the institutional structure of production.
>
> —Ronald Coase

Historical and Current Frontiers and Their Importance in Economic Development and Resource Use

Frontiers have always been a source of optimism and economic mobility. With low population densities and rich endowments of land and other valuable resources, frontiers have spawned history's principal migrations, and they continue to do so today. In nineteenth-century North America Horace Greeley and others encouraged those with an entrepreneurial spark to go to the western frontier in order to take advantage of the bountiful opportunities it offered:

> If any young man is about to commence in the world, with little in his circumstances to prepossess him in favor of one section above another, we say to him publicly and privately, Go to the West; there your capacities are sure to be appreciated, and your industry and energy rewarded.[1]

Noted historian of the western frontier Frederick Jackson Turner also pointed to the economic advantages of the frontier: "To the peasant and artisan of the Old World, bound by the chains of social class, as old as custom and as inevitable as fate, the West offered an exit into a free life and greater well-being among the bounties of nature, into the midst of resources that demanded manly exertion, and that gave in return the chance for indefinite ascent in the scale of social advance."[2] Research on the characteristics of migrants to the North American frontier and their subsequent economic welfare shows that new settlers typically were young risk-takers, with low opportunity costs, who sought the speculative opportunities rising frontier land values offered.[3] Once on the frontier, these early settlers appear to have accumulated wealth more rapidly than did their counterparts who remained behind in more settled regions.[4] The West was so attractive for migration and new opportunities that it was referred to by later scholars as a safety valve, drawing labor to the frontier to maintain wages in urbanized, settled parts of the country, providing new, low-cost sources of raw materials as inputs for production, and generating consumer demand for an industrializing U.S. economy (Danhof 1936, 1941; Shafer 1937).

Although, the safety-valve thesis has been challenged, the mythology and the optimism associated with the western frontier in shaping the country are unquestionable. When the U.S. Census Bureau announced that the frontier had closed in 1890, the United States seemed a smaller, less-promising country as a result, resources seemed in short supply, and shortly there after, the economy plunged into one of the deepest recessions in its history.[5] Indeed, as Lawrence Friedman noted, "By 1900, if one can speak about so slippery a thing as dominant public opinion, that opinion saw a narrowing sky, a dead frontier, life as a struggle for position, competition as a zero-sum game, the economy as a prize to be divided, not a ladder stretching out beyond the horizon" (1985, 338).

In the late twentieth century, the important role of frontiers for economic and social advancement remains as an outlet for risk takers and the less privileged, especially in developing countries. Frontier regions offer one of the few opportunities for individuals to start anew, outside the constraints of more settled regions, to acquire experience, capital, and wealth. As such, frontiers are important social and economic phenomena. We examine the characteristics of those who first migrate to the frontier and how those individuals fare from this migration. Frontiers also, paradoxically, are the sites of some of the most pressing, current environmental problems on the planet, and hence their management looms as a major policy issue.

Frontiers of one sort or another exist in many areas of the world where labor-to-land ratios are low.[6] Although we focus on the Brazilian Amazon, other frontiers are found in many parts of rural Africa and Asia, as well as in Latin America and sections of North America, where the implications of this study also apply. Populations are migrating to the Amazon lowlands in Bolivia, Ecuador, Columbia, and Venezuela.[7] Settlers are moving into previously sparsely populated parts of Nepal, Thailand's northeast, the Philippines' uplands, across islands in Indonesia, the Northwest Frontier Territory of Pakistan, Myanmar, Laos, and elsewhere.[8] Further, there are migrating populations in Africa, some to more remote areas and others to regions previously abandoned due to past military conflicts.[9] Access to low-cost land and new agricultural opportunities prompt much of this migration. Many of these frontier destinations also are experiencing high levels of deforestation, soil erosion, desertification, and the associated loss of critical habitats. Additionally, especially in Brazil, violent conflict among land claimants has attracted worldwide attention.[10]

To generate the potential wealth associated with the frontier and to avoid costly and environmentally damaging resource-use practices, property rights must be assigned routinely as settlement occurs. Otherwise, the wealth of the frontier will be dissipated through competition for control of frontier land. The tragedy of the commons will emerge with wasteful, short-term exploitation of natural resources and violence among competing claimants.[11]

Although property rights can develop through informal agreements among frontier settlers, at some point rising population densities, higher land values, and intensified competitive rivalries likely will make these arrangements ineffective, and the more formal property institutions provided by government will become necessary. Titling policies, however, should take into account the existence of indigenous practices where they are well established (such as in parts of Africa), and where they do not exist, governments must move quickly to avoid losses associated with competitive, common-pool production.[12]

With secure tenure, wider markets can develop to channel land to its highest-valued use and allow early settlers to capture higher capital gains from land sales. While speculation has been viewed negatively by many historians of the frontier, speculative land sales have been a critical source of wealth for poor migrants.[13] Further, with well-defined property rights, investment is promoted because individuals have security of control and can use their land as collateral to access capital markets.[14] If property rights to land are enforced, uncertainty of control is reduced, allowing individuals to focus on current and future production options, rather than on an imperative to rush exploitation, which is characteristic of open-access, competitive conditions and which typically diminishes future returns. Indeed, property rights security is necessary if rain forest endowments and other critical habitats are to be protected through set asides.

How quickly and effectively government policy develops depends upon political and bureaucratic conditions. Unfortunately, property institutions that provide incentives for settlers to adopt rational land-use practices that maximize the value of frontier resources and minimize the dissipation of economic rents may not be the outcome of the political process.

Property rights not only grant resource access and use privileges, but also assign wealth and political influence. Accordingly, their allocation and enforcement involve distributional concerns, which often are politically contentious. With many competing demands and agendas, political debates over the nature and assignment of property rights may take a long time to resolve and involve many compromises.[15] These compromises and the adoption of conflicting policies, however, result in incomplete and confused property rights to frontier lands. Further, if the distribution of the assigned property rights is viewed as being too skewed or in some sense unfair, then political pressures will arise for a reallocation of land—land reform. Land reform, however, can weaken the property rights structure, reducing the incentive to invest and limiting the gains from exchange.

Bureaucracies, especially land allocation and titling agencies, also are involved in the rights assignment on the frontier. Bureaucratic constraints, such as budget allocations and staffing levels, influence the provision of property rights to land. Agencies respond to competing political pressures in directing resources to land allocation issues, and bureaucratic officials have their own agendas.[16] These factors suggest that the political and bureaucratic assignment of property rights to frontier lands may be neither straightforward nor smooth.

Indeed, government development and resource-management policies throughout the world have been subject to harsh criticism, and as we will see, many government programs have had adverse consequences in the Brazilian Amazon.[17] Deacon (1994, 1995), for example, links government policies and government instability to deforestation rates across countries. Bunker (1985a), Gillis and Repetto (1988, 5–26), Repetto (1988), Binswanger (1989), and Mahar (1989) are critical of government development subsidies and land-tenuring policies that have distorted incentives and encouraged the rapid deforestation of rain forest stands in Brazil and elsewhere.[18] There are ample reasons, then, for concern about whether or not governments will provide well-defined and enforced property rights on the frontier at the optimal time.

In this book, we examine the process and impact of institutional development in Brazil. We primarily focus on the eastern Amazon state of Pará, the second largest in Brazil, between 1970 and 1996. We also examine an earlier frontier in the southern state of Paraná between 1940 and 1970 to see if conditions on the current Amazon frontier are similar to those that occurred before. We are interested in the politics of frontier settlement, land reform (redistribution), the nature of land laws, and land-titling practices. We are concerned with the timeliness and completeness of the property rights that are assigned and how they are enforced by private means and government agencies. We want to see how politics molds government policies, and in turn, how those policies affect the allocation and use of land in this environmentally-sensitive region. Using census data and other primary and secondary sources for each of the two frontiers with observations at the *município* (county) level, we examine government jurisdictions, settlement and titling policies, and the extent of titled land. We develop an analytical model that links the value of land to distance from the market and use that model to predict the effects of land value on the demand for, and supply of, title, as well as to show the impact of title on investment and land value.

It is important to emphasize what our study covers and what it does not. We focus on migration to the economic (agricultural) frontier and the subsequent development of property rights on the frontier as land values rise. We also examine how secure tenure affects land use and land values. Migration to the agricultural frontier involves most of the rural population movement in Brazil and affects most of the frontier land. Inequality of landownership in Brazil fuels frontier migration, and the determinants of violent conflicts among large and small land claimants and their spillover effects on land values are part of our study.

We do not examine the comparatively smaller and more localized mineral frontiers in Brazil. Nor does our study include the land claims of the indigenous native population. Issues involving native lands claims are interesting in their own right, but beyond the scope of this study. Based on the latest census figures, the native Indian population of Brazil is approximately 0.16 percent of the total national population of 146 million. Indian land reserves, however, cover approximately 12 percent of Brazilian land, and much of that is in the Amazon. In the Amazon, about 990,000 square kilometers are in Indian reserves. Most of this land is remote and beyond the economic frontier, at least at this point. With so much land and a small native population to defend it, tensions have risen as encroachment has occurred by other claimants, generally miners. So long as the reserves are largely inaccessible, conflict between the native population and those who seek land for farms will be relatively limited.[19]

Figure 1 is a map of Brazil that shows the states of Brazil, including the two frontier states that we examine.

Pará and Paraná are ideal regions to study frontiers. Paraná was the site of the rapid settlement of unoccupied government land initiated by a coffee boom after 1940.[20] As migration from the Atlantic states of Rio de Janeiro, São Paulo, and others to Paraná grew, the population of the state rose from approximately 1.2 million in 1940 to nearly 7 million by 1970. Between 1940 and 1960, the amount of agricultural land almost doubled, and the number of farms increased more than fourfold. A migration from southern Brazil to the Amazon has taken place in a similar manner, largely

Fig. 1.   Brazil and the states of Paraná and Pará

since the late 1960s, facilitated by the Transamazon and Belém-Brasília Highways.[21] Between 1970 and 1985, the population of Pará grew from just over 2 million to more than 4 million. The amount of land in farms doubled in the 1960s and again in the 1970s, and the number of farms rose sharply (IBGE 1990a, 183; 1991a, 180–83).

As we describe in chapter 7, the migration to Paraná was quite similar to that which occurred in North America in the nineteenth century. Movement to the frontier primarily was based on spontaneous, private decisions, as individuals migrated to claim open government land. The process by and large was unexceptional, much like the history of frontier settlement in the United States.[22] It did not attract much international attention. In contrast, migration to the Amazon has been quite controversial. The rapid cutting and burning of parts of the Amazon rain forest have raised international concerns about the safety and longevity of this uniquely valuable natural habitat. There also are concerns about soil depletion and other environmental costs of settlement.[23] Violent conflicts among claimants, especially between large farmers and ranchers and squatters, add to a commonly-held view of the Amazon as a region of chaotic conditions and wasteful destruction of irreplaceable resource endowments.[24] Finally, because settlement of the Amazon often has been initiated by conflicting government policies, ranging from formal colonization projects for small farmers in the 1970s and 1980s to subsidized cattle ranching by large farmers in the 1980s, critical policy reviews have questioned the motivations and outcomes of government actions.[25]

In general, there is a sense that the settlement of the Amazon frontier is occurring in a different manner from other earlier frontiers, one that entails high resource and human costs. There is a similar worry that this characterization applies to other contemporary frontiers elsewhere in Latin America and other developing areas of the world. Unfortunately, the amount of empirical evidence to support, moderate, or dismiss these concerns about the Amazon frontier is surprisingly sparse. Although the literature on the Amazon is a large one, our understanding of the settlement of that frontier, particularly of the institutional structure that underlies it, has remained very limited. This volume provides detailed new information on the political development and impact of property rights on the Amazon frontier.

Our analysis of government policies using census data on tenure and land use across time in Paraná and Pará provides a comparative framework for investigation. These data reveal much greater variation in land value, tenure, and investment than is possible to observe with household survey data, which do not exist over such a long period or for comparable frontier regions. As such, we can determine how quickly and completely governments provided property rights to land as relative prices changed on earlier and current Brazilian frontiers. We supplement the aggregate analysis with investigation of household survey data that we have collected between 1992 and 1996. The surveys were collected from six frontier sites in Pará near the communities of Altamira, Tucumã, São Felix, Tailândia, and Paragominas (Reunidas and Nova Aliança). These communities include both state and federal government jurisdictions; some sites were planned colonies, whereas others were invasion sites. Accordingly, it is possible to test for a variety of jurisdiction and land policy effects on the provision of property rights to land.

In our analysis, we examine the characteristics of those who first migrated to the region (age, education, wealth, origin, previous experience), the number of migrations they made as the frontier shifted, whether they planned to sell or stay at the site, their land tenure, land value, production practices, and investments. Additionally, we analyze the nature of property rights to land, how individuals obtain property rights, and the impact of titles on land use, investment, and land value. We also address the sources of violent conflict over land, which occurs primarily between large farmers and squatters who invade their lands. For this analysis, we add survey material from the municípios of Paragominas, Marabá, Rio Maria, Conceição do Araguaia, and Parauapebas.

Figure 2 is a map of Pará that shows the location of the survey sites. Our research shows that title is a vital institution in promoting investment and in expanding markets. It increases land values and wealth significantly in a region that has many poor settlers. Title also gives individuals a longer-term perspective or planning horizon that is essential for the maintenance of rain forest endowments. But our research also shows that the provision and enforcement of title are not smooth processes. Politics and bureaucratic concerns in some cases delay the assignment of title, whereas in other cases, titles are provided before they are warranted by local conditions. Additionally, there is an incongruity between civil law, which provides for the sanctity of title and is enforced by the courts and the police, and constitutional law, enforced by the federal government, which adds a beneficial-use requirement as a condition for title enforcement. This constitutional provision is part of land reform in Brazil, a country characterized by highly skewed landownership and wealth.

Constitutional law and land reform policies are implemented by INCRA, the National Institute for Colonization and Agrarian Reform. Following a squatter invasion of allegedly unused private lands, squatters lobby INCRA to intervene on their behalf. Agency intervention involves a determination of whether the farmer has clear, legal title, and whether or not the farm is being used productively (usually, whether it is cleared of forest). If the assessment is that the farm is not in productive use, INCRA may expropriate the land for redistribution to squatters. Regardless of the validity of the distributional goal, these conflicting policies naturally lead to insecure property rights, related wasteful land use, and potential violence.[26]

These activities are all part of the complex process of frontier settlement, institution formation, and resource use that we examine on the Amazon frontier of Brazil. Because these conditions are replicated elsewhere in whole or in part, they have important implications for economic growth and resource use on frontiers in other parts of the world.[27]

The Role of Property Rights in Resource Use and Wealth on the Frontier

Frontiers have the potential to provide for the improved economic and social welfare of settlers, but whether or how they will do so depends upon

Fig. 2.   The state of Pará

the property rights regime and how flexible that regime is to fluid, new economic conditions that emerge.[28] If property rights are clearly assigned and enforced, individuals can exploit frontier resources in ways that maximize their wealth and that can reduce environmental problems.

Frontiers also have the potential to be the site of conflicts over property rights and associated wasteful practices because, by definition, they are a place where formal legal and government institutions are largely absent. The provision of government infrastructure and services, such as land titles and enforcement mechanisms (judiciary and police force), is socially costly and is provided over time as land values rise. But just how smooth the process will be and how complete the property rights assigned are will depend upon political conditions and the nature of the land and other natural resources over which rights are to be defined. The incentives and actions of politicians, bureaucrats, judges, and the police will affect the ways in which rights are assigned and enforced.

Property rights consist of three elements: (a) the right to use the asset (*usus*), (b) the right to appropriate the returns from the asset (*usus fructus*), and (c) the right to change its form, substance, and location (*abusus*). Each of these attributes implies exclusivity, and through them individual owners become residual claimants; that is, they have the rights to bear the consequences from resource use, investment, and exchange. The flexible right of transfer induces an owner to operate with a long-term planning horizon and, thus, to show concern for the efficient use and allocation of resources over time.

Accordingly, recognized property rights in land are an essential aspect of market expansion on the frontier. As noted by Demsetz (1967), the promotion of market formation is one of the primary outcomes of a property rights regime. With secure rights to land and the existence of land markets, price signals will direct land to those who will place it in its highest-valued use at any point in time. This may involve consolidation of frontier plots and their subsequent transfer from initial settlers to those who arrive later with more farming experience and access to capital.[29] The more broadly understood and accepted the property right, the more extensive will be the market for frontier land. This condition enhances the wealth of frontier settlers because it extends the number of potential buyers who are willing to pay more for the land than are other people on the frontier. Land often is the major (and only) asset held by early migrants, and their ability to claim and sell land and then move on to settle, claim, and sell, yet again and again, is a critical element in social and economic advancement. Through this process, eventually individuals acquire enough wealth to stay on site, develop it, and to become permanent farmers. This process suggests a life-cycle dimension to frontier settlement, whereby relatively young individuals with little education, wealth, or options move to the frontier as entrepreneurial or risk-taking land speculators.[30]

Experience on historical frontiers in North America shows that land speculation and the associated earning of capital gains in land sales were critical sources of wealth generation (Swerienga 1970; Curti 1959). Similarly, on Brazilian frontiers, Ozório de Almeida's (1992) longitudinal study of 400 farmers in eight colonization projects between 1981 and 1991 indicates that settlers acquired capital and wealth over the period, improving their economic condition, relative to others with similar characteristics elsewhere in Brazil. Schneider (1994, 9–15) also finds a positive relationship between farm turnover and economic performance. He points to a Food and Agriculture Organization (FAO) study that found incomes in northern INCRA settlement projects to be four times the minimum wage in Brazil. The assets of these settlers grew with repeated migrations and sales. Although land consolidation occurs through the process of land exchange, the landownership distribution in the Amazon remains more equal than elsewhere in Brazil. In sum, Schneider concludes that frontier settlement provides a path for improved economic and social status (1994, 12). Our household surveys in six sites in Pará, described in chapters 5 and 6, support these conclusions about the positive role of land sales on the frontier, made possible by arrangements for secure property rights.

Clear and recognized property rights to frontier land not only assist settlers in attracting buyers, but the land markets that they support promote consolidation of plots to take advantage of any economies of scale in agriculture that might develop as land values and land use changes on the frontier.[31] The plots initially cleared by frontier settlers necessarily are small, often well under 50 hectares. These early farmers have very limited labor and, often, minimal farming experience, and forest clearing and soil preparation are extremely difficult. Moreover, on remote frontiers, there are few markets for agricultural output, so that initial settlers engage in rudimentary, subsistence agriculture. But as transportation costs decline and population densities rise, local markets for farm products develop, and with sufficient improvements in roads and other forms of transportation, opportunities arise for specialization and the export of production to even more remote markets. Such production likely involves some minimal economies of scale as well as experience in farming and in commercial sales that initial settlers on the frontier probably lack. By transferring land from original settlers to more experienced arrivals, market sales prove beneficial to both parties.[32]

Another advantage of recognized and enforced property rights on the frontier is that they allow settlers to focus scarce labor and other inputs on clearing, farming, and other productive activities, rather than on defending their land claims. Subsistence farmers with limited resources can afford few distractions. Any circumstances that lead to the diversion of labor from agricultural pursuits to defensive ones, such as clearing swaths of land (that otherwise would be left in forest) to demarcate holdings and to allow for routine patrolling, reduces production and potential wealth. Indeed, defensive efforts could be so taxing that they would make frontier farming untenable. In the aggregate, violent conflict over land dissipates resource rents, and the associated uncertainty of control reduces land exchanges, investment, and land values. Unfortunately, violent conflict occurs in parts of the Amazon. We examine the political and institutional sources of that conflict and its effect on land values, investment, and deforestation in chapter 8.

In addition to these advantages, secure property rights promote land-specific investment in at least two ways. One is that they allow for longer-term planning horizons because landowners have the assurance that their preferences will be implemented and that they will capture the returns from their investment activity. There will be little or no dissipation of the increased resource rents from investment due to competition for control. Absent a recognized property rights structure, however, short-time horizons dominate, and resource exploitation is more rapid and excessive than is socially optimal.[33] These open-access conditions were labeled "the tragedy of the commons" by Garrett Hardin nearly 30 years ago.[34] Under such circumstances, the private and social net returns from production diverge, and the private incentives created by the commons are the source of many of the environmental and wasteful resource-use problems encountered on frontiers today, including the depletion of valuable rain forest stands, the overgrazing of natural pastures, and the rapid exhaustion of soil nutrients.[35]

Recognized title also promotes investment by providing collateral, providing landowners access to capital markets. Frontier settlers typically are poor, and land is their most important asset. Its use as collateral facilitates more substantial capital-intensive investments in irrigation, pasture improvements, planting of permanent crops (such as orchards), and timber management. The important roles of title and collateral in economic development is shown by Feder and Onchan (1987) and Feder and Feeny (1991) for small farmers in Thailand. In their analysis of household survey data for 206 small landholders in Pará, Alston, Libecap, and Schneider (1996b) find that title is a powerful determinant of investment among these settlers on the Amazon frontier. With investment measured as the percentage of farmland in pasture and permanent crops, having title adds between 21 and 48 percentage points, depending on the site, to the portion of a farm in such uses.

In the United States, many of the potential problems of the common pool on the nineteenth-century frontier were avoided by the rapid and complete assignment of property rights to agricultural and mineral lands by the federal government. Beginning with the Land Ordinance of 1785, the objective of government land policy was to make frontier land available to individual claimants at low cost, with transfers from government to private ownership concluded as rapidly as possible. The Jeffersonian goal of creating a nation of small, self-reliant farmers was accomplished, at least in the North, east of the 100th meridian.[36] The agricultural frontier expanded with the formation of successful farming communities, and agricultural productivity rose through the development of rich frontier lands and later through the adoption of new farming techniques. Similarly, mineral rights on the American frontier were provided smoothly and quickly through the Mining Law of 1872.[37]

The assignment of property rights to land on the American frontier was important not only for allocating ownership and assigning the benefits and costs of land use (and thereby avoiding the tragedy of the commons), but the land laws also created precedents for property rights to other assets. If rights to the most valuable asset, land, on the agricultural or mining frontier were clearly defined and securely enforced by government, then expectations were that property rights would be provided for other assets. Indeed, Hughes (1977) argued that the assignment and guarantee of private rights to frontier agricultural land was one of the most significant, if underappreciated, achievements of early U.S. land law. Secure rights to land encouraged the development of markets for all assets and thereby promoted economic growth in the United States.

On the twentieth-century Amazon frontier described in this book, however, the record of governments in providing formal property rights or supporting locally devised arrangements to resolve common-pool problems is more problematical. The process by which property rights are assigned and enforced by government to frontier lands is complex, and the rights that emerge are often incomplete. The conflicting objectives of frontier land policies, their effects on the rapid and effective titling of land, and the resulting economic impact on investment and land value are the subjects of this volume.

A Model of Frontier Settlement and the Demand for and Supply of Property Rights

The relationship between the frontier and the demand for and supply of property rights is outlined in figure 3. The figure describes the nature of the frontier and provides a framework for analyzing the characteristics of early settlers and the development of property rights arrangements. The horizontal axis is distance from market, the most important determinant of transportation costs, which in turn are the principal determinants in defining the location of the frontier. The vertical axis is the net present value of land use. Moving away from market centers, transportation costs rise, reducing the net profitability of economic activities. The increase in transportation costs also leads to the selection of activities that have high value per unit of transportation costs, usually extractive, resource-extensive activities, such as slash-and-burn agriculture, logging, and mining. As distance increases, transportation costs rise, and at some point settlement and economic activities are not viable. For example, at the lower right of figure 3, the economic rents from very remote land do not cover the opportunity costs of the marginal laborer. The land is not occupied and remains beyond the economic frontier.

The economic frontier can be defined as that region or border where

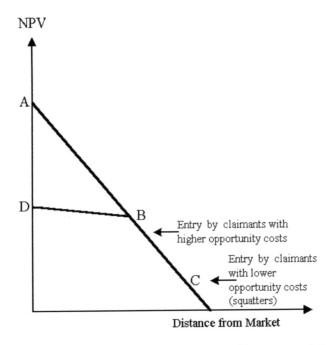

Fig. 3.   Emergence of land rent and the demand for property rights

the returns from land occupation and use just cover the opportunity costs for those with few other options. This region begins at point C in the figure. To the right of that point, transportation costs are so high that the net returns from settlement and land use are negative. The land remains unsettled because there is no incentive to migrate to the area. It remains too remote and costly to support economic activities. Those settlers who first occupy the frontier at point C are individuals with little education and wealth and who typically are young. Such individuals have a longer period to recoup the significant investment involved in migration and settlement.

Among early settlers, informal land allocation and use practices dominate. Land values are too low to justify formal documentation of individual land claims or to justify costly conflict among claimants. With abundant, cheap land, conflicting claims are avoided by the voluntary movement of one of the contending claimants to another area. Rudimentary methods of denoting individual holdings are sufficient to divide land, and informal, temporary conflict resolution mechanisms are sufficient to address occasional disputes.[38] Moreover, low resource values on the frontier typically mean that the resident population will be small and very homogeneous with respect to education, wealth, age, sex, and expectations for land allocation and use. Small numbers of homogeneous individuals provide conditions for successful collective action. Individuals will understand, appreciate, and support local, informal land institutions. Since land claims are uncontested, local land markets can develop among frontier residents, whereby exchanges occur without title. Through these exchanges, some consolidation of holdings occurs, and some settlers move on to new frontiers.

As land values rise over time due to new settlement following the construction of roads and introduction of other forms of transportation improvements, informal property rights institutions and conflict resolution mechanisms no longer will be sufficient to allow claimants to appropriate potential land rents.[39] In the framework of figure 3, closer to the market (to the left of point C), transport costs are lower, settlement is greater, locational rents are higher, and competition for the land increases. With greater competition, private enforcement costs rise. Moreover, increased migration to the frontier brings more heterogeneous individuals to the scene. These new claimants may not understand or recognize local land property regimes. Efforts to negotiate new, local property arrangements among existing and new claimants under remote and fluid frontier conditions will be plagued by high transactions costs of negotiation, especially when there is limited information about the value of the assets being claimed or traded (as would be the case for frontier land in the absence of much price data), free riding, and monitoring problems (also a problem in the presence of dense forests that hide boundaries and conceal infringement or trespass).[40]

In the aggregate, these problems suggest that early frontier property rights will be limited in scope and based on local, informal arrangements. But they will be difficult to maintain as additional migrants appear on the scene who have different experiences and expectations regarding the allocation and use of frontier lands. Violation of local rules, trespassing on previous land claims, and the absence of permanent conflict-resolution institutions, such as courts and police, ultimately lead to dissatisfaction with existing local arrangements. If they break down, resources will be diverted from production to defensive and predatory activities as competition for control ensues.[41] As a result, starting at point B, settlers will begin to feel the uncertainty of tenure associated with conflict over land claims. This uncertainty will dampen any investment plans and encourage more rapid land use activities.

Those wishing to make long-term investments to raise productivity or take advantage of new commercial opportunities, such as planting permanent crops, investing in untried field crops, and improving pastures, now that land is more scarce, will require tenure assurances. Secure tenure, as represented by formal, enforceable title, will provide collateral for accessing capital markets for such investments and facilitate land sales to those with higher opportunity costs and greater education, wealth, and farming experience. These are the people most likely to be aware of new investment opportunities and to have experience in implementing them. By promoting investment and the transfer of land as necessary, titling will maximize land rents. Higher land rents are represented by line AB in the figure.

If secure property rights are not provided, land transfers will not take place as readily, and individuals will focus on short-term, existing farm activities, forgoing investment, limiting sales opportunities, and channeling productive resources to defending their claims or seizing those of others. These alternative conditions lead to a lower rental stream, which is indicated by line BD in the figure.

The value of secure property rights, then, is the vertical difference between lines AB and BD, the appropriable change in rent made available with secure property rights. For land to the left of point B, increased investment and higher land values will occur if tenure services are provided. Hence, individual claimants will have incentives to lobby for government provision of formal tenure and enforcement services for land to the left of point B in the figure and will invest up to the difference in the two rental streams to secure favorable tenure institutions. The more difficult it is to obtain formal property rights, the more potential rents will be dissipated in efforts to secure them. The complexities of the political process suggest that the smooth, low-cost provision of property rights on the frontier will be the unusual, rather than the common, case.[42]

Indeed, political conditions and bureaucratic initiatives will determine how quickly and effectively governments respond to the demands for more precise and enforced property rights. Yet as we have discussed, there is no guarantee that the political process will provide for an effective and timely property rights regime as the frontier develops (see Libecap 1989, 10–28). What actually happens depends upon political bargaining in the process of creating, modifying, and enforcing property laws. Property rights arrangements affect the distribution of wealth and political influence as well as incentives for production. Politicians, judges, and bureaucrats face competing constituents and political agendas. Accordingly, it is easy to understand why disagreements can occur, why political bargaining can result in compromise and the establishment of rights structures that diverge from the pattern required for a fully effective institutional arrangement.

The Political Provision of Property Rights

Government policy will determine who receives title (through the allocation formula), when it is assigned (through marking and survey policies, pricing, and other settlement requirements), whether it is secure (through enforcement practices and conditions), and whether and how conflicts are adjudicated through the police and courts. Each of these attributes of the property rights system will be determined through the political process. The assignment and enforcement of property rights involves an assignment of wealth and political power that no politician can take lightly. Politicians have multiple constituents to respond to and limited budgets to allocate. Their decisions are made so as to maximize reelection prospects or otherwise to promote the advancement of their political careers. Because political conditions change and new influential constituent groups emerge, politicians must be very flexible and adept in responding to new political opportunities or threats. As Peltzman (1976) has suggested, these factors mean that no constituent group will receive all that it wants; political decisions will be made so as to balance expected political costs with expected political benefits with politicians acting as brokers among competing parties. Further, fluid political conditions suggest that politicians will have short time horizons, making political agreements with other politicians and with constituent groups with short-run objectives in mind. Shifting political coalitions suggest that making long-term commitments will be difficult.

Of course, these short-term political pressures exist by degree, with some politicians more secure than others. But in general, they pose problems for the development and support of permanent property rights institutions. Politicians largely determine statutes, and constitutional law and pervasive social customs may provide longer-term protection for property rights. Incongruent civil and constitutional law and local customs raise problems for the security of property rights, as Feder and Feeny (1991) point out. As we will see in the case of Brazil, there is an incongruity, but it is between constitutional and civil law, rather than between formal law and informal practices, which were the concern of Feder and Feeny. In Brazil, civil law protects the sanctity of title, but constitutional law adds beneficial-use requirements as a condition of title enforcement. These constitutional provisions were added in response to populist pressures for land reform. As we show, the beneficial-use requirement introduces uncertainty of enforcement and as such, encourages violent conflict over land in Brazil. This conflict, in turn, reduces investment and land values, and results in injuries and deaths. All of these results reduce welfare in a country with a rapidly growing population and ambitious economic development goals.

Property rights to frontier lands determine the wealth distribution, and their allocation is designed to address a variety of political goals. These range from satisfying private demands for access to valuable new mineral deposits, agricultural lands, and timber stands to responding to domestic and international pressures for the creation of environmental and Indian reserves. Accordingly, as frontier lands become valuable there will be competing claims for them. In some cases, politicians will not be able to balance those claims effectively and property rights will be left unclear and insecure. Unfortunately, these same conditions encourage the dissipation of frontier land rents.

The formal provision of property rights signifies legal endorsement of a property allocation, and exclusivity means that some claimants will be denied property rights to frontier land. If those groups who otherwise might be denied land are sufficiently politically influential, they may be able to block the smooth and timely provision of tenure services on the frontier. That is, distributional concerns play an important role in how politicians respond to demands for property rights as settlement on the frontier increases. To secure multiple political goals, politicians may assign some frontier lands to claimants other than those who currently occupy the land or attach covenants that limit resource use, tax its returns, or add conditions for title enforcement. These adjustments or attenuations of property rights can be viewed as side payments crafted by politicians to compensate various constituents. But these political side payments affect the nature of the property rights that are assigned and enforced on the frontier. As described in this book, we observed the tension between the efficiency gains from clearly defined and enforced property rights and equity concerns on Brazilian frontiers. These tensions are the source of costly and violent conflict over land, and they complicate the process of institutional development.

Additionally, the timeliness and extent to which formal property rights are provided and enforced on the frontier depend upon bureaucratic agencies that may have longer-term objectives and different political constituents than do current politicians. If bureaucrats have job tenure, they may be relatively insulated from the immediate political pressures facing politicians or at least, subject to different political demands. Bureaucratic officials who seek to advance within the bureaucracy and who seek broader administrative mandates and greater budget and staffing allocations, may have interests very closely tied to those of politicians. Politicians will decide budgets and staffing and enact legislation that determines bureaucratic roles. In this way, the interests of senior bureaucrats may coincide with the interests of politicians. The rank-and-file bureaucracy, however, may have different allegiances, and information and monitoring problems may limit how effectively senior officials can manage those below them in the administration of land policy.[43] Even aside from these agency and incentive problems, bureaucratic agencies are subject to budget and staffing constraints in how they respond to demands for tenure services.

An added consideration is the existence of multiple, competing government agencies with conflicting constituencies and objectives for frontier lands. Land title agencies may have different policies than do environmental agencies or agencies that are charged with supporting indigenous populations. Agencies that administer to particular land uses, such as mining, agriculture, or forestry, also may have conflicting policies that affect the provision of secure property rights to frontier resources.

Another institution that affects the nature and security of property regimes is the judiciary. Judges are assigned the role of arbitrating among competing parties and in interpreting property and land use laws. Judges have the authority to order the police to enforce title or to define settlement conditions among competing parties. How judges respond depends upon the selection process (election or appointment, and by whom and for how long), whether or not jurisdictions are well defined, and the nature of the law—are the various bodies of law, civil and constitutional for example, consistent so that judges have clear direction in enforcing property rights?

This discussion of why governments may not smoothly or quickly provide complete property rights when they begin to be demanded (at point B in fig. 3) assumes that governmental jurisdiction is not an issue. But it may be. That is, competing national governments may lead to confused or unenforced property rights to valuable resources.[44] Even when national jurisdictions are not at issue, competing governmental jurisdictions within a country may lead to conflicting policies. For example, if jurisdiction to frontier land is contested among states or between the federal and state governments, then there will be confusion as to which government can provide title, and conflicting titles likely will be issued. As we describe in chapter 3 in the case of Brazil, there *are* competing government jurisdictions, with state land agencies adopting policies that contend with those of federal land agencies. Overlapping jurisdictions and the corresponding issuing of multiple titles to the same lands brings confusion, potential violence, and a delay in the provision of secure property rights on the frontier. We examine these problems directly by considering how competing jurisdictions between the federal government and the Paraná and Pará state governments have affected the provision of definite titles on Brazilian frontiers. In total, these conditions mean, at best, a holdup in the provision and enforcement of secure tenure and, at worst, the blocking of effective property rights on the frontier, with associated losses in resource rents and welfare.

Politicians, bureaucracies, and judges face conflicting demands from many different parties for rights to frontier lands, including smallholders who are part of formal (federal or state government) colonization efforts, squatters, and large ranchers. Each seek the police power of the state to enforce their claims. There also are likely to be third parties, such as financial institutions and other debt holders, who have a stake in the assignment and security of property rights. Although private claimants may bargain early among themselves for the establishment of informal rights arrangements, as the frontier develops they must form interest groups to lobby in the political arena to secure formal state definition and enforcement of their property rights or to obtain a forced redistribution of land from others.

For instance in Brazil, squatters organize for land reform and expropriation of private farms through the Movement of Landless Workers (MST). Besides pressuring the federal land reform agency, INCRA, to intervene in land conflicts, the MST also lobbies the Brazilian Congress for favorable land reform statutes. Similarly, large landowners are organized through the Rural Democratic Union (UDR). The UDR is active in both state and federal politics in efforts to obtain strict government enforcement of the property rights of its members. Indeed, as we show in chapter 3, organization of squatters in Brazil is an essential ingredient if they are to attract the attention of the federal land agency, INCRA, in establishing a settlement project and in the provision of infrastructure and credit.

There are, then, multiple parties involved in political negotiations over the assignment and enforcement of property rights on the frontier. The role of government in resolving competing interests and in providing property rights that support efficient resource use is further complicated by peculiarities of the political process. That is, in the political arena, transactions and information costs are likely to be higher than in markets.[45] Whereas markets provide residual claimants who benefit from new information and promote the formation of institutions, such as commodities markets, to provide such information, politics can reward the suppression of information. In politics there are fewer institutions to counter such actions.[46] High information costs about the effects of uncertain property rights on the frontier, affect constituent mobilization and bargaining with politicians, bureaucrats, and judges over property issues.

Moreover, political actions create a path dependency in the provision and enforcement of property rights. Statutes that spell out the conditions for obtaining rights to land create constituencies who, in turn, lobby for either the maintenance of those statutory provisions or for their modification to make the law even more beneficial. Groups with vested interests are likely to have advantages in political bargaining, relative to other groups, because of lower costs of collective action. Their current position in the system binds them together to make them a relatively cohesive bargaining group. They also have beneficial ties to established political processes and leaders. These advantages make vested interests effective political lobbyists. In the case of property rights, these advantages can intensify distributional tensions that threaten the long-term viability of the property system.

Ultimately, distributional issues become the key issue in political debate over the provision of property rights on the frontier. Under a property rights system, some parties, by definition, must be excluded. Property rights create owners and nonowners. Nevertheless, the system of property rights provides the basis for wealth creation through the expansion of markets, investment, and reduced resource use in private defensive or predatory activities, releasing inputs for productive use. Owners become the economic agents with decision-making authority, and they have the greatest stake in the property arrangement and the wealth it can generate. If the economic system is perceived as reasonably open, that is, if nonowners can accumulate capital (human or physical) and buy land or other important assets, they too will have a stake in the system. Under these circumstances, distributional concerns (the kinds of most concern to politicians) will not detract from the property rights system. Most members of society, owners and nonowners alike, will see it as benefiting them and worthy of political support through legislation, judicial rulings, and police activity.

If the property system, however, is perceived to be closed; that is, if nonowners have few practical means of becoming owners (either through legal restrictions or through the size of the capital accumulation necessary to acquire land, such as would be the case with a very skewed distribution of landholdings), then owners and nonowners will have different incentives to maintain the property system. Indeed, some parties may prefer an incomplete specification of property rights because such an arrangement allows for greater redistribution. In the political arena, politicians will receive demands from those who seek clear endorsement of their land claims and those who seek redistribution. The tension between wealth creation through secure property rights and redistribution to redress a skewed distribution of wealth and political power will be high. Under these circumstances, the outcome of political competition between those who demand secure property rights and those who demand redistribution or land reform is contentious and uncertain. As political debates drag on and political mandates change, valuable assets, such as frontier land, may remain in open access.

A final problem arises for some frontier resources, particularly water and migratory animal species, if the nature of the resource raises the costs of defining and enforcing property rights. Ronald Coase has commented that "the reason that some activities are not the subject of contracts is exactly the same reason why some contracts are commonly unsatisfactory—it would cost too much to put the matter right" (1960, 39). Whether or not the more complete defining of property rights on the frontier is socially beneficial depends on the magnitude of the potential common-pool losses, the nature of the costs to resolve them, and the costs of defining and enforcing property rights. All of these factors suggest that property rights will not evolve smoothly or routinely on the frontier and that resource use issues and environmental problems will be a characteristic of frontier settlement.

An Introduction to the Brazilian Amazon Frontier and the Outline of the Book

Despite considerable media attention and growth of a large literature on the problems associated with Amazon settlement, the development of the region is still in its infancy. Recent estimates indicate that only about 6 percent of the Amazon rain forest has been settled and deforested.[47] Major migration to the area began in the late 1960s, accelerated in the early 1970s, and then waned in the 1980s with a slump in the overall Brazilian economy. More significant movement to the Amazon appeared to be occurring once again in the mid-1990s. This record of settlement means that much of the Amazon rain forest and other natural resources remain relatively untouched. It also means, however, that there will be many new frontiers in the Amazon as migration intensifies. Most of the land that is open to private settlement and claiming is in the hands of the state and federal governments. Hence, government policies will play a central role in how the development of the Amazon proceeds. How smoothly and completely those governments provide property rights institutions will be key in determining whether the potential wealth of the Amazon is captured by the settlers or dissipated away in competition for control of the land. Property rights institutions also will determine whether frontier settlement can occur with a minimum of environmental damage and whether important parts of the rain forest endowment can be preserved.

As noted earlier, the existing literature provides a mixed score card for the Brazilian government in the management of the frontier. Ozório de

Almeida (1992) and Schneider (1994) are reasonably positive in terms of their evaluation of the impact of frontier settlement on the welfare of smallholders. Schneider also emphasizes the opportunities that remain for the development of effective government policies to mitigate environmental damage. Gillis and Repetto (1988), Spears (1988), Binswanger (1989), and Mahar (1989), however, are critical of government policies both for a failure to provide well-defined property rights and for encouraging deforestation as a means of staking claims to land. They also object to past government subsidies for particular settlement and land use activities, such as road construction and ranching. Fortunately, most of these subsidies have long since been dropped. Additionally, concerns about the extent of deforestation and the benefits of Amazon settlement in the face of feared high environmental costs are raised by Goodland (1985), Fearnside (1985, 1986), Cowell (1990), Serrão, Nepstad, and Walker (1996), and Smith et al. (1996). Whether settlement policies benefit smallholders through the development of permanent farms or leave them as itinerant, landless peasants, squeezed out by land consolidation, is questioned by Bunker (1985a), Bakx (1990), and Walker and Homma (1996).

Most authors agree that timely, low-cost, and clearly enforced property rights institutions are essential for the effective management of the Amazon frontier, both to advance the well-being of migrants to the region and to safeguard its valuable natural habitats. Yet, many potential problems loom. There are large numbers of heterogeneous, competing claimants for frontier lands. These include small farmers recruited from southern Brazil under formal colonization programs, squatters who have arrived from northeastern Brazil, large farmers who in some cases have developed profitable ranches and in other cases have holdings that remain largely in forest. There also are traditional Brazil nut lease holders with *aforamento* concessions, miners, and loggers.[48] Major inflows of these heterogeneous groups suggests that the kinds of local, indigenous property systems cited by Rudel (1993, 1995) and emphasized by Ostrom (1990) as effective in addressing potential common-pool problems will not be a solution in the Brazilian Amazon. Instead, the provision and enforcement of title by government as frontier land values rise will be the primary way in which the losses of the common pool are to be avoided. Absent clear property rights, competition for control of frontier land will lead to the sources of rent dissipation cited earlier—uncertainty, violence, limited land markets, short time horizons, and little investment in the future—and thus rapid deforestation and soil mining. Not only will these conditions intensify environmental costs, but the poor who migrate to the frontier will not have their expectations for economic and social advancement realized. Political tensions will mount.

As we show, there are important grounds for concern about the likely effectiveness of government policies in the provision of property rights regimes. The problems are political ones, and these problems are apt to be replicated in every other frontier region of the world, with similar potential consequences. In the case of Brazil, there are conflicting jurisdictions between state and federal governments that have delayed the assignment of clear property rights to land. Moreover, we document titling policies that are not optimal. That is, INCRA provides too few titles in areas where land values are high, and ITERPA, the Pará state land agency, provides titles too extensively in areas where land values are low. The undertitling by INCRA appears to be caused by its being underfunded, understaffed, and subject to fluctuating federal government political concerns. INCRA also is tied up in resolving land disputes, most often in intervening in squatter invasions of large farms. The overtitling by ITERPA appears to be in response to local, state election pressures, with candidates promising titles prior to upcoming elections. Both of these conditions suggest that INCRA and ITERPA do not strictly follow the optimal sequence of the provision of title as described in figure 3. Because we also document the importance of title in encouraging investment and raising land values, the welfare consequences of the delayed or sporadic provision of title can be enormous for the comparatively poor Amazon migrant population.

Further, as we describe, there is a serious incongruity between civil or statutory law that guarantees the sanctity of title and is enforced by the courts and the police and constitutional law that adds beneficial use as a condition for title enforcement. Forested land is viewed as unproductive, and hence forested areas of large farms are vulnerable to invasion by squatters under constitutional provisions for land reform. INCRA, the country's land reform agency, has the responsibility to enforce these constitutional requirements by intervening on behalf of squatters to expropriate "unproductive" land. The implications for the maintenance of the rain forest are clear.[49] Additionally, since there is uncertainty as to if or how INCRA will respond to a particular property dispute, violent conflict between farmers and squatters occurs. Violence appears to be a tool of squatter organizations in forcing INCRA's hand, when the agency has many demands on its resources for settlement, the provision of title, and land reform or redistribution. Land redistribution seeks to place land in the hands of small farmers. But there is little evidence as to how effective this effort is in terms of permanently changing the skewed land and wealth distribution in Brazil. What is clear, however, is that redistribution and the threat of redistribution serve to weaken the security of property rights and thereby reduce the incentive for long-term investment and reduce the gains from trade. As we show later in the volume, land-specific investment is a major contributor to land value and individual wealth on the frontier.

In this book, we detail these issues. We analyze how property rights affect investment and land values and, in turn, how investment and land values affect the demand for property rights. The supply of property rights to land, however, is through the political process. We examine the history of land policy in Brazil to show the legacy it provides for current property rights assignment and enforcement. Further we examine the sources of violent conflict and investigate the effects of violence and land redistribution on investment, land values, and the provision of title.

The outline of the book is as follows: Chapter 2 provides a history of land policy and land reform in Brazil. Chapter 3 outlines the current institutional arrangement for the assignment of property rights on the frontier, identifies the land agencies involved, discusses current land reform policies and their impact on frontier property rights, and points to the sources of potential conflict over land. Chapter 4 provides a framework for analyzing settlement, the provision of property rights, their impact on land values, and the occurrence of violence on the frontier. This framework is then used in the chapters that follow with empirical analyses. Chapters 5 and 6 use survey data to examine the characteristics of settlers on the Amazon frontier at six sites in the state of Pará and analyze the interaction among land values, investment, and titling at those sites. The politics involved in the supply of title are addressed in these chapters, and the analysis suggests that governments are unlikely to provide and enforce title at the optimal time. Chapter 7 continues this analysis through use of Brazilian census data to obtain a broader sense of the interplay among title, land values, and investment, and the role of politics in the provision of title on an earlier frontier in Paraná with the current frontier in Pará. Chapter 8 examines the sources of violence and the impact of violence on frontier land values and investment. Chapter 9 provides concluding comments and a discussion of the relevance of the results of the study for other frontiers.

NOTES

1. New York Herald Tribune, 1858, as quoted in Hale 1950, 195, and presented in Conley and Galenson 1998.

2. Turner 1947, 261, as presented in Conley and Galenson 1998. Throughout this book we use the notion of the economic frontier as a shifting phenomenon that occurs when land values become sufficiently high (due to falling transportation costs, higher output prices, new valuable resource discoveries) to attract the first

new settlers or claimants to previously unoccupied land. Migration to the economic frontier is prompted by the desire of settlers to improve their economic position—to become wealthier, to obtain a new start in life. Many voluntary migrations historically have been stimulated by such desires. The evidence from North America (Conley and Galenson 1998; Ferrie 1997) indicates that migrants improved their wealth position by moving to the frontier, relative to their counterparts who remained in more settled regions. This experience appears to be replicated in Brazil. Hence, we view the frontier settlement process as a generally positive phenomenon. Nevertheless, there can be a downside to this process, particularly if existing occupants are pushed aside without compensation, or worse. Environmental damage may result in the absence of property rights and consideration of longer-term time horizons in resource use. Externalities, such as the pollution of streams from mining activities, are an example. For a discussion of this view of the frontier, see essays by White and Limerick in Grossman 1994. They emphasize the distributional and environmental consequences of the frontier migration in North American.

3. For discussion of the nineteenth-century North American frontier and the characteristics of the settlers who migrated to it, see Bogue 1963; Curti 1959; and Swerienga 1970.

4. Current research is examining the performance and wealth accumulation of those on the frontier relative to those who stayed behind. For example, see Conley and Galenson 1997; Ferrie 1997; and Schaefer 1985, 1987.

5. In 1890, the U.S. Bureau of the Census announced that the frontier was closed: "Up to and including 1880, the country had a frontier of settlement, but at present the unsettled area has been so broken into isolated bodies of settlement that there can hardly be said to be a frontier line. In the discussion of its extent and its westward movement it can not, therefore, any longer have a place in the census reports" (U.S. Department of the Interior, Bureau of the Census 1892, xviii). See Olson 1961 for discussions of impending shortages. The economic depression of 1893 through 1897 was a serious one, and it was followed by yet another in 1907.

6. Frontiers can be defined in many ways. Shortly, we define the economic frontier that is the focus of our analysis. A very low labor-to-land ratio is a necessary condition for any settlement frontier.

7. For discussion of frontier settlement and the role of local tenure institutions in allocating land and in moderating resource use, see Rudel 1993, 1995.

8. Migration and the development of tenure institutions in the Philippines is discussed by James and Roumassett 1984 and Eder 1990. The role of tenure institutions in Thailand is analyzed by Feder and Onchan 1987 and Feder and Feeny 1991.

9. The impact of tenure institutions in Ghana is discussed by Besley 1995.

10. See New York Times, April 21, 1996, 8; and O'Grady 1995. Issues of violence are examined by Skaperdas 1992 and in Garfinkel and Skaperdas 1996. See also Human Rights Watch 1991 for a report on Brazil.

11. For discussion of the commons problem, see Gordon 1954; Hardin 1968; Cheung 1970; Johnson and Libecap 1982; and Lueck 1995.

12. Indigenous tenure institutions are locally recognized and often informal property rights arrangements that are assembled by the existing population. Throughout its history, much of the Brazilian frontier has involved unoccupied land. Hence, migrants to the region have had to devise their own practices. But when immigration has been very rapid, drawing individuals from diverse areas, no basis has existed for the development of durable local property rules. Under those conditions, government becomes the only source of property rights. For analysis of indigenous tenure institutions in parts of Africa, see Migot-Adholla et. al. 1991; and Place and Hazell 1993. Libecap and Johnson 1980 and Johnson and Libecap 1980, in examining property rights and land use on southwestern U.S. Indian reservations, discuss the problems that arise when formal government tenuring policies conflict with local practices.

13. For discussion of speculation on the North American frontier, see Swerienga 1970.

14. The importance of title for investment is shown empirically by Feder and Onchan 1987 for Thailand and by Alston, Libecap, and Schneider 1996b for Brazil.

15. Even in a comparatively simple setting, the unitization of American oilfields, the assignment of unit shares among producing firms are an assignment of property rights to oil field rents. The negotiations can take 15 years or more, even while extensive dissipation of rents is occurring. See Libecap and Wiggins 1985; and Wiggins and Libecap 1985.

16. See Johnson and Libecap 1994 for discussion of bureaucratic incentives and behavior in another context.

17. For critical discussion of government policies, see Gillis and Repetto 1988; and Repetto 1988. For criticism of Brazilian policies, see Binswanger 1989; and Mahar 1989.

18. Binswanger 1989, 5–8, for instance, points to land use requirements in Brazil that effectively require clearing as a means of enforcing title. Forest land is considered "unused" and, hence, vulnerable to invasion by squatters. This issue is addressed in our research.

19. Description of conflicts involving Indian reserves as well as other related data can be found in <http://www.nativeweb.org/abayayala/cultures/brazil/cimi/>.

20. Frontier land owned by the state was made available to private claiming via land grants or occupation. As we show in subsequent chapters, land grants and small farm claimants often were in conflict on Brazilian frontiers.

21. The literature on Amazon settlement is a large one, and we reference many of the works throughout this book. One volume is Schmink and Wood 1992. Stone (1996, 1) points out that road construction over the last 30 years has provided access to vast areas of the Amazon, attracting migrants to the frontier.

22. Although there clearly were violent conflicts between native Indian tribes and the U.S. Army, the broad pattern of western agricultural and mining settlement by millions of private claimants was routine and for the most part, peaceful.

23. Schneider 1994, 1–2, provides estimates of population growth and deforestation in the Amazon in general.

24. For example, see Human Rights Watch 1991.

25. For example, critical discussion of settlement policies is found in the readings edited by Schmink and Wood (1984, 1992).

26. The political economy of land reform in Brazil is discussed by Mueller (1994). Widespread violence over land is asserted by Onis (1992). Our analysis indicates that violent conflict over land is not ubiquitous, but rather is localized in specific regions.

27. Violence over land occurs in other Latin American countries due to tension between the conflicting goals of secure property rights to promote investment and wealth redistribution. For general discussion, see Skaperdas 1992. For implications in development, see Dinar and Keck 1997; and Binswanger, Deininger, and Feder 1995.

28. A brief citation cannot do justice to the range of the literature. Work on the role of institutional factors in economic development includes Bardhan 1989; Ostrom 1990; Feder and Feeny 1991; and Besley 1995. See also related work by Douglass North (1981, 1990); Alston, Eggertsson, and North (1996); Furubotn and Richter (1993); Eggertsson (1990); and Williamson and Winter (1991). Feder and Feeny provide the most detailed discussion of emerging property rights systems and their impact on resource allocation and use during economic development. For Brazil, see Alston, Libecap, and Schneider 1995a, 1995b, 1996a, 1996b; and Alston, Libecap, and Mueller 1998a. For more historical studies and contemporary natural resource problems, see Libecap 1989.

29. Of course, if some socially valuable uses are not easily tradable and do not have prices, then land may not be allocated to those activities. This condition would characterize possible externalities, such as the potential contribution of rain forest endowments in the absorption of carbon dioxide in the atmosphere or in the provision of habitats for yet unknown species of plants and animals. Although these issues are of broad international interest, their relative empirical significance remains to be demonstrated. In any event, our focus is on agricultural settlement of the frontier and the role property rights play in that process.

30. Bakx (1990) questions whether the process works in a way to advantage settlers in the western Amazon. Alston, Libecap, and Schneider (1995a), however, find support for individual advancement and a life cycle of claiming and settlement in Pará.

31. Basic economies of scale in agriculture are described by Halcrow (1980, 111–16). The degree to which economies of scale exist in a development context of course is an empirical issue. Sources of possible economies of scale in livestock raising in Latin America are discussed in Lovell 1986, 41. In subsistence agriculture that characterizes initial frontier settlement, economies of scale may not apply. Indeed, many studies of less-developed areas find few size advantages (see Carlson, Zilberman, and Miranowski 1993; Binswanger and Deininger 1993; Cornia 1985; and Kawagoe, Hayami, and Ruttan 1985). But as population densities increase, transportation costs fall, and commercial opportunities grow, new agricultural production becomes possible, often with some economies of scale. Economies of scale may also describe ranching, which is growing in the Amazon, even in the

absence of government subsidies. See Schneider 1994 and Mattos and Uhl 1994. In our field studies, we observe considerable consolidation of plots, which would suggest at least some economies of scale in commercial production.

32. Again, we are not making strong claims about the existence of economies of scale, only that our observation is that among frontier settlers there is a shift from subsistence farming on very small plots by the initial settlers to more market-oriented production on consolidated plots as population densities grow.

33. That is, total output or harvest by all parties on the frontier exceeds the social-wealth-maximization point, where social and private marginal costs equal social and private marginal returns.

34. See Hardin 1968. Here, the term commons is used to describe a condition of open access. It is not meant to describe a viable common-property institution. For a discussion of the costs of the commons under different settings and methods for addressing them, see Johnson and Libecap 1982; Libecap 1989, 10–28; Ostrom 1990; and Lueck 1995.

35. Slash-and-burn agriculture, often associated with frontier settlement, may or may not be due to open-access conditions. Most often, slash-and-burn agriculture occurs when land values are very low, when population densities are minimal, when transportation costs are high, and when property rights are informal. Slash-and-burn agriculture describes a stage of frontier production. As noted below, as transportation costs fall and commercial opportunities increase, the property rights system becomes more formalized and agricultural activities more permanent. The open-access conditions described here reflect resource uses when the smooth development of a property rights structure is blocked. Secure property rights are a necessary, but not sufficient, condition for slower rates of production or harvest. Price expectations also determine production and harvest incentives.

36. For discussion of U.S. land policies, see Gates 1968; and Kanazawa 1996. A comparison of U.S. and Brazilian land polices is provided by Alston, Libecap, and Mueller (1997a).

37. For discussion of mineral rights, see Libecap 1978, 1989.

38. Libecap's (1978, 1979) studies of the nineteenth-century mining frontier in the American West reveal early miners to be "good humored" with reliance upon informal mining camp rules to assign mining claims. There is little evidence of violence.

39. Rising product prices also increase the returns from frontier settlement, but we focus on transportation costs in the figure.

40. Olson 1965 describes the problems of negotiation among heterogeneous parties.

41. For discussion of the role of potential violence in the allocation of resources, see Umbeck 1977, 1981. Rent-dissipating violence among competing claimants is possible (Skaperdas 1992; Garfinkel and Skaperdas 1996).

42. North 1990 emphasizes this point.

43. The problems of bureaucracy, especially when the rank and file differ in motivation from senior officials and politicians, are discussed by Johnson and Libecap (1994).

44. Fisheries are a notorious example. For discussion of the problems of international cooperation, see Keohane and Ostrom 1995.

45. For an opposing view that stresses similarities between markets and political processes, see Wittman 1995.

46. For example, Johnson and Libecap (1994) argue that federal employee unions benefit from stressing the myth that any serious reform of the government bureaucracy in the United States will lead to the re-adoption of patronage practices. Although this would be very unlikely given the absence of interest among politicians for such an action, representatives of government employee unions repeatedly make the claim to discredit reform efforts. There is no well-organized counterconstituency to refute such charges since the gains from bureaucratic reform are broadly spread throughout the economy.

47. The estimates of deforestation vary dramatically. See Anderson et al. 1996, 36–39, where 6 percent is above most of the estimates given for the late 1980s.

48. For discussion of the many different types of property rights claimants and possibilities on the frontier, see Monteiro 1980.

49. See for example Onis 1992, 7, 63, for discussion of the role of deforestation in strengthening title.

CHAPTER 2

A History of Land Policy in Brazil: The Assignment of Property Rights to Land and Land Reform

The Role of Land Policy and Reform in the Settlement of Frontiers in Brazil

We begin our analysis of frontier settlement and property rights in Brazil with an examination of the history of Brazilian land settlement policy and land reform initiatives. Since the nineteenth century, government land has been open for private claiming and occupation. Government land policies have had an important impact on how property rights to land are allocated and enforced in Brazil.

We focus on land reform in this chapter for three reasons. First, this is a book about property rights, and any coercive redistribution of land through land reform necessarily weakens private property rights. Hence, we are concerned with how land reform measures developed and how they affected the security of tenure, associated land values, and incentives to invest. These latter issues are addressed directly in chapter 8. Land reform is a critical political issue in most of Latin America and in other developing countries. How it has developed in Brazil has implications for other countries. Indeed, policies for more secure land tenure and policies for a more equal division of land-based wealth reflect the long-standing tension, found in almost every country, between the efficiency objectives of property rights and distributional goals. A very skewed wealth distribution creates social conditions that may weaken the security of property rights. At the same time, however, aggressive land redistribution also weakens property rights, leading to the loss of the incentive advantages they provide for socially beneficial economic behavior.[1]

A second and related reason for examining land policy and land reform is that property rights are political institutions. Accordingly, an understanding of how they develop and are maintained within the political arena in the face of competing demands for redistribution provides insights into the political process by which property institutions in general are created and modified.

Finally, we are concerned with land reform issues because they directly affected the settlement of the Amazon region, beginning in the late 1960s. As we describe, an outcome of the debate over land redistribution in southern Brazil was a shift of attention to the largely unoccupied lands in the north. The adoption of directed colonization efforts by the federal and state governments seems to have changed the nature of the frontier settlement process in the Amazon from what existed in earlier frontiers in Brazil. We examine this hypothesis directly in chapter 7.

With the exception of the Amazon, by the 1960s, most of the land in Brazil had been transferred to private hands. Indeed, the Amazon is the last frontier in Brazil, with only about 13 percent of its total area occupied by farms in 1985, the date of the last census (IBGE 1985). The current process of occupation of public land in the Amazon, however, is not a new phenomenon. It represents the last stage of a long process of frontier settlement that started with the European discovery of Brazil. Unlike in the United States, in Brazil the system of landownership and use evolved very slowly. The early institutions for disposing of public land persisted for over 300 years, and only by the end of the nineteenth century did land become a commodity transacted in markets.

Throughout much of its history, Brazil has had a highly concentrated ownership structure characterized by large, often unproductive properties known as latifundia. The subsequent period of accelerated occupation of government land during the first decades of the twentieth century reinforced and even exacerbated the skewed ownership structure, making Brazil one of the countries with the highest levels of land concentration in the world. The resulting coexistence of large idle farms and large numbers of landless peasants has made land redistribution or reform a major issue in Brazil since the 1960s. Although the idea of land redistribution through expropriation of latifundia by the government has been considered socially and, in some cases, economically appealing at different times, it has always been a politically sensitive issue. Furthermore, land reform efforts have consistently failed to reduce the levels of landownership concentration. Owners of latifundia have been politically powerful, and they have successfully resisted the expropriation of their lands. As a result, the tension between the efficiency gains from secure property rights to land and the distributional goals from land reform have been long standing.

In this chapter we describe the evolution of land policy in Brazil. The first section describes the occupation of land from the discovery of Brazil through the colonial and imperial periods, and up to the first half of the twentieth century. Throughout these 450 years, landownership was highly concentrated even though, for most of this time, land was abundant and relatively sparsely settled by world standards. In the second section we describe the history of land reform in Brazil. Land reform became more of a policy issue in 1950, by which time much of the public land had been occupied and only remote frontier regions remained. Land reform was seen as the solution to many land-related economic and social problems that were previously attenuated by the existence of abundant claimable public land. At several times over the past four decades, the Brazilian government attempted large land reform programs. In each of these attempts there was a perception that land reform would yield important social benefits, yet each effort at reform was either blocked in its planning phase or diluted in the implementation phase. The analysis of these events highlights the important role played by politics in the provision of property rights in Brazil and provides the background for the analysis of the current land policy issues in the subsequent chapters.

The Occupation of Public Land in Brazil from Historical Times to Present

Brazil was discovered in 1500 by the Portuguese. One of the first issues faced by the Portuguese Crown was how to occupy the new colony. The first land policy (1532) was a system called *capitanias hereditárias* (hereditary provinces), by which Brazil was divided into 14 sections with boundaries drawn westward from points every 50 leagues along the coast. Each province was given to a captain, who was in charge of providing governmental structures and who had complete authority over land within his *capitania*. This system had worked well in the Portuguese colonization of the Madeira Islands in the Atlantic, but the lack of any significant source of revenue to be gained from the *capitanias* in Brazil made them very unappealing to both the captains and to potential settlers (Junqueira 1976, 13). As a result, six of the captains did not even bother to take possession of their lands, and the others had very little incentive to invest in their settlement (Moog 1955, 147). The Crown revoked the system in 1548 after only 16 years and assigned a general governor for the whole colony.

Settlement of Brazil was slow during the sixteenth century because the initial exploration found no precious metals, and there existed an attractive alternative opportunity for profit from the monopoly of the sea route to the East Indies. Although this condition justified the relative neglect of the colony by the Portuguese Crown, it was necessary to promote some settlement in order to guarantee the possession of Brazil (Simonsen 1937, 78, 89; Lima 1954, 33). The right of possession resulted from discovery, but only actual settlement would make it possible to keep interlopers, such as the French and the Dutch, from occupying portions of the colony. Additionally, in the early part of the sixteenth century, Portugal was a country with a small total population and relatively low population densities, factors that further hindered the task of settling a colony of the size of Brazil.[2]

Given the lack of interest in settlement, the Portuguese Crown turned to the strategy of offering large grants with relatively unencumbered tenure. These grants, called *sesmarias,* gave full property rights over a plot of land to the grantee, with the sole condition being that the land be cultivated.[3] The cultivation clause reflected the intention of the Crown that the grantee use and not merely hoard the land grant. This qualifier has persisted throughout the land laws in Brazilian history and has been consistently unenforceable. Further, as we will see, the *beneficial* use requirement contributes to conflict over land and tenure insecurity today. In this early period, however, none of the *sesmarias* reverted to the Crown, despite the fact that in many cases, their lands were largely untouched (Junqueira 1976, 31).

During the sixteenth century, sugar production along the northeast coast of Brazil became profitable, and coincidentally, it became necessary to own capital and slaves in order to petition for a *sesmaria.* The sugar mills were nearly autonomous units, and they resulted in little settlement. Most inputs and consumption goods were locally produced, and there was little development of an internal market. In the interior of Brazil, cattle ranches were started, but they involved large amounts of land and few settlers. Thus, by the eighteenth century, after two centuries of colonization, the population of Brazil stood only at 300,000. Most of the population was concentrated along the coast, and interior land values remained comparatively low. Under these circumstances of cheap land, formalized property rights to land were not a major concern.

This condition changed only slightly in the early nineteenth century with new ore discoveries that brought new migrants to Brazil. By 1800, the population of the colony had increased to 3,250,000 over the past hundred years (Furtado 1961, 93). Even so, most of the mining population was concentrated in mining camps, and the land near the populated centers was in large estates that were only fractionally cultivated (Simonsen 1937, 87). Small subsistence farmers squatted on more remote land that had not been granted as a *sesmaria.* Because land was abundant, only a limited market developed, and the *sesmaria* system remained the principal mechanism for transferring land until Brazilian independence in 1822.

The new independent government abolished the *sesmaria* system, but it did not put any new land allocation laws into place until 1850. For the first 28 years of independence, the disposal of government land occurred through claiming by occupation (the right of *posse,* which exists today). Expansion of holdings through informal occupation or *posse* contributed to the growth of the latifundia, because the owners of large estates had the capital and other resources to occupy and defend additional land claims (Smith 1990, 348; Dean 1971, 608–9).

The absence of an elaborate land allocation system is understandable, given low land values due to vast available tracts of land and sparse settlement. Under these circumstances, there was little incentive for individual claimants to organize and push for changes in the land laws to provide more formal property rights.[4] However, toward the middle of the nineteenth century, land values escalated in the coffee-producing regions of southeast Brazil as the export of coffee mushroomed. By 1840 coffee represented over 40 percent of the total value of exports. Unlike sugar production, coffee production was accessible to smaller entrepreneurs, because it required less fixed capital than did sugar. Further, given the huge worldwide demand for coffee, producers brought large amounts of land into production.

With the increase in the value of land and the lack of formal property rights, conflict over land became more common. The nearly complete lack of land surveys, although formally required for *sesmarias,* and the arbitrary nature and size of the *posses,* provided natural ingredients for disputes to arise once land prices appreciated. Parliamentary debates during the 1840s indicate that growing land disputes were a major concern.[5] These conflicts involved not only large landholders against small claimants, but also disputes among large landholders. The resort to violence as a means of land allocation is reflected by a statement from a member of parliament who noted the common use of private gangs by large landholders to "intimidate and commit violence in order to usurp land or defend land already usurped."[6] As land values rose, the costs of defending claims increased just as the benefits of ownership increased.

Higher land values also created a demand for a change in institutional arrangements concerning property rights in order to alter the private costs and benefits of owning land. As a result of the political pressure to clarify property rights as competition for control increased, the Land Law of 1850 was passed. This statute legalized *posses* or informal squatter claims and revalidated all *sesmarias* obtained to that date. The statute, however, forbade further land acquisitions through occupation or squatting. After 1850, land could be acquired only through purchase.

Enactment of the law reflected the political influence of landed elites and their desire to limit infringement on their holdings by squatters. The sequence of low land values and an absence of formal property rights, followed by a rise in land values, greater conflict among competing claimants, and then, a demand for government-enforced titles, will be observed repeatedly on the frontier throughout Brazilian history, as we discuss in subsequent chapters.

After 1850, the Brazilian frontier began to move more rapidly than before, with continued expansion of the coffee economy and greater European immigration. To facilitate settlement and the transfer of property rights to land from the government to private claimants the government provided large grants to colonization companies and increasingly used direct sales to individual claimants. In 1889, with the proclamation of the Republic, the jurisdiction over public land was transferred to the states, and the federal government retained control only over the boundaries of the country and over the territories. Although each state adopted its own legislation pertaining to public land, there were no radical deviations from the basic principles of the law of 1850 (Lima 1954, 29).

To encourage settlement in the late nineteenth and early twentieth centuries, Brazilian states aggressively sold land and issued land grants, often without resolving conflicting land claims. Through these efforts large areas were alienated (Smith 1954, 485).

As frontier migration increased and as the states attempted to promote development through the provision of tenure and the formation of farms, problems were encountered in determining which lands remained in the public domain and which ones were held by large colonization companies and other private holders. Many earlier land grants had not been carefully surveyed; moreover, past settlement policies had not been consistent, so that many private claims were not titled or had competing titles.

As the sale of land, colonization, and frontier migration proceeded, the stock of public land in each of the states fell. Using available census data, table 1 shows the percentage of land in each region that was in private farms from 1920 to 1985. In 1920, when the first census was taken, much of the land in the South and Southeast had already been transferred to private hands.[7] The rate of growth of the ratios in the table indicates the extent and pace of settlement. The Amazon (the North) is an outlier with virtually no increase in settlement from 1920 to 1970. This is why the Amazon began to be perceived in the 1960s as the last frontier in Brazil. In other areas, especially in the South and Southeast, over 50 percent of the land was placed in private farms by 1940.

The progression of the frontier in the twentieth century has been to the west and the north. As the agricultural frontier has passed, the demand for land has increased, and along with it, the demand for title from the state and federal governments. Despite the confused nature of previous land policies, title appears to have been provided in a more or less routine manner. We illustrate this phenomenon when we examine frontier settlement in the state of Paraná between 1940 and 1970 in chapter 7 below.

The History of Land Reform in Brazil

The transfer of vast amounts of public land to private ownership over the twentieth century did not reverse the high levels of landownership concentration inherited from previous centuries through the granting of *sesmarias* and the formation of latifundia. Table 2 shows that the Gini coefficient of landownership distribution for Brazil in 1960, when most of land in the major agricultural states had already been occupied, was 0.842, among the highest in the world.

Beginning in the 1930s, the Brazilian government recognized that a combination of frontier settlement and land reform would be a way to boost agricultural production, address rural labor displacement by mechanization and modernization of agriculture, and reduce political tension over the skewed distribution of land and wealth. In 1938 the Land and Settlement Division of the federal government was created (INCRA 1984, 645). Initially, land policy took the path of least resistance: aggressive disposal of the public domain. However, as more of the stock of public land in each state was privatized, attention shifted to the latifundia, which in

TABLE 1. Ratios of Occupied Land to Total Land (in percentages)

| | Total Area in Farms | | | | | | |
	1920	1940	1950	1960	1970	1980	1985
Brazil	20.6	23.2	27.2	29.3	34.6	42.9	44.1
North	6.0	7.1	6.5	6.6	6.5	11.6	12.6
Northeast	23.2	27.6	37.6	40.6	47.9	57.0	59.3
Southeast	49.4	62.1	66.4	68.8	75.2	79.5	79.2
South	47.7	54.9	61.6	67.8	79.0	83.3	83.3
Center-West	23.6	21.4	28.5	31.9	43.4	60.3	61.9

Source: Fundação Instituto Brasileiro de Geografia e Estatístico (IBGE), Censo Agropecuário, 1920–85.

TABLE 2. Gini Coefficient of Landownership Distribution in Brazil

Region	1960	1970	1975	1980	1985
Brazil	0.842	0.844	0.850	0.853	0.854
North	0.944	0.839	0.865	0.830	0.795
Northeast	0.846	0.855	0.858	0.858	0.865
Southeast	0.771	0.761	0.754	0.763	0.766
South	0.727	0.727	0.725	0.735	0.744
Center-West	0.845	0.856	0.851	0.840	0.836

Source: Hoffman 1982 and C. C. Mueller 1987.

many cases were held by absentee owners and not placed into production. The coexistence of these unproductive areas with large contingents of landless peasants made the idea of land redistribution naturally appealing to many politicians. In the mid-1940s, the land policy debate focused on the redistribution of land not placed in socially beneficial use. As available government land (*terra devoluta*) declined further over time, the emphasis on *beneficial* use as a means of maintaining title and property rights to land grew. Defining productive use became a source of uncertainty and conflict, as we explore later. The model of land reform that emerged in the policy debate involved the expropriation of unproductive latifundia, with no or only partial compensation, and the redistribution of land to those who were willing and capable to make it productive. The 1946 constitution allowed for the possibility of expropriation of land for a "social function," when it was not being used to contribute to social welfare. This new provision made it possible for a latifundium to be expropriated simply on the basis that the land was being left idle. Although land reform debates generated intense controversy, there was little implementation throughout the 1950s (Rua 1992, 51). More intense adoption of land redistribution policies awaited the 1960s.

Beginning in the 1960s, and continuing through today, there has been a growing perception that land reform in Brazil is critically needed to reduce social tension in the country based on a very inequitable distribution of wealth. The justification for land reform has varied over time, but the issue has consistently remained on the policy agenda for over 30 years. Although various redistribution schemes were attempted, a glance at the Gini coefficients in table 2 indicates that none of these attempts has been very successful. In each case, land reform has been successfully blocked, reversed, or diluted at initiation or implementation by political coalitions of large landowners. Absent sufficient compensation for their lost lands (assembling such funds has not been politically possible), it has not been in the interest of large landowners to support coercive land redistribution schemes. Because of their dominant political position, large landowners have been able to thwart land reform until recently.

In the mid-1990s land reform efforts have been more aggressive. The apparent shift in political support away from landowners to squatters has resulted from well-organized squatter groups. These groups have forced the government to pay more attention to their demands. It is useful to summarize the development of land reform programs in Brazil since the 1960s as a means of understanding policies toward redistribution and how they might impact property rights on the frontier.

Land Reform under the Military Regime: 1964–84

By the 1960s there emerged a consensus among politicians and intellectuals in Brazil, as well as among foreign lending agencies such as the World Bank, that a series of structural reforms were needed to reduce political tension and to promote economic growth. In particular, there was concern about the rural population exodus to urban areas, leading to congestion, pollution, and other social problems; conflicts over land as holdings became more concentrated (notice that table 2 reveals a gradual increase in ownership concentration in Brazil); and a perception that agricultural production was too low. Land reform or redistribution was seen as a solution for each of these three problems: redistributing land to the landless would abate the rural exodus, halt land conflicts, and increase agricultural output.

From 1961 to 1964 numerous reform projects were proposed, but they went nowhere. Many were impractical; all were resisted by large landowners (Prado 1979, 87). Even so, despite entrenched opposition by landowners, the question was no longer whether there should be land reform, but what form it would take. The main issue involved the form of compensation for the expropriated landowner. The constitution required that the payment should be in cash, in advance, and at a fair price—conditions that would make a extensive land reform very costly. As an alternative, the president proposed that the government would decide on the value of expropriated land and that compensation would be made with 20-year government bonds, policy options opposed by many landowners. Nevertheless, there was a broad consensus that land redistribution was necessary to avoid violent conflict within the country, at a time when the spread of communism was feared by many political interests throughout Latin America.

Perceiving a general political paralysis over a variety of issues, the military staged a coup in 1964. The coup was a reaction to the whole economic, political and social state of the country, but an inability to enact a land reform program was a key stimulus. The new military regime immediately began organizing a land reform program of its own, giving the issue precedence over many other tasks of setting up a new government. The belief was that land reform was urgently needed, including expropriation of latifundia, in order to increase the productivity of agriculture and to increase rural employment, thus leading to a stable rural middle class. Furthermore, land reform would stimulate the economy and reduce social tension by promoting migration from swelling cities, by increasing the size of internal markets for industrial goods, and by providing much-needed hard currency through the export of primary goods. Economic growth, then, was a major justification for land reform.

One of the main steps in the new government's land reform program was to amend the constitution to allow the compensation of an expropriated farm with government bonds, similar to the project proposed by the previous government. This measure was strongly resisted by landowners and their representatives in Congress. After much bargaining, the parties passed an amendment to the constitution in 1964 that stipulated that agricultural bonds for expropriations would be indexed against inflation and that land improvements would be paid in advance in cash. This amendment mitigated the punitiveness of expropriations and reduced political opposition. But it also raised the budgeted cost of land reform. Despite a military dictatorship, Congress still was able to mold the final form of land reform policies.

Congress also passed the Land Statute (Estatuto da Terra) in 1964. This law regulated the rights and obligations of the government to establish a land and agricultural policy, and it remains today the fundamental law regulating land settlement, tenuring, and redistribution policy in Brazil, except for the changes made in the Constitution of 1988. As one would expect given the value of the asset at stake, many of the provisions of the Land Statute were molded by special interests in Congress. For example, "rural enterprises" were to be exempt from expropriation and high taxation, and these enterprises were defined in the statute as a farm that achieved a minimum specified rural productivity. This provision and its vague definition resulted from the insistence of the representatives of landowners. They apparently believed that implementation could be directed in their favor.

As the military government tried to implement land reform under the Land Statute it encountered enormous practical difficulties and achieved few results. This outcome was in part due to a lack of experience and qualified human resources, however, opposition from landowners, their congressmen, and even from within the administration contributed greatly to derailing the process. As a consequence, in order to facilitate expropriations, the government once again amended the constitution in 1969. It removed the provision for advance payment of compensation and added a requirement that compensation value was to be set by the government, or if the owner preferred, to be set equal to the land value declared for tax purposes, which was notoriously underestimated.

The amendment was adopted after the military government dismissed Congress in 1968 and began to rule by decree. This move toward a more authoritarian regime marked the beginning of a new era in the political decision-making process for land reform. It was believed that with the pernicious influence of political interests extricated, the government would be able to implement policies based on purely technical criteria. Given the military government's commitment to land reform, the (at least temporary) removal of congressional interest groups from policy formation, and the existence of all the necessary constitutional provisions, one would have expected that substantive land reform would be undertaken.

This was not the outcome, however. The Gini coefficients presented in table 2 show no trend toward a more equal distribution of landholdings in Brazil. The removal of congressional politicians from the decision-making process did not lead to an end of the difficulties in producing and implementing land redistribution policy (Rua 1992; Bunker 1985a). The obstructive conflicts, bargaining, and negotiation that previously occurred between the bureaucracy (administration) and the politicians (Congress), now occurred among different sectors within the administration. These interbureaucratic disputes filled the vacuum left by the absence of Congress with the heads and staff of different agencies and ministries pursuing their own preferences or those of the interests they represented. Once again, given the value of the land assets at stake and the political and social positions they underwrote, the result could hardly have been different.

Although major decisions regarding land reform were determined by the military leadership, implementation and administration were delegated to the large bureaucracy that reflected various stakeholders in land issues, including councils, ministries, departments, secretariats, and a variety of more peripheral agencies. This delegation of authority provided considerable latitude for competing constituent groups to influence land reform. In the end, this new arena for policy debate had the same effect of impeding land reform as the previous period, when politicians were directly involved.

Of importance for our purposes in examining the Amazon frontier, the lack of progress of land reform in southern Brazil by the late 1960s led to a shift in emphasis to settling landless peasants on public land in the Amazon rather than on expropriated land in the central regions of the country (see Rua 1992). As before, this represented a path of least resistance, given the difficulties involved in expropriating and redistributing private land when there was no consensus on compensation. Further, the shift to Amazon colonization complemented nicely another major concern of the military government—firming Brazil's claim to the region.

Since colonial times, the Amazon had been viewed as a area of immense potential wealth. In 1953, the government established a federal agency (SPVEA—Superintendência do Plano de Valorização Economica da Amazônia) to promote the economic use of the Amazon, and in 1960, the Belém-Brasília Highway linked the region to the rest of Brazil. It was only after the military regime came to power, with the occupation of the Amazon as one of their principal goals, that the federal government's presence in the region became significant.

Developing the Amazon not only guaranteed Brazilian sovereignty over the region, an issue very dear to the military ideology, but also made it possible to tap into its potential wealth, thereby contributing to rapid economic development and modernization of the country. Reaching these goals meant encouraging new flows of migrants and capital into the region. This process also could reduce competition for land in central and southern Brazil.

In 1966, SPVEA was replaced by SUDAM (Superintendência do Desenvolvimento da Amazônia). This administrative change represented the start of Operation Amazônia. SUDAM was in charge of organizing and coordinating the federal development of the Amazon region. SUDAM stimulated investment by private entrepreneurs in the Amazon through fiscal incentives. In 1971, Operation Amazônia was accelerated with the creation of the Program of National Integration (PIN) that sought to integrate the Amazon into the Brazilian economy through the construction of several highways within the region as well as the start of what was to be an impressive settlement effort based on a series of colonization projects. The Transamazon Highway, begun in 1970, opened access to vast areas of land.

To coordinate land tenure–related issues throughout Brazil and to implement the occupation policy in the Amazon, especially settlement along the Transamazon Highway, the federal government created INCRA (National Institute for Colonization and Agrarian Reform). INCRA initially planned to settle 100,000 landless families from elsewhere in Brazil in the Amazon region.

To achieve this ambitious goal the federal government enacted Military Decree Law 1164 in 1971. Decree 1164 extended federal jurisdiction by fiat over a 100-kilometer strip of land on both sides of federal highways, federal highways under construction, or highways planned in the Amazon. This expansion occurred at the expense of the state governments, which lost considerable portions of public land under their jurisdiction.[8]

Despite a seeming will to colonize and populate the Amazon, it became clear by 1975 that the government's colonization programs fell far short of their objectives. In part, the failure resulted from an uncontrolled migratory flow of settlers, many from the impoverished Northeast region. INCRA was unable to cope with the demand for demarcation of individual plots, recording claims, formally surveying, providing title, and provision of other promised services, such as infrastructure, education, health care, seeds, and fertilizers (see Moran 1975, 1981; Ianni 1979; Fearnside 1986).

In 1975, the government reevaluated its policy toward the Amazon and announced the Poloamazonia program together with Second Development Plan for the Amazon. The new plan represented a shift from government to private colonization, as well as an emphasis on large-scale agricultural and cattle enterprises. This program expanded the earlier fiscal incentives managed by SUDAM.

The incentives attracted several enterprises to the region, but many of the large holdings that arose under this scheme were not put into productive use because of high transportation costs. For example, Gasques and Yokomizo (1986) reported that of a sample of 29 SUDAM-subsidized cattle ranches with an average size of 16,334 hectares, 14 sold no cattle at all, and only 2 reached more that 50 percent of their target between 1974 and 1985.

These large tracts of land, held largely uncultivated and unused, together with the large contingent of landless peasants left stranded on the frontier due to the government's policy reversal, presented the ingredients underlying subsequent land invasions and conflicts. In order to settle these conflicts INCRA was forced in many cases to step in and expropriate the disputed farms. During the last half of the 1970s and early 1980s INCRA increasingly was put into the reactive policy position of responding to land conflicts through expropriation and the creation of settlement projects on the disputed land. Formal colonization projects faded into the background. As we discuss in chapters 3 and 8, the resulting use of invasions by organized groups of squatters as a means to force INCRA to respond became the de facto land reform policy of the 1990s.

The first half of the 1980s brought the start of a decade-long period of macroeconomic crisis in Brazil with profound consequences for Amazon land settlement policy in general and for land reform in particular. The occupation of the Amazon as a means of solving the problem of landownership concentration was abandoned, at least temporarily. Interest in the occupation of the Amazon waned, although tension over land distribution increased, as did demands for the provision of titles. Land reform concerns also grew elsewhere in Brazil.

In a last attempt to address land redistribution and resolve chronic disputes between owners and squatters in the southeastern region of the Amazon, the military government created a new land agency, GETAT (Executive Group for the Land of the Araguaia-Tocantins Region). This new agency took over land-titling and reform issues from INCRA in certain parts of Pará. GETAT was under direct military control and thus more insulated from the competing interests within the civilian bureaucracy. The agency expropriated enough contested properties for subsequent distribution to squatters that the creation of a similar agency for another region of the Amazon, GEBAM (Executive Group for the Land in the Lower Amazon) seemed appropriate.

The creation of GETAT, giving it jurisdiction over an area that was previously under INCRA's jurisdiction, however, underscored the inability of the military to overcome the influence of interest groups against land reform within the existing government. INCRA, for example, was more concerned with distributing government land to farmers (often large ones) who could expand agricultural production than with the expropriation and partition of large holdings among many small, landless squatters. INCRA was under the minister of finance at the time, who was the main spokesman for modernization of agriculture instead of land reform. Rather than opposing the special interests within INCRA, the military government thought it would be easier and more effective to establish GETAT and GEBAM, agencies whose decision-making process was not influenced by other demands. The difficulties that even an authoritarian regime had to overcome to implement land reform reflects the importance of political and bureaucratic factors in the provision of property rights to land in Brazil.

Table 3 summarizes land reform success by region across Brazil from 1940 through 1985. The table (panels A and B) shows the share of total farms occupied by squatters and the share of total farm area occupied by squatters as reported in the census. It is clear that the most settled regions, the South and Southeast, have had comparatively small percentages of farms or farmland held by squatters (those without title). These are the regions where agribusiness has developed and where consolidation of farms has occurred. It is also evident that for Brazil as a whole, the percentage of farms and percentage of farmland held by squatters has remained relatively constant since 1970, despite various land reform efforts. The North (Amazon) stands out as the region with consistently high portions of farms and farm area occupied by squatters, especially since 1970, when major migration to the region began. The data suggest that the federal government (through INCRA) has focused more on settlement and encouraging migration to the region than on titling. We discuss the implications of this observation later in the volume. It indicates, however, that the government has not moved quickly to provide formal property rights to small farmers on the Amazon frontier. As we later show, title is critical for accessing capital, promoting long-term investment, and thereby raising land values.

The National Plan for Land Reform

In 1985, the transition from the military regime to a civilian government was completed with the (indirect) election of a large coalition from the previous political opposition and dissenters from the shattered government party of the military regime. Among the main instruments of the new government to attack various social and economic problems in Brazil was the PNRA (National Plan for Land Reform), which was a new ambitious land reform program. Whereas in the 1960s and 1970s the major justification for land reform had been economic benefits to promote agricultural production, develop internal markets, and reduce urban unemployment, by the mid-1980s the modernization of agriculture in central and southern Brazil had so increased the supply of food that it diminished the salience of the economic argument.

Although the PNRA did promise economic benefits, the justification for land reform was social justice. The rapid development of the country in general and the modernization of agriculture in particular had affected a large portion of the rural population. It became necessary, the argument

TABLE 3. **Share of Total Number of Farms and Farm Area Occupied by Squatters by Region (in percentages)**

Region	1940	1950	1960	1970	1975	1980	1985
			A. Farms Occupied by Squatters by Region				
Brazil	6	10	11	16	19	17	18
North	13	25	33	47	54	44	34
Northeast	10	15	16	21	23	20	23
Southeast	3	4	4	7	6	6	8
South	3	8	8	9	8	8	9
Center-West	18	25	18	20	21	15	12

Region	1940	1950	1960	1970	1975	1980	1985
			B. Farm Area				
Brazil	3	4	4	7	7	6	5
North	3	3	7	25	27	26	14
Northeast	1	3	2	6	5	4	4
Southeast	2	2	2	4	2	2	3
South	1	3	3	4	3	3	3
Center-West	7	9	5	8	7	5	2

Source: Fundação Instituto Brasileiro de Geographia e Estatístico (IBGE), *Censo Agropecuário,* 1940–85.

ran, to reintegrate these landless peasants through the provision of land as a means to participate in the economy (Graziano 1991, 16). As their numbers grew, the landless became an increasingly influential political constituency, which, as we describe, was organized by the rise of peasant unions and other sympathetic groups. The problem of unemployed, poor, rural workers became increasingly visible as the number of invasions of private property and related conflicts with landowners multiplied throughout the country. There was a growing perception that land reform, if perhaps no longer a necessary condition for economic development, was nevertheless an important measure to reduce social tension.

In May 1985, the PNRA was presented by the government as a proposal for debate. The objective of the plan was to "change the landownership structure of the country, distributing and redistributing land, eliminating progressively latifundia and minifundia and assuring a regime of possession and use of land that fulfills the principles of social justice and the increase of productivity, so as to guarantee the socioeconomic realization and the right to citizenship of the rural worker."[9] Settlement of 7.1 million rural workers by the year 2000 (1.4 million from 1985 to 1989) was the specific policy target. The land was to come from the stock of 409.5 million hectares of latifundia, according to INCRA's statistics, and the 71.7 million hectares of land belonging to the government. In terms of property rights security, the PNRA differed from previous attempts at land reform in Brazil by explicitly stating that expropriations of private property were to be the main instrument for reaching its objectives. Previous land reform attempts were either conceived or diverted to emphasize other instruments, such as colonization and other forms of distribution of government lands. The government designated areas of social conflict, high concentration of ownership, good aptitude for agriculture, and existing infrastructure as having priority for expropriations.

The Land Statue of 1964 was still the fundamental law that governed agrarian policy, and through that law, the financing of the PNRA was to be done through the use of TDAs (titles of agrarian debt) to pay for the expropriation of the land. The problem of valuing land and improvements for compensation remained from before. If market prices had to be paid for the land, however, the resources available would not allow a large-scale reform. Costs were expected to be reduced, however, through proclamations that designated certain areas as having priority for land reform. These proclamations were envisioned as reducing the value of all land in those areas.

Additionally, the National Program for Land Reform attempted to obtain the cooperation of the judiciary in lowering the costs of expropriations. Landowners in Brazil typically had been able to contest compensation for expropriations in the courts by arguing either that their farms were productive (and thus could not be expropriated) or that an increase in the value of the offered compensation was justified. Because Brazilian courts have had a strong tradition of private property rights, which is expressed in the Civil Code, judges tended to be sympathetic to such pleas.[10] While the Land Statue required that a "just price" was to be paid for expropriated land, the PNRA suggested that the courts penalize the owner for not using the land in determining compensation.

The commitment of the government to actually follow through with the PNRA was expressed through the creation of a ministry to implement the reform, MIRAD (Ministry of Land Reform and Development). Whereas previous land reform attempts had been assigned to various departments, secretariats or agencies, such as INCRA, the creation of MIRAD placed land reform at a high hierarchical level within the government. Although this did not guarantee that the ministry would actually be powerful within the executive branch of the Brazilian government, especially in terms of independence and resources, it did provide a signal of commitment, because ministries were thought to be more independent of constituent pressures than were lower-level agencies. Additionally, the individuals named as minister of land reform and president of INCRA were strongly in favor of land reform (see Ribeiro 1987; Gomes da Silva 1987).

The fact that the new government proposed a massive land reform as one of its major programs reveals that, not only did it perceive that the reform could deliver important social and economic benefits, but also that it would attract sufficient support from powerful interest groups to be politically viable. The reason for this assessment was that Brazil was going through a process of redemocratization and institutional change after years of military rule, and officials in the new government believed that there was widespread demand for "social justice." But also, during the years of military rule information about constituent demands became harder to come by, so that miscalculations were possible.

Subsequent political reaction indicates that the government miscalculated support for land reform under the PNRA. Indeed, as soon as the proposal was presented in May 1985 and the various interest groups mobilized, it became clear to the government that the opposition to the program far outweighed any political backing it would generate (Ribeiro 1987).

INCRA and MIRAD sought to justify the PNRA to generate a favorable political climate. To allay the fears of landowners, it was emphasized that the proposed reform was based on the Land Statute and thus would not expropriate any productive properties. Public opinion tended to sympathize with the need for land reform in Brazil. There was a widespread belief that landownership in Brazil was too concentrated in the form of latifundia, many of which were thought not to be in production (Graziano 1991, 13; Gomes da Silva 1987, 108; Veiga 1990, 83). At the same time, however, public opinion appears to have been extremely sensitive to any suggestion that land reform might entail the expropriation of productive farms.

Even with this effort to build a consensus, strong reaction developed against the PNRA from several different quarters. As one would expect, a direct campaign against the program was initiated by the organizations that represented the interests of rural producers and landowners, the two largest being CNA (National Confederation of Agriculture) and SBR (Brazilian Rural Society). These organizations were made up of large farmers who were most likely to be directly affected by the PNRA.

More surprising to advocates was the opposition expressed by most of the small rural producers and landowners, who in principle would have no reason to fear land reform. Presumably, the concerns of this group were based on the feared weakening of property rights to land as expropriations took place and uncertainty as to the operational definitions to be used in deciding which properties would be expropriated. To organize the political opposition to land reform under the PNRA, a new organization was formed, the UDR (Rural Democratic Union) whose mandate was to promote the interests of farmers and landowners in Congress. The UDR developed into an effective, well-organized force with extensive resources, and it openly advocated the use of violence against squatter invasions or any other threats against private land.

Another unanticipated and important source of opposition that quickly manifested itself against the PNRA came from within the government's own coalition in Congress. Although both of the major parties that formed the coalition officially supported the program, each of them had entrenched landowning interests in their constituencies. Out of the 84 large landowners in Congress, who together held nearly 5 million of the 850 million hectares of land in Brazil, 45 were from the government's coalition (CEDI 1986, 48). Even within the executive branch, support waned as the opposition grew, with few of the ministers openly defending the program. Soon, the president's own advisers became convinced that the PNRA was a political mistake (Veiga 1990, 117).

In response to the reaction against the proposal, the president's resolve for land reform faltered. Not only had there been an unexpected reaction against the PNRA, but the support from the groups who stood to benefit the most was very weak. The president had counted on rural workers for support; they were numerous and had become increasingly organized. One advocacy organization was CONTAG (the National Confederation of Workers in Agriculture), which had formed in 1979 (Graziano da Silva 1985, 45–49). The Catholic Church had also officially thrown its weight in support of land reform. Finally, the most radical advocacy group was the MST (Landless Peasants Movement), an organization independent from the rural unions that organized squatter invasions of unproductive land throughout the country.

Once the proposal had been presented, it became clear that whatever support the rural workers were going to provide was no match for the opposition from the landowners and farmers. Furthermore, the support of the rural workers was not unconditionally or enthusiastically given. All previous land reform attempts had included promises similar to this program, yet none of them had materialized. Consequently the rural workers were cautious about backing the PNRA and did so only critically, pointing out the points where they thought it had not gone far enough (Leal 1985, 38).

In response to pressure from the landowning interests, the president went against the wishes of the agencies that would have implemented land reform, MIRAD and INCRA, by making several last-minute changes to the PNRA. In the final version of the land redistribution scheme, the president did not assign priority areas for land reform, nor did he change the standards for a farm to be considered productive. This last-minute reversion to the status quo enabled landowners subsequently to use the courts to successfully prevent expropriations.[11] One week after the signing of the plan, the president of INCRA resigned, and the minister of land reform was replaced shortly thereafter. Despite these changes, the PNRA had very ambitious goals of settling 250,000 families on 7.6 million hectares of expropriated land by 1987. INCRA fell far short of the target: only 21,367 families were settled on 714,000 expropriated hectares plus 100,000 hectares that INCRA already owned.

Land Reform and the Constitution of 1988

Following the introduction of the National Program for Land Reform in 1985 the aggregate performance of the Brazilian economy worsened, and land reform ceased being a major issue as politicians turned to efforts to revive the economy. Renewed emphasis was placed on redistribution with the drafting of a new constitution in 1987. The prevailing constitution dated from 1969, during the military period, and was not well suited for the new institutional and political environment. In drafting the new constitution, it was clear to all interested parties that the new document would define the future of land reform through the manner in which it defined property rights to land, productive use, and the conditions for expropriation.

The task of drafting the constitution fell to the current members of Congress, instead of a specially appointed committee. As a result, interest groups on both sides of the land reform debate lobbied actively to mold the document in their behalf. Land reform turned out to be one of the most disputed of the many topics debated throughout the writing of the constitution. The public at large was also interested: in a 1987 poll land reform ranked third out of fifteen topics that should be given priority by the constitution.[12]

It is noteworthy that early in the process, Congress decided that there should be a chapter specifically about land reform and land policy. The process for drafting the constitution mandated that each specific topic originate in a subcommittee and, after being approved, be passed to its parent committee (the Committee of Economic Order in the case of land reform). From here, the product was sent to a final committee, which joined the various projects of the parent committees. This entire document would then be open to amendments by the floor (composed of all senators and representatives in the Congress) after which the constitution would be put to a vote. A second voting round would correct errors and omissions, as well as allow additional amendments, before a final vote was held.

The entire process of constitution drafting took over a year and a half, ending in October 1988.[13] The land reform chapter of the new constitution was particularly troublesome. The votes in the various committees were always close, and the process was constantly followed from the galleries by members of rural worker groups (CONTAG and MST) and landowners (UDR), as well as much lobbying behind the scenes. The main point of contention centered on the exemption of productive properties from expropriation. The congressmen who defended the interests of landowners tried to minimize the obligations of landowners for their land to be considered productive and thus not be subject to expropriation. Those in favor of land reform believed that the text should make the expropriation process as unencumbered and expeditious as possible. Neither side dominated the process with the upper hand switching numerous times between interests in favor of, and interests opposed to, land reform.

Politicians attempted bargaining, negotiation, and logrolling, but the issue was too contentious and no deals were struck (Gomes da Silva 1989). At one point in the process, President Sarney passed a decree abolishing INCRA and instituting a new land reform decree. This move by the president fundamentally changed the rules that regulated the process of expropriations and, as such, affected the debate over the constitution. The new decree made expropriations much more vulnerable to appeals in court and created a much less propitious legal, technical, and political atmosphere for land reform.

It appears that the intention of the president's decree was to influence the drafting of the land reform chapter in the constitution. Before his decree, the status quo point from which the bargaining in Congress started included the laws and administrative and court rulings in the Land Statute of 1964 along with subsequent changes made by the PNRA. The drafting process stipulated that if an absolute majority did not approve a topic, then it would be excluded from the final version of the constitution, and the law would revert to the status quo. During much of the constitutional negotiation, the land reform chapter seemed to be heading this way. Neither side was able to muster an absolute majority, and negotiations reached no accords. By changing the current law for land reform, the president was changing the status quo. Because this new status quo was much less desirable to the proreform side, they made concessions so as to avoid leaving land reform out of the constitution and subject to the new unfavorable environment.[14]

The new decree altered bargaining positions, and a deal was struck in committee. However, the committee left one contentious point to be decided on the floor, specifically, Article 190 of the land reform chapter. This article stated: "The law will guarantee special treatment to productive properties and will establish the criteria for the fulfillment of its social function, *the unattainment of which will allow its expropriation in the terms of Article 218* (emphasis added)." The final vote involved deciding whether the phrase in italics would be left in the final version or removed.

For a property to fulfill its social function, according to Article 191, it has to simultaneously satisfy four requirements:

1. Adequate and rational use;
2. Adequate use of the natural resources available and preservation of the environment;
3. Observance of the dispositions which regulate labor relations; and
4. Exploitation that favors the well-being of the proprietors and workers.

Because these requirements were very generally stated, the actual standards for productive use would be interpreted by the courts. Court rulings would determine the practical effect of the new standards on expropriations and land reform. Nevertheless, the vote on the removal of the phrase highlighted in Article 190 of the new constitution was considered crucial since the phrase implied that even if a property was productive it could be expropriated, as long as at least one of the requirements of its social function was not met. Without the phrase, land reform would be much more difficult to accomplish because constitutional protection of productive properties created the potential for judicial restrictions on expropriation.

The final vote did not produce an absolute majority to keep the phrase, and it was removed. As a result, the proreform groups considered the chances of land reform in Brazil through the new constitution drastically reduced. This assessment set the stage for a more aggressive push for land redistribution involving the use of violence by advocates. These actions affected the security of property rights on the Amazon frontier.

Conclusion

In the years that followed the adoption of the constitution of 1988, land reform was once again overshadowed by other issues. Each successive government instituted a land reform program, but none was given priority. Before the new constitution, INCRA settled a yearly average of 22,861 families from 1986 to 1988 in new farms as part of land redistribution. But the average fell to 10,526 from 1989 to 1994.[15] Using the Food and Agriculture Organization's estimate of 2.5 million landless families in 1996, it would take over 100 years to settle the landless in new farms even at the higher pace of the pre-1988 constitution.[16] Testimony to the low priority given to land reform is the halving of INCRA's staff in 1991. In addition, INCRA was judicially prevented from expropriating any farms from 1990 to early 1993. It was also relatively easy for landowners to reverse expropriations in court, and until 1993 Congress had not passed legislation to facilitate expropriations. In the meantime INCRA had to limit itself to the negotiated purchase of land for the few settlements it did perform (INCRA 1992, 7). With over three decades of failed experiences, a consensus emerged among academics and politicians that large-scale land reform based on massive land redistribution would never happen in Brazil.[17] Nevertheless, the growing problems of landless peasants and associated tensions over landownership created an environment that threatened the security of property rights to land.

In the face of this administrative inaction, the landless peasants became increasingly organized, particularly through the MST. The MST was founded in 1984 in the wake of the democratization of the country and the revival of land reform in the PNRA. The MST had been conducting land invasions throughout the entire period. Until 1994, however, these invasions had been isolated events with little obvious impact on land reform. As the movement grew and perfected its strategy, it gradually became clear that something more fundamental was in the making.

Against all predictions, the MST, and other squatter groups that followed its example, revived the issue of land reform in the political agenda by 1994 to a point perhaps never reached in Brazilian history. The new strategy involved the invasion of private land and the use of violence to attract domestic and international attention to the skewed distribution of landholdings. By embarrassing congressional politicians, the president, and INCRA officials, such violence could force INCRA to intervene on behalf of squatters and expropriate private land. This strategy has shifted the locus of action from INCRA and the government to squatter organizations, such as the MST. The growing use of violence to provoke expropriation has broad implications for the distribution of land and wealth in Brazil and possibly on the level of wealth, at least in frontier areas, by affecting the security of property rights, land values, and the incentives for investment. In the next chapter, we analyze current land policies in Brazil and the political economy of squatter-led land reform. In chapter 4 we discuss the use of violence as a strategic weapon in conflicts over land on the frontier. Finally, we model and examine the determinants and impact of violence in land conflicts in chapter 8.

NOTES

1. For a discussion of these advantages, see Libecap 1989.

2. Lima 1954, 19. In the early fifteenth century Portugal faced depopulation of its countryside.

3. A tithe also had to be paid to the Order of Christ, but this tithe was equivalent to a land tax and not a feudal encumbrance, since it was fixed and predictable. See Junqueira 1976, 24–26.

4. Davis and North 1971; Libecap 1978. We are not arguing that demand side factors alone determine property rights, but only that during this period the rental stream from land did not warrant much demand for secure property rights. As we will discuss later, supply factors play an important role once land values increase.

5. For discussion, see Dean 1971.

6. Quoted in Dean 1971, 611. In the American context, see Umbeck 1981.

7. When considering these ratios it must be borne in mind that some of the land in the state is in urban areas, coastal regions, lakes, and roads that never become farms.

8. Foweraker 1981, 100. In Pará, for example, this meant that in 1985 only 29.7 percent of public land was under jurisdiction of the state's land agency ITERPA,

while 43.4 percent was under INCRA's jurisdiction. The remaining 26.9 percent was under the jurisdiction of other federal agencies such as the air force, the forestry service, and the Indian agency. See Oliveira and Silva 1986, 47.

9. See Leal 1985, 77–120, for a transcription of the proposal of the PNRA. Graziano da Silva 1985 provides a summary of the proposal. Graziano 1991 critiques the numbers in the proposal.

10. Fachin 1991. It has also been argued that another reason why INCRA frequently loses its court cases and is forced to increase the value of the compensation paid to expropriated landowners is that it has too few attorneys, who are badly prepared. INCRA cannot simply hire attorneys, since it is a civil servant job subject to a public entrance exam. The salary is not capable of attracting the more able candidates. In contrast landowners have high values at stake and can hire specialized lawyers. This view was expressed to us in interviews with INCRA staff in Brasília and Belém. See also Mandim 1995.

11. See Gomes da Silva 1987, chap. 5, for an analysis of the full scope of these changes.

12. Land reform ranked behind free education and wealth distribution. *Jornal do Brasil* September 13, 1987, cited in Gomes da Silva 1989.

13. Mueller (1994) analyzes the political economy of the writing of the constitution of 1988; Gomes da Silva (1989) describes day-to-day events.

14. One year after its abolition with the new constitution already in place, INCRA was reinstated and once again put in charge of land reform. This supports our hypothesis about the rationale for the decree that abolished INCRA. Once the chapter on land reform had been completed, there was no reason not to reinstate INCRA. This action was preferable to incurring the costs of creating a new agency to fulfill those same duties.

15. Data from INCRA 1996.

16. The Food and Agriculture Organization estimates 2.5 million families of landless peasants in Brazil in 1996 (IBRD/IDA 1997, 4).

17. See Rossi 1997 and *Folha de São Paulo,* September 24, 1995, 8.

CHAPTER 3

Current Land Policies: The Politics and Economics of Property Rights Distribution, Enforcement, and Land Reform

Introduction

In the previous chapter we outlined the history of land reform in Brazil. That history is important because it not only molds current policies, but shapes the institutions that define and enforce property rights to land on the Amazon frontier. Property rights are political institutions, and land reform policies are determined in the political arena. Past policies for both land distribution and land reform have created expectations and constituents for the policies that exist today. In this chapter we continue the discussion of the institutions that specify and enforce property rights on the frontier. We emphasize the political and bureaucratic factors in the provision of property rights and arbitration of conflicts. In the first four sections we describe the major players in land reform and the frontier settlement process: INCRA, landless peasants, landowners, and the courts. In the final section, we describe some new approaches to land reform that may provide better ways of dealing with the problem of landless peasants and high levels of land concentration. In the conclusion, we discuss the state land agency, ITERPA, and its role in the provision of title on the frontier.

INCRA and Expropriations

INCRA, the National Institute for Colonization and Agrarian Reform, is the main governmental organization in charge of implementing land policy. In the previous chapter we briefly discussed the history of INCRA. INCRA was established in 1970 under the military government with a mission to oversee land reform and the settlement of landless peasants. Over time, as the government's land policy objectives changed, so did the activities of INCRA. During the 1970s it concentrated on creating planned colonization projects in the Amazon. This involved numerous tasks: (1) distinguishing private land from public land (*discriminação*); (2) registering public land in its name (*arrecadação*); (3) selling and granting land; (4) demarcation and mapping; (5) creating a list of potential beneficiaries as well as a list of all the farms in the country (*cadastro*); (6) providing provisional titles initially and permanent titles subsequently; (7) providing infrastructure (in practice this involved mostly building roads); (8) providing credit and technical assistance; (9) collecting payment from the beneficiaries; and (10) concluding projects as they matured. Other tasks of INCRA not directly related to colonization included the collection of the rural land tax and the expropriation of private land.

Early on it was realized within the agency that it was impossible to fulfill all of these goals. Not only did settlement of the Amazon present a much greater challenge than had been foreseen, but the large flows of spontaneous migration quickly swamped INCRA's capacity to provide services, such as surveying, recording, and titling lands. INCRA was not even able to maintain a trustworthy cadastre of all the rural properties, much less accomplish other more demanding entitling tasks. The consequent logistical and political difficulties in determining the true ownership of land occupied by settlers and the high costs of surveying created long delays in the provision of title.

When the government changed its strategy in the late 1970s and opted instead to focus on large-scale agricultural projects instead of colonization, most settlers and squatters in the Amazon were left with uncertain tenure to the land they occupied. Much of the land was unsurveyed and untitled and had competing claimants. Moreover, there was also little agricultural credit because of a lack of title and collateral and because of the riskiness of investment in the region. The policies of INCRA in the 1970s set the stage for many of the land-related problems that became increasingly visible in the 1980s.[1]

With the PNRA (National Plan for Land Reform of 1985, discussed in the previous chapter), INCRA inaugurated a new model of land redistribution based on the expropriation of private properties. INCRA recognized that reform could not be accomplished merely by settling landless peasants on the remote frontier. Lacking infrastructure and access to markets, frontier colonies were apt to fail. The considerable private land not in use, yet relatively close to markets, provided an alternative. Such properties could be expropriated and assigned to small settlers with a greater likelihood of success.

The process of expropriation and reallocation naturally was not smooth. Landowners organized politically to block government expropriations. Further, a limited budget and restrictive legal rules and procedures designed to protect private property rights from arbitrary government action slowed the agency. Finally, INCRA increasingly found itself responding to agendas set by squatters, rather than methodically selecting the farms to be expropriated and choosing which peasants to settle on the expropriated land.

The shift of agenda setting from the agency to squatters occurred as INCRA allowed squatters to retain the private lands they invaded. Following an invasion INCRA would intervene to resolve the ensuing conflict between the farm owner and trespassers by expropriating the property and reallocating it to the squatters. As this pattern of behavior by INCRA became clear, peasants concluded that rather than waiting to be settled in a formal colonization project, which could take decades, they could expedite the process by invading a farm. The subsequent conflict and violence, however, embarrassed the office of the president and forced INCRA to intervene. In a time of limited budgets for expropriations, squatters could force agency action by seizing the initiative through invasion and the strategic use of violence. Both landowners and INCRA realized the new strategy of the landless peasants and in turn reacted. The result was the establishment of a new scenario of land reform in Brazil. The "game" that is played by squatters and farmers in their fight for land will be discussed in chapter 4 and modeled and tested in chapter 8.

Given the central role played by expropriations in the current model of land reform, it is useful to examine in detail the rules and procedures involved. According to the constitution, a rural property that is not fulfilling its social function can be expropriated by the federal government. A property fulfills its social function essentially when it is "rationally and adequately used." The constitutional provision was complemented in 1993 by Law No. 8629, defined criteria for determining beneficial use.

Adequate use, according to this new law, requires that at least 80 percent of the land be productive above certain defined levels. In forested regions, such as the Amazon, a key element is deforestation. But the standards are necessarily vague and vary according to land types. There is considerable room for disagreement and for resorting to the judicial system for determination of whether the property meets the specified criteria.

Besides land use requirements, expropriations are based on farm size. The size of a property is measured in regional units called *módulos,* which are equal to the area needed by a family to make a living cultivating subsistence crops. A small property is defined as from 1 to 4 *módulos,* a medium property from 4 to 15, and a large property above 15. Small and medium properties are not susceptible to expropriation so long as their owner possesses no other land.

According to the law of 1993, expropriation must be "just," that is, involving "a compensation that allows the expropriated landowner to replace the value of the good lost in the name of social interest" (Law No. 8629, Art. 12). The landowner is paid in TDAs (titles of agrarian debt) for the farm and in cash for the value of any improvements made on the land. The federal government's budget determines the annual volume of TDAs available for expropriation. Indeed, TDAs are a large part of INCRA's operating budget. In 1995, they accounted for 56 percent of INCRA's total budget of approximately U.S.$1.3 billion (Tribunal de Contas da União 1996, 44). Before 1992, TDAs had been highly discounted due to high default probability by the government. Since 1992 the Treasury has administered the TDAs, and because they can be used for purchases in the privatization program, they have regained some credibility, although they are still heavily discounted in the market. The TDAs are indexed against inflation and are redeemable in yearly installments, starting in the second year after the expropriation and continuing for 5, 10, 15, or 20 years, depending on the size of the property, with larger properties being compensated over a longer period.

An expropriation starts with an inspection of the targeted farm by a delegation from INCRA. Article 2 of Law No. 8629 of 1993 allows INCRA to enter a property for inspection after notifying the owner.[2] Currently most of the farms visited by INCRA are already occupied by squatters. If the farm is deemed unproductive and fulfills other requirements for being expropriable, a decree will be signed by the president declaring the property as being of social interest and authorizing INCRA to propose the expropriation. The act by which the title of the land is passed from the farmer to INCRA is called *imissão de posse* (transfer of title), and it must be confirmed by a federal court. It is at this point that a landowner can contest the expropriation either on grounds of productivity or on the value of the compensation. These court challenges increase the time it takes for the *imissão de posse* to be concluded, in some cases by many years, and in other cases, prevent the expropriation from being completed.[3]

In response to complaints by squatter groups and their supporters in Congress, a law was passed in August 1996 to remove these obstacles from INCRA's expropriation procedures. The law, known as *rito sumário,* established that after the inspection of the farm and its expropriation, the *imissão de posse* must occur within 48 hours. The landowner may still go to court to discuss the price of the farm, but the expropriation is completed.

With possession of the property, INCRA initiates a land reform settlement project. The official procedure is for INCRA to select and settle several families of landless peasants, who have registered with INCRA beforehand. In practice the land is usually given to the squatters whose invasion prompted the expropriation. Creating an official project requires that some infrastructure be built, and the cost must be included in the following year's INCRA budget. These budget requirements may lead to additional delays in the formal settlement (IBRD/IDA 1997, 17). If INCRA is low on resources, the investments for infrastructure will be reduced or put off to the future. Further, it is not uncommon for the settlement project to be abandoned by INCRA after the initial settlement, because INCRA's performance is judged not by the quality of the final settlement project but rather on the number of families *initially settled.* Once the expropriation is legal and the peasants are on the land, INCRA can claim to have settled those families and can use its resources to expropriate other contested farms instead of following through with investments in each project.[4] We return to this issue in chapter 9, where we discuss the incentives of the peasants' union (MST) and INCRA to devote resources to titling. If they are not so motivated, then land reform efforts may leave property rights insecure for small, as well as large, holders.

Ironically, having title facilitates the expropriation of a farm by INCRA because it allows the agency to negotiate with a legally recognized owner. In practice this becomes a difficult issue because of the large number of properties with doubtful titles, especially in those states where the process of land privatization in the past was done without surveying or attention to discovering if anybody claimed the land before the government sold or granted it.[5] If a property does not have a title, or if the title is flawed, INCRA sorts out the situation in a process called regularization (*regularização*). If the land is found to have no true owner, INCRA will consider it to be public land and use it for land reform. In many cases, INCRA allows the person who claims to have title to buy the portion of the farm that was made productive plus a multiple of the area in unused land. The residual is used by INCRA to settle landless peasants.

For example, when we surveyed farmers in Parauapebas in November 1996, INCRA was regularizing several farms that had been invaded. Most of the farmers in this region did not have legitimate title but had been on the land for over 10 years. Typically only a small fraction of the land on each farm had been cleared of forest. INCRA regularized all the farms that had been invaded. Each farmer was allowed to purchase the cleared area plus 1.5 times that amount. The squatters were settled on the remaining land or moved to other land if not enough remained. The farmers viewed this process favorably, as long as the price of the land was reasonable, because it not only allowed them to finally get title but it solved their problems with the squatters.

In order to understand the motivation of INCRA in land settlement, titling, and land reform, it is necessary to look at the interests of the president. Land reform in Brazil has always been seen as a duty of the president, who determines the specific program to be followed and goals to be achieved. More importantly, the president influences the conditions that determine INCRA's likely success. The most critical instruments controlled by the president are (1) the size of INCRA's budget; (2) the head of the agency; and (3) his personal political support of the agency.

Table 4 shows INCRA's budget. Most notable is the increase in resources since 1994.[6] Additionally, there has been considerable turnover within the agency since the end of the military regime. There were 4 different heads in the first two years of the Fernando Henrique Cardoso administration and more than 19 from 1990 to 1996.[7] Whenever INCRA appears not to be meeting the president's goals and a land reform issue embarrasses the president, the head is replaced. Finally, the president's political support for INCRA is not easily measurable, but a dramatic example of a change in support was the creation, abolition, and recreation of the Ministry of Land Reform in 1985 through 1996 after two episodes of fatal violence over land that occurred in Rondônia and Pará. In both instances INCRA remained the executor of land redistribution, but the new minister of land reform provided the direction and performed the important political tasks of pushing the program forward. Before the creation of the Ministry of Land Reform in 1996, INCRA was under the jurisdiction of the Ministry of Agriculture. This ministry typically had been sympathetic to large landowners and thus provided, at best, only weak political support for INCRA's efforts. By creating a Ministry of Land Reform, President Cardoso signaled his commitment to redistribution and his goal of settling 280,000 families from 1994 to 1998 (see table 4). In contrast, the Collor administration (1990) was an example of a lack of political support for INCRA. Collor reduced the staff of INCRA by 50 percent as part of an overall program to cut the number of civil servants.

Landless Peasants and Settlement Projects

The high levels of land concentration in Brazil has always meant a large contingent of landless peasants. The modernization of agriculture and the congestion of the large cities have resulted in an increase in landlessness. In 1996 the MST estimated at least five million families fit this category. They were defined as rural wage workers, day laborers in agriculture, sharecroppers and renters, owners of properties of less than five hectares, and sons and daughters of families that owned less than 30 hectares.[8] The number of landless peasants includes families residing on invaded sites.

Table 5 shows the number of families directly involved in invasions from 1991 to 1995. This is the most visible part of the five million landless, and they are the most likely beneficiaries of land reform. The fate of those who invade also has a strong demonstration effect that can lead to further invasions of private land.

Beginning in the 1970s and 1980s, squatters invaded idle or unproductive privately owned farms and managed to convince INCRA to expropriate the land in their favor. However, it was only during the first half of the 1990s that organized groups of landless peasants adopted the strategy of using invasions as part of a large-scale, coordinated offensive to obtain land and to force INCRA to be more active in their behalf. The most important group of landless peasants is the MST, formed in 1984 from groups who had occupied farms in southern Brazil. The MST had been the driving force behind the revival of land reform in Brazil in the 1990s. As the MST became more organized, it became increasingly successful in converting occupations into actual expropriations. By 1996 the union was organized in 22 of the 26 states in the country and claimed to have helped approximately 140,000 peasants obtain land in its 12 years of existence.[9]

Despite the fact that the MST is by far the most important and most visible organization of landless peasants, it is by no means the only one. There are several smaller groups usually confined to certain regions that have adopted tactics similar to those of the MST. Some of these are groups

TABLE 4.   INCRA's Budget and Number of Families Settled

Year	Number of Families Settled	Budget (in millions of US dollars)
1986	12,211	N.A.
1987	32,790	N.A.
1988	23,583	N.A.
1989	13,470	76
1990	2,875	393
1991	14,393	1,209
1992	23,630	323
1993	4,268	368
1994	4,523	443
1995	42,912	1,314
1996	60,000[a]	1,500[b]
1997	80,000[a]	2,600[b]
1998	100,000[a]	N.A.

Note: N.A. = not available
Source: IBDR/IDA 1997, 16.
[a]Targets for the Fernando Henrique Cardoso administration
[b]estimates

of dissidents from the MST, others are organized by local rural worker unions (*sindicatos de trabalhadores rurais*), and others are isolated groups brought together for the invasion of a particular farm. Out of the 198 occupations in Brazil in 1995, the MST organized 89. Although this represents only 45 percent of all invasions, the MST occupations were generally larger than the average since 20,500 (65 percent) of the 31,400 families involved in all occupations were associated with the MST.[10]

The MST is not a political party and is not linked to any party, although it does sympathize and interact with the Labor Party (PT). In different municípios it will seek political support from whatever sources are most promising. Given the MST's high level of organization and ability to mobilize a large number of voters, there have been instances throughout Brazil when local politicians of the most diverse parties, including those on the right, have supported particular farm occupations. This ability to garner local support is only part of the political force behind the MST's influence.

Another part of its influence involves an ability to extract concessions from the federal government by encouraging invasions and conflicts that embarrass public officials by signaling failure in land reform. Apart from the attention raised by land invasions, a wide range of other instruments, such as invasions of public offices, marches, meetings, media appearances by the leaders, and a web page have formed a successful marketing campaign that has kept the issue at the top of the political agenda.

The MST is financed from a wide variety of sources. The peasants who participate in an invasion pay a fee to buy supplies, such as the plastic sheets to make the tents in which they camp. The peasants who have already been settled pay a small part of their production each year to the MST. Those in the process of being settled and who are currently receiving credit from INCRA contribute with 1 or 2 percent of the credit received.

TABLE 5. Number of Occupations and Landless Families Involved

Year	Number of Occupations	Number of Families in Occupations
1991	77	14,720
1992	81	15,538
1993	89	19,092
1994	119	20,516
1995	198	31,400
1996	167[a]	44,647[a]

Source: Comissão Pastoral da Terra (Pastoral Land Commission) and MST as cited in *Folha de São Paulo*, 24 September 1995. 12.

[a]Only the invasions by the MST

In 1996 this was the source of approximately U.S.$4 million of the total estimated U.S.$20 million received by the MST.[11] Each local group also tries to secure support and resources from local politicians and organizations. Additionally, the MST receives donations from a series of foreign organizations, mostly religious groups. The money collected is used to finance invasions, to pay salaries and travel expenses for the leaders and militants who organize the invasions, and to publish their newspaper.

Rather than having a single head, the MST has a dispersed group of 15 leaders, of which only a few make public appearances. This is allegedly done due to the constant risk of being arrested. These leaders follow general guidelines determined by a national coordination committee composed of 65 members from each of the states. The hierarchy consists of state coordinators, state directors, regional division heads, and finally camp coordinators. The camps are the basic form of organization in an invasion. Each camp is managed by approximately seven people. Most of these are local leaders of the group of landless peasants, but the MST will usually send one or more trained militants to help organize the group. Each camp leader has a directive to oversee a different activity: education, food, health, security, production, and conflict negotiation.

The camp is set up in a neutral zone, usually a roadside or an area provided by a sympathizer. This structure allows the group to organize and await the right moment to start the invasion. MST leaders chose the property to be invaded, taking into consideration its tenure and productivity. Naturally the choice is made so as to maximize the chances that the invasion will result in an expropriation and eventually a settlement project.

Another consideration of MST is the location of the farm. The proximity to a local town is an important concern for landless peasants because this determines their ability to produce for the market and the quality of life they will lead. Although there is plenty of remote land that could be occupied with little resistance, especially in the Amazon, this land is not the object of MST invasions or of other well-organized groups. Groups with greater bargaining power, like the MST, are more likely to invade properties that are close to transportation and markets (hence, of higher value).

Squatters may remain camped for a long time before the invasion. Moreover, there will be considerable time after an invasion before events unfold and the squatters learn whether or not an expropriation will occur. Squatters may be evicted by the farmer or by the police immediately after the invasion, or the situation may drag on for years. If evicted, they usually camp once again in a neutral zone to prepare a new invasion, perhaps in the same area. If an expropriation occurs, the farm will be divided into individual plots.

Discipline in the typical MST camps is strict. There is a well-specified daily routine with different tasks for each person. Behavior is monitored and deviations may be punished with expulsion. The children are educated, and all members are indoctrinated with slogans and songs about the MST. Members must obtain permission to leave the camp even for limited periods of time. These strict requirements help ensure that MST invasions are well organized and that the squatters involved are apt to become active farmers rather than land speculators. Of course not all invasions involve such discipline and organization, especially those not organized by the MST. Many persons participate in invasions who have no intention of settling on the land. It appears that paradoxically, invasions with a high likelihood of success result in more subsequent land turnover among squatters.

The initial invasion is not generally accompanied by violence because most invaded farms are not productive and the owner does not live on the land. Violence tends to occur when the owner tries to evict the squatters, either through his own means or with the help of the police (the evictions will be discussed below). A crucial aspect of an invasion is the negotiation and bargaining with INCRA and the farmer. This involves knowing when to leave the farm voluntarily, when to resist, how to publicize the invasion, and how to apply additional pressure, for example, invading an INCRA office or blocking a road. Groups that invade without organization and careful planning have a much lower chance of obtaining the land.[12]

The MST owes much of its success to the knowledge it has acquired of how to play this game. With a large number of invasions occurring throughout the country, it is necessary to know how to lobby for INCRA's attention. Even after an expropriation this remains an important concern. Because the expropriation ends the confrontation with the landowner, INCRA will tend to set that particular settlement project aside to concentrate on other conflicts. In order to obtain the credit and other resources they have been promised, the settlers have to continue pressuring INCRA. Many invasions of INCRA offices have been done with this intent.[13]

The growing number of invasions and conflicts typically have led INCRA and the government to two different reactions. The first has been to step up the pace of land reform, increasing the number of expropriations and settlement projects. The other has been to try to convince the landless peasants, and in particular the MST, to cease invasions. This is done both by threatening them with the law, because invasions are a criminal act, and by negotiating. The problem with a hard-line approach is that landless peasants are typically very poor and have little to lose, so there is little to threaten them with but force. However, precisely because they are among the poorest classes in society, public opinion legitimates their movement, and it becomes politically sensitive to deal with them harshly. Negotiations, on the other hand, have not led to a reduction in the number of invasions.

The MST has a clear notion that the reason the government is dealing with them and meeting many of their demands is precisely because the invasions cause the government political discomfort. Thus they have never accepted government proposals to settle thousands of families in exchange for a period of truce with no invasions. As one of the MST leaders stated in an interview, occupations are "the only way to make the government, which seems like a paralyzed turtle, act."[14]

Once a farm has been expropriated, INCRA implements a settlement project. INCRA divides the area into plots and assigns them to specific families. INCRA, the local city or county government, and other federal and state agencies may construct some infrastructure, such as roads, dams, a school, and a health post. The settlers receive two types of credit. The first, meant to help them get established, is divided into credit for food during the first three to six months, credit for purchasing tools and equipment for six months, and credit for housing in a lump sum worth approximately U.S.$1,800 in 1995 (Tribunal de Contas da União 1996, 59). The second type comes from PROCERA (Special Program for Land Reform Credit), which is funded both from INCRA's budget and by resources earmarked by law from several constitutional funds. This credit is highly subsidized, with a fixed interest rate. In 1995 the nominal rate was 12 percent per year, on which a 50 percent discount was given, so that the actual rate charged was 6 percent. The interest rate is usually below the level of inflation. The total amount of PROCERA credit given in 1995 was U.S.$106.5 million, which benefited 34,489 families, with the maximum amount per family at U.S.$7,500 (Tribunal de Contas da União 1996, 60–61). These resources are subject to political and bureaucratic delays— thus the need for settlers to remain organized even during this phase.

With land expropriated and demarcated, INCRA is to provide settlers with provisional titles or licenses to occupy that serve to document property rights while a definitive title is being prepared. In practice INCRA may delay providing provisional titles and take several years or more to distribute definitive titles. The settlers' property rights are secure with the provisional titles, but they cannot receive credit from banks. Since they receive credit from INCRA, this may not be a significant problem in the initial phases.

Table 3 indicates very high levels of squatting in the Amazon region over time, even though INCRA has been active in settlements and expropriation. This evidence suggests that INCRA may be very tardy in providing titles. Our survey results support this conjecture. In chapter 9 we explore why it might be in INCRA's interest not to provide titles.

According to Law No. 8629 of 1993, which complements the constitution, the beneficiaries of settlement projects cannot sell the land they receive for 10 years. In fact, this restriction is not observed, and there is an intense turnover of plots, a process that we have observed in our surveys in the Amazon. This phenomenon was observed early, beginning with the colonization projects of the 1970s as well as with spontaneous settlements on public land. Even without an official property right document, settlers frequently bought and sold plots of land. Squatters on public land sell their right to be granted the land, and squatters on private land sell their rights to be compensated for any improvements made in case they are evicted by the owner. Most land reform plans speak of "fixing the worker" to the land; however, squatters and settlers tend to move around considerably, buying and selling land, before settling down for good (as will be further explored in chap. 5).

To illustrate the level of turnover of small rural properties, consider the results from surveys conducted on two sites: one in late 1992 and a follow-up in early 1993 in Colônia Reunidas (a land reform settlement) and Colônia Nova Aliança (an invaded site), both in Pará. In the six-month period between the two surveys, 15 percent of the settlers in Colônia Reunidas and 32 percent in Colônia Nova Aliança sold their plots. A much-quoted study of settlement projects by the FAO and INCRA cites the high rate of turnover of the settlers as one of the greatest problems to be overcome if land settlement and reform is to result in permanent small farms (FAO/UNDP/MARA 1992). In the projects located in the Amazon, the number of original settlers was often less than 50 percent of the current occupants after only a few years. In some cases settlers were unable to make a living on the land and decided to move elsewhere. In other cases, however, the settlers sold because others arrived in the community after clearing and improvements had occurred and were willing to pay more for the land. It appears that higher-quality land and closeness to towns increases the likelihood that the original squatters will sell their plots and move elsewhere.

We visited a settlement project 15 miles from the town of Parauapebas in the state of Pará in 1996. It was being implemented on a recently expropriated farm of 12,000 hectares. Two hundred forty-eight families camped in a central area waiting for INCRA to demarcate and allocate the plots. Because of its desirable location, an active market developed even before the plots had been assigned. We learned that some of the families in the project already owned property in town and that other claimants were just fronts financed to stay in the project to receive the property rights to a plot. INCRA had provided credit, allowing some of the settlers to build houses. Public opinion in town about these sales was mixed. Some people felt that it was unjust to reward invaders who had violated the law while other landless peasants in the area who obeyed the law received nothing. Clearly, however, the lesson for the uncompensated landless was *to invade another farm in order to claim similar benefits.*

Many of the landowners interviewed mentioned that they no longer received any credit assistance from the government and were going through hard times, whereas for squatters there was help from the government. Some of the farmers noted that they were benefiting indirectly because they owned most of the businesses in town where the squatters purchased goods and supplies with their credit. All indications are that this settlement project will follow the path of many other projects with a consolidation of the plots into the hands of a smaller number of owners. The Colônia Reunidas project in Paragominas, which we surveyed in 1993, was also located close to town and was already at an advanced stage of this process, with most of the original settlers having sold to larger farmers and business owners.

The fact that much of the land in settlement projects where conditions are good tends to end up in the hands of prosperous townspeople casts doubt on the wisdom of sticking with the current model of land reform.[15] The cost of settling one family in 1995, including land, improvements, infrastructure, services, and credit, was estimated at U.S.\$30,000.[16] Although this is less than the estimated U.S.\$40,000 it takes to create a job in the service sector or the U.S.\$80,000 in industry, it still implies that settling 2.5 million landless families would require some U.S.\$75 billion.[17] This huge investment will not be politically sustainable if the land subsequently is transferred back to larger holders.

Landowners and Unproductive Properties

The law that governs the process of expropriation clearly states that productive land cannot be subject to expropriation. Standards for productivity vary but in general are not very high. In the Amazon region simply clearing the forest is considered productive use. Even in the rest of Brazil, a farm that is even partially put into cultivation is normally safe from expropriation. In practice, the standard for what is productive has not been much of an issue because there are plenty of properties that are unquestionably unproductive.

Table 6 shows that of the 370 million hectares in farms in 1985, 285 million hectares (77 percent) were latifundia, defined as not productive according to INCRA's criteria and thus subject to expropriation. A question that naturally arises is, why have landowners in Brazil held onto land and not put it to use?

A frequent explanation has been that land bestows political power and hence is valuable, even if not put into production due to poor soil or high transportation costs.[18] Although this claim may have had some validity for the past, the political power of the landed elite has declined significantly with the rise of business and industry in Brazil. A more likely explanation for holding unproductive land is that real assets, like land, are a good hedges in economies experiencing high rates of inflation.[19]

Brandão (1992), in an analysis of land prices from 1966 to 1984, shows that land was an attractive investment compared to other assets, particularly during the 1970s. A study by the Getúlio Vargas Foundation found that in the more recent period from 1985 to 1995, however, land declined in value.[20] The drop in land values was sharpest after the stabilization of the economy in 1994. The decline in land prices was also caused by other factors, including conflict over ownership, reforms that weakened the security of property rights, high interest rates, and scarcity of rural credit.

Rural credit in particular has been one of the main determinants of land prices (Brandão 1992; Rezende 1982). During the 1970s the government increased dramatically the amount of subsidized rural credit (Monteiro 1995, 14). As a result land prices rose sharply. During the 1980s the government allocated less for rural credit and also indexed the interest rates, yet rural credit remained attractive to many because they anticipated little or no enforcement of the debt obligation. In 1996 the overdue rural credit debt in the Banco do Brasil was approximately U.S.$10.2 billion, 69 percent of which belonged to owners of large properties.[21] In addition

TABLE 6.   Land Area and Use in Brazil

Land Category	Million Hectares
Total area of Brazil	850
Area registered by INCRA	600
Public land	250
Area in farms	370
Area in Latifundia	285
Properties above 100 thousand hectares (265)	32.5

Source: INCRA and IBGE 1996, as cited in the MST Home page, <http://www.sanet.com.br~semterra/situacao.htm> 15 March 1997.

there were several other subsidies to landowners, such as the SUDAM and Superintendency for Development of the Northeast (SUDENE) programs that gave fiscal incentives for firms and individuals to set up farms and ranches in the North and the Northeast respectively. Naturally, these subsidies were capitalized into the value of the land, raising prices above the level justified by the land's agricultural return. With the sharp rise in interest rates since 1994, as one of the instruments of the macro stabilization program, and with the removal of most forms of subsidies, rural credit has become tremendously expensive. No doubt this has contributed significantly to the recent fall in land prices.

The link between subsidized rural credit and the prevalence of unproductive land can be seen by looking at an extreme example: the abuse of the SUDAM program by firms and farmers who set up "ghost" ranches in the Amazon as a means to receive the subsidies (Gasques and Yokomizo 1986; Tendrih 1989). The program gave incentives for firms and individuals to propose agricultural and ranching projects in order to receive subsidies. At the same time, there was little or no incentive to establish a bona fide operation, particularly in remote frontier areas where transportation and production costs were high. To a lesser degree, the same process occurred wherever there was subsidized credit. It seems likely that the rural credit was totally or partially diverted to nonfarm uses that were more profitable than agriculture—thus the prevalence of so much idle land. We anticipate that as rural credit in Brazil in the late 1990s declines, the stock of unproductive properties will also decline.

Another important factor in the propensity to hold unproductive land is the Brazilian land tax, know as ITR (rural territorial tax), which has been systematically evaded by most landowners. The government conceived the land tax as a major instrument for land reform in the Land Statute of 1964, complementary to the use of expropriations. Despite several changes in its rules, the ITR never managed to achieve its purpose. During some periods the tax rates were set too low, and during others the value of the land used to calculate the tax was notoriously underestimated because value was declared by the owner. Even when these problems were solved, many landowners simply did not pay the tax. Curbing evasion was difficult politically and logistically. While only 32 percent of the landowners with properties up to 100 hectares in size evaded the ITR in 1995, 74 percent of those with properties from 1,000 to 50,000 hectares evaded the tax, with the number going up to 94 percent for properties from 50,000 to 500,000 hectares.[22] The total amount of money collected through ITR in Brazil in 1995 was slightly less than U.S.$100 million, an amount that represented only 0.03 percent of the federal government's budget revenue and only 0.21 percent of the total amount collected in net taxes (Tribunal de Contas da União 1996, 46).

In December 1996 the Brazilian Congress approved a new land tax law that sharply raised the tax for unproductive properties. The tax rate for unproductive property above 5,000 hectares was set at 20 percent of assessed value. That law provided owners of latifundia with an incentive to either use or sell the land to someone willing to make it productive. One of the purposes of the law is to reduce the price of land and thereby reduce the cost to INCRA of obtaining land for settlement projects. Other articles in the law sought to assure that owners declared the true value of the land for tax purposes. In addition, the law made evasion more difficult.[23] It is still too early to tell if this law will achieve its goals, or if it will simply be a dead letter, as so many of its predecessors have been.

Given the traditional political influence of landowners in Congress, it is significant that such a stringent law was passed. As was noted in the previous chapter, landowners consistently have blocked land reform, but it now appears that the balance of power in the political arena between the groups for and against reform is more equal. The landless have become more organized, while the landowners have become less well organized. The MST and other peasant groups have been able to mobilize votes and funds, whereas the UDR (see chap. 2), founded as a means to defend the landowners' interests in the drafting of the constitution in 1988, no longer existed by the end of 1993. Although still operative, two other landowner organizations, the CNA (National Confederation of Agriculture) and the SBR (Brazilian Rural Society), lost political strength, perhaps due to the deterioration in land values and, hence, ranchers' wealth. This decline was mirrored with diminished effectiveness in Congress of the representatives of the farmers and landowners (*bancada ruralista*) (see Oliveira 1995, 10).

Although declining land values in the 1990s may have helped to reduce the wealth and power of landowners, it is too soon to count them out as a political force, for they may be remobilizing. In 1996 a group of landowners who had been involved in a prolonged and intense dispute with squatters in the state of São Paulo resurrected the UDR.[24] The farmers realized that only by reorganizing politically could they hope to counter the pressure applied by the MST on INCRA, the states' land agencies, the state governments, and public opinion.[25] The origin of the dispute was a court decision in 1985 declaring that a considerable amount of land in the western part of the state was illegally occupied by the existing farmers and hence "public." In addition, many of the farms were considered unproductive by the criteria of the region.

The future of land reform in Brazil will, as it has in the past, depend on the relative political influence of both sides. The landowners are struggling to reorganize and counteract the offensive from the landless peasants. However, high interest rates, limited availability of credit, and low land prices suggest that their resources are limited.

One must recognize that landowners are not homogeneous. Productive farmers are generally members of the CNA and SBR. They produce for the market, both locally and abroad, and are not threatened by land invasions or reform because their property rights are secure. They are concerned instead with general agricultural policy, for example rural credit, interest rates, and exchange rates. Members of the UDR, by contrast, are frequently owners of latifundia and subject to the threat of invasion. This separation of interests across the landowning groups may make it more difficult to regain the level of influence they had in the past.

With the lack of credit, threat of invasions and expropriation, higher land taxes, and flat prices, owning land, especially idle land, has become much less attractive. Many landowners have thus decided to sell,[26] and as a consequence land prices have fallen dramatically. Given the slump in the market, selling land to INCRA has become a more attractive option than before. INCRA is aware that low prices provide a good opportunity to obtain land cheaply for reform.

The willingness of owners to sell also increases the likelihood of corrupt deals with INCRA staff or government officials, in which land is sold to INCRA at above-market prices.[27] The landowner may invite a group of peasants to invade property in order to convince INCRA to purchase it; having a farm invaded may increase the price because INCRA wants to avoid violence and associated publicity. Although the current situation has given increased incentives for corruption, most landowners still consider expropriation undesirable because it typically involves physical and mental distress, a long bureaucratic process of negotiation with INCRA, costly legal proceedings, and below-market compensation.

The Courts, Property Rights to Land, Evictions, and Land Reform

Because of the nature of rural conflicts in Brazil and the historical importance of private property rights, the courts play an important role as arbitrators in land disputes. The judicial branch is involved with conflicts in three different ways: the local courts issue eviction warrants; the federal courts review expropriations contested by landowners; and federal and local courts may determine whether criminal acts have occurred during conflicts over land.

In the 1970s and 1980s many invasions occurred without opposition by the landowner. In some instances the owner was unaware of the presence of squatters. More typically, owners ignored squatters' presence and evicted them only when land prices increased.

Landowners generally initiate evictions with a mixture of threats and offers of compensation for improvements. In some cases owners have hired gunmen to "clean" the area. In the 1990s with the increase of the number of invasions on farms closer to towns, landowners responded with efforts to evict as soon as the invasion occurred. Because these farms were adjacent to markets, they were more valuable and generally occupied by the owner, who was well aware of any squatter activity. Further, recent invasions organized by MST have been covered by the news media in order to pressure INCRA to act. Accordingly, the owners have been made all too familiar with these situations.

Instead of removing squatters privately, landowners can go to the local court and request a warrant to have the squatters evicted by police. Judges issue a warrant, called a "reintegration of possession" (*reintegração de posse*), when property (not just land) is taken. The purpose of this judicial instrument in the Civil Code is to protect property rights and to prevent damages that may be difficult to remedy if a solution has to await regular judicial proceedings (Dutra 1992, 132).

The landowner must pay a fee and incur the expenses of a lawyer to obtain a reintegration of possession. Landowners in Parauapebas in Pará in 1996 told us that the average expense of obtaining a reintegration of possession was approximately U.S.$5,000. Hence, landowners will take such action only if the land is valuable enough to warrant resisting squatter occupation and potential expropriation.

Reintegration of possessions are an important part of rural conflicts because police eviction of squatters to implement the court's ruling is when violence frequently occurs. Many times squatters leave peacefully when evicted (often to return later), but in other cases they resist. It is common for the farmer to hire additional hands to assist in the eviction, because the police are generally ill equipped and underpaid.

Upon receiving a request for a reintegration of possession, a judge follows the procedure in the Civil Code that is the basis of Brazilian statutory law. Formally, a request for a reintegration of possession involves only the question of an individual's property being taken by another; it is not seen as a question of land reform or of social justice.

As discussed above, the Brazilian constitution only guarantees the property rights to land if that land fulfills its social function—is productive. Invaded farms are typically not productive. The local judge, however, does not take these issues into consideration when a reintegration of possession is requested. The issue of whether the farm may be expropriated is beyond the court's jurisdiction. Only INCRA can propose an expropriation, although the courts may become involved subsequently in determining whether or not INCRA's actions are justified.

Several authors and policymakers suggest that the local courts should be made to view a reintegration of possession as an integral part of a larger social issue instead of a simple question of formal property rights (see Dutra 1992; Fachin 1991; Pinheiro 1992). It is alleged that if judges refused to grant a warrant to properties that were not in beneficial use, then the number of squatter evictions by landowners, and hence the amount of violence, would fall dramatically. A law that would force judges to consider land use before granting a warrant for eviction was sent to Congress in 1996, but it was not voted on (Rothenburg, Lima, and Gugliano 1996). The notion was that if judges were required to consider squatter claims, they might not issue eviction orders. At a minimum, the proponents reasoned that allowing more judicial discretion would slow the eviction process and possibly lead to less violence.

Oliveira (1991, 4) has gone further and suggested that the judiciary should take over the task of expropriation, with judges expropriating unproductive properties. In some cases, judges have refused to grant a reintegration of possession when they fear that there is imminent danger of violence. But, the typical scenario is for judges to issue warrants upon request when property is invaded. It is not the case, as some have reasoned, that judges have been captured by landowners. Judges in Brazil tend to be politically insulated because they are selected on the basis of a public entry exam open to all suitably qualified individuals, and they hold their office for life.

Although reintegrations of possession are issued by local courts, the *federal* judicial branch gets involved in rural conflicts when a landowner contests an expropriation by INCRA. Approximately 95 percent of expropriations are contested by landowners.[28] Landowners can either argue that the farms fulfill their social function, and thus could not be legally expropriated, or that the price offered by INCRA is too low. Another legal tactic is for lawyers to claim that the inspection by INCRA was not done properly, or that the notification of the expropriation was not handed directly to the owner of the land, which invalidates the whole process. The lawyers who specialize in this type of suit have been extremely successful.[29]

It is common for the courts to uphold an expropriation, but also common to reset the price at a higher value. INCRA in turn may appeal the valuation set by the court. As time goes by and INCRA does not compensate the landowner, the cost of the expropriation increases due to late fees, lawyer charges, interest, adjustment for inflation, and compensation for lost profits. Eventually, these costs reach exorbitant levels that are practically unpayable. For example, in 1987 INCRA valued a farm of 7,000 hectares in the state of São Paulo at U.S.$900,000. By 1996 INCRA owed the owner of that farm U.S.$385 million, which it will naturally never be able to pay.[30] In 1997 INCRA owed U.S.$1.063 billion in compensation for 212 farms expropriated in the 1970s and 1980s.[31]

Judicial wrangling over expropriated farms can take years, and this process restricts dramatically the ability of INCRA to obtain land for settlement projects. These delays may change with the *rito sumário* law passed in 1996. Under this law INCRA must receive the land 48 hours after an expropriation, although landowners can still contest the proposed compensation.

Courts may also get involved through criminal proceedings that emanate from violence. If a squatter, farmer, policeman, or gunman is killed in a conflict, the case must be investigated by the district or state attorney (Ministério Público) and tried in local courts. The attorney's office is also supposed to try lesser crimes such as threats, disruption of peace, cattle theft, or possession of illegal weapons, but these crimes are often ignored. By its discretion over what it deems criminal, the courts are able to influence the way a conflict unfolds. Accordingly, the position taken by the local court will be an important variable in the model of rural conflict presented in chapter 8.

The news media, many academics, INCRA, and the Ministry for Land Reform view the courts as largely responsible for rural conflict because of their supposed negligence in prosecuting landowners accused of crimes.[32] These groups argue that the failure to prosecute fosters more violence in other conflicts. Indeed, while there were 1,630 deaths associated with land conflicts over the period 1964 to 1990, courts heard only 24 cases involving 36 deaths, and only half resulted in a conviction (Comissão Pastoral da Terra 1990, 33–34). Even in the internationally publicized murder of Chico Mendes the case took over two years and the two men charged eventually escaped from jail. With the increased attention on land reform in the mid-1990s, the performance of the courts should improve, but, with the escalation of land invasions, the courts will be overwhelmed. Some scholars advocate the establishment of an exclusive set of courts (*justiça agrária*), with judges specialized in agrarian law, as a means to ameliorate rural conflicts.[33]

New Models of Land Reform

In this section we will briefly describe how the current formal and informal institutions discussed above influence land conflicts. We will then turn to proposed solutions to the problem of land reform. In short, an inconsistent set of property rights for owners and squatters causes land conflict in the Brazilian Amazon. The existing laws do not clearly assign and enforce the property rights of either party, and as a result there is dissipation of land rents through physical violence and legal disputes.

The government and INCRA must be aware that by responding to invasions by expropriating land and settling squatters, they provide incentives for more invasions. It must be clear that by increasing expropriations, they encourage further invasions because of the large number of peasants who desire land. Nevertheless, so long as the performance of INCRA continues to be measured by the number of farms expropriated and number of families immediately settled, it is politically rational for the agency to retain its current policy despite a recognition that it is counterproductive.

The problem with following the current, politically imposed path is the risk that conflicts will get out of hand. Aware of this, the federal government has been looking for alternative models of land reform, that is, new ways to deal with the problem of excessive concentration of ownership and landless peasants. Although currently the government is politically constrained from switching to a completely new approach, it has been adopting new policies on a experimental basis or as a complement to the main land reform instruments.

One important change that could dramatically affect the future of land reform in Brazil is the new rural land tax law passed in 1996, which, as we have indicated, raised the tax rate for large, unproductive farms to 20 percent of the value of the land per year and was accompanied by a promise of strict enforcement. In principle, a well-structured land tax should be sufficient to reduce excessive land concentration, although in the past it has been logistically and politically very difficult to enforce and to collect the tax. The poor performance of the tax historically accounts for the suspicion with which many proreform activists view attempts at reform through fiscal instruments. They do not oppose the tax but insist that it is not a substitute for expropriations as the main instrument of land reform. Potentially, the tax can increase the supply of land for redistribution by making it less attractive to hold idle land, as well as by increasing the financial resources available to INCRA for expropriations.

As an alternative to expropriations, INCRA has instituted a pilot program, financed and assisted by the World Bank, through which community associations of landless peasants, or peasants with too little land, are financed to purchase land.[34] Rather than INCRA going through contentious expropriation procedures and paternalistically implementing a settlement project, an organized group of peasants presents a project to INCRA. The peasants select a farm and negotiate its purchase directly with a landowner. Once the land is purchased, the new owners decide on the internal allocation of land and payment obligations. INCRA and the state agencies finance, advise, and monitor the final negotiations. The difference between this market-assisted approach and conventional land reform is that it is designed to give the peasants an incentive to be efficient and cost-effective because the loans have to be repaid. Further, these projects could avoid the long delays associated with expropriations because only willing landowners would be involved. Although this project is still an experiment that may run into many difficulties, it does try to avoid some of the main problems inherent in the current approach.

Another alternative for the problem of landless peasants would be to foster the use of renting and sharecropping contracts. Most approaches to land reform have focused on redistributive solutions where in one way or another landless families come to own a plot of land.[35] But it is not the case that landless peasants must become a landowners in order to improve their standard of living. If land can be rented at a reasonable price and under reasonable conditions, including credit, technical assistance, and other necessary inputs, a landless family can prosper along with the landowner.

Unfortunately, the current set of laws in Brazil make share contracts and other rental contracts highly risky for the landowners because such contracts can be a cause for expropriations.[36] To encourage landowners of currently idle land to rent it to the landless, the laws must be changed so as to specify and enforce the property rights of the landowner in a clear and transparent manner. The advantage of rental arrangements is that they could quickly match large numbers of landless peasants with land.

Concluding Remarks

This chapter completes our summary of land distribution and land reform policies, federal agencies, and political constituencies in Brazil. It is important to understand them because they provide the institutional setting through which property rights to land are assigned or competed for on the Amazon frontier.

Before proceeding to an analysis of frontier settlement, we turn to one additional land agency, ITERPA, the state land agency in Pará. ITERPA has jurisdiction over all state government lands open to private claiming in Pará. As such, it can initiate colonization projects and grant titles, but it cannot expropriate farms, a mandate left only to INCRA. ITERPA (Land Institute of Pará) was created in 1975 to allocate state lands to private claimants as the frontier moved across Pará. Further, in the mid-1970s there were conflicting private claims to land in Pará, and as land values rose with acceleration of Operation Amazônia and the start of PIN (Program of National Integration), these conflicts became more intense. Part of ITERPA's mission was to resolve local disputes and clarify property rights to land under state jurisdiction (IDESP 1986).

ITERPA's major function, however, is to transfer and title rural plots of less than 100 hectares. Most of the titling of small plots is done in colonization or settlement projects (IDESP 1986). In Parauapebas, for example, where we conducted some of our surveys, ITERPA was promising the farmers' union that it would send a crew to title the approximately 700 settlers in Colônia Jader Barbalho, a colony it had created in 1988. Lobbying in a manner similar to that observed for INCRA, the farmer's union of Parauapebas has been pressuring ITERPA to proceed with the titling for several years so that the settlers could apply for credit from the Bank of Amazônia (BASA). Like INCRA, ITERPA has been chronically underfunded in the 1990s and therefore less able to respond to titling demands. In August 1997 the farmers' union informed us that they were optimistic that titles would be given next year since it would be an election year and the distribution of titles by the governor is a typical form of campaigning in Brazil. The same is true of the donation of plots. As we describe in chapter 6, ITERPA seems to be more responsive to local political pressures than is INCRA. This seems understandable since INCRA is more remote, headquartered in Brasília, and is a federal agency, subject to many different constituents.

Because ITERPA is a state agency and its president and budget are controlled by the governor, it is natural that the agency is used politically, being subject to capture by several different interest groups. Although the local INCRA offices in each state are also subject to the same kind of pressure, they are more insulated since they must respond to the central INCRA office in Brasília, which, as was argued above, has the mandate of actually promoting land reform and resolving most land-related problems on federal lands.

Another main function of ITERPA is the sale of state land. The process starts when a potential buyer requests the purchase of public land in the state's domain. The buyer must describe the economic use that is planned for the land, including environmental aspects. ITERPA will certify that the land is actually unoccupied and not claimed by anyone else. The maximum that can be sold is 3,000 hectares, although in practice buyers have often purchased contiguous plots totaling more than 3,000 hectares under different names or using fronts. The buyer receives a provisional title as soon as the project is approved and a definitive title after at least half of the project is implemented and the land paid for. In practice these steps are not always followed. ITERPA tends not to monitor projects closely, and sales are made with little control since the state often needs the money. It is also clear that political influence affects sales (Silva 1987, 8).

During the 1970s there were jurisdictional conflicts between ITERPA and INCRA, with each agency claiming desirable areas and pushing problematic areas to the other's responsibility (Pinto 1980). During the 1980s, as INCRA moved from colonization to land reform, these jurisdictional conflicts became less prevalent. In 1987 the jurisdiction of most of the land in Pará was returned to the state, and INCRA limited itself to areas where it had already started colonization or settlement projects, plus all areas where it decided to implement land reform. ITERPA has been very slow in assuming the functions performed previously by INCRA (Éleres 1996).

It is clear from the summaries of land reform agencies and practices in Brazil that the process of obtaining and enforcing property rights to land on the frontier is a complex one. It not only involves settlement and claiming land, but issues of potential redistribution. We now turn to analyses of who the frontier migrants are, the contribution of clear property rights (through title) to land value and investment, the political provision of property rights, and the problems inherent with controversial distributional issues.

NOTES

1. For discussion of INCRA's colonization effort see Moran 1975, 1981; Ianni 1979; Foweraker 1981.

2. The Supreme Court annulled several expropriations in 1996 because the owner was not personally notified that a visit would occur (*Folha de São Paulo,* August 1, 1996, 6). A landowner can thus avoid an expropriation by not being found by the person delivering the notification. This requirement illustrates the complexity of the judicial rules involved.

3. From May to August 1996, 134 expropriation decrees were signed, and there were no *imissões de posse* (*Folha de São Paulo,* August 29, 1996, 9).

4. This has led to much confusion as to the government's claims regarding its accomplishments. In 1995 the government claimed to have settled over 42,000 families; the MST stated that the real number was around 12,000 families. Clearly each side has a different definition of what is a settled family.

5. In the state of Pará, for example, from 1961 to 1967 thousands of irregular titles were issued by the state government, covering over 3 million hectares of land, without surveys or demarcation. This created many problems a decade later when the value of land started to rise and the original claimants appeared (Pinto 1980, 123–25).

6. The size of the budget is not necessarily a reliable indication of the commit-

ment toward land reform. The workings of the federal budget in Brazil are very complex and understood by few. For example, INCRA's budget has in the past been used by congressmen as a means to distribute pork to their constituencies, as we learned in conversation with INCRA staff in Brasília. The construction of a road or a bridge can be claimed to be necessary for a settlement project and included in INCRA's budget.

7. *Veja,* April 24, 1996, 40–43.

8. *Folha de São Paulo,* April 22, 1996, 7.

9. MST homepage <http://www.sanet.com.br>, March 15, 1997.

10. *Folha de São Paulo,* September 24, 1995, 12.

11. *Folha de São Paulo,* March 9, 1997, at <http://www.uol.com.br/fsp/brasil>. Having its own homepage indicates the sophistication of the MST.

12. This claim was expressed to us by both INCRA staff in Pará and leaders of the local rural worker *sindicatos* in Marabá.

13. See, for example, *Jornal do Brasil,* December 19, 1996, at <http://www.jb.com.br/08950520.html>.

14. *O Globo* (Rio de Janeiro), October 1995, 12.

15. In part, the issue depends on the objective of land reform. Whether or not settlers sell their plots, their wealth increases. But most policymakers believe a successful land reform entails the settlers remaining on their plots.

16. INCRA 1995, cited in <http://www.sanet.com.br/~semterra/custo.htm>.

17. Statistics from *Veja,* April 24, 1997, 40–43.

18. For example, Abramovay (1985a, 17) states that in Brazil "land is an essential piece, one of the bases of conservative power."

19. Monteiro and Amin 1994, 24; *Veja,* April 24, 1996, 40–43.

20. Quoted in *Veja,* August 14, 1996, 81.

21. *Veja,* August 14, 1996, 82.

22. *Veja,* August 14, 1996, 82.

23. *Jornal do Brasil,* December 19, 1996, at <http:www.jb.com.br/brasil.html#Congresso>.

24. The region under dispute is known as the Pontal do Paranpanema and has been one of the most tense regions in terms of rural conflicts in the 1990s, together with the south of Pará.

25. Farmers and landowners in other states have followed suit and established offices of the UDR. See *Folha de São Paulo,* January 31, 1997, at <http://www.uol.com.br/fsp/brasil/fc310124.htm>.

26. *Agroanalysis,* January 1977, 18–22.

27. *Folha de São Paulo,* February 3, 1997, at <http://www.uol.com.br/fsp/brasil/fc030220.htm>.

28. *Veja,* August 14, 1997, 80–83.

29. See *Folha de São Paulo,* November 27, 1995, 9, for an interview with a famous lawyer specializing in expropriation cases.

30. *Veja,* August 14, 1996, 83; and *Folha de São Paulo,* October 3, 1995, 12.

31. *Folha de São Paulo,* January 20, 1997, at <http://www.uol.com.br/fsp/brasil/fc200112.htm>.

32. See any of the yearly publications by the Pastoral Land Commission, which monitors land conflicts in Brazil. See also Pinheiro 1992 for the report of a Congressional Inquiry Commission's report on the causes of rural violence in Brazil.

33. In February 1997 the minister of land reform stated that "ending impunity is an attribution constitutionally delegated to the states" (quoted in Gondim and Salomon 1997, 6). For the minister and INCRA this mudslinging may be seen as an attempt to absolve themselves of blame. For the views of academics and the media, see Rothenburg, Lima, and Gugliano 1996, 3; and Pinheiro 1992.

34. For the project appraisal report see IBRD/IDA 1997.

35. The minister of land reform did mention the intention to pass a rural land renting law in an interview in 1996 (speech at the Universidade de Brasília July 11, 1996). However, as this has less political impact than other redistributive methods, little has been done.

36. In 1985 when the PNRA (see chap. 2) was announced, there was a wave of eviction of renters and sharecroppers by landowners who feared losing their land to the peasants on their land.

CHAPTER 4

A Framework for Analyzing Settlement, Property Rights, and Violence on the Brazilian Amazon Frontier

In the previous two chapters, we discussed the history of land policy and the Brazilian government's role in promoting land settlement as an integral part of land reform. Both actions directly affect the assignment and enforcement of property rights to land. Settlement policies include tenure provisions, and how they are implemented and enforced determines the allocation of property rights on the frontier. Land reform policies, especially expropriations, may weaken property rights, depending on how reform occurs.

Land reform can be viewed broadly as any policy that promotes the acquisition of land by the landless. Land reform policies include expropriation, colonization, and titling. Expropriation entails the partially compensated taking of land from the landowners and giving it to the landless. Colonization is the subsidized migration and settlement of landless. Titling represents the formal recognition of ownership by the government through the provision of court-enforceable documents. In the past 30 years the government has been active on all three fronts, although the emphasis has changed over time as political pressures have shifted.

In the initial development phase of the Amazon—the mid-1960s through the 1970s—the government relied primarily on extensive settlement through colonization projects on frontiers as a reform policy. The data on land occupation by squatters that we presented in chapter 2, however, suggests that the government has not uniformly provided titles to those who have settled in the Amazon. Recall that table 3 revealed that the North (Amazon) has consistently had higher levels of squatting than other regions of Brazil. The high percentages of farms and farmland occupied by squatters (those without title) through 1985 indicates that the Amazon has not been titled as routinely as elsewhere (even when other regions were frontiers). We return to this issue later in the volume. Recently, the government has placed less emphasis on recruiting settlers for colonies in the

Amazon and turned to an active expropriation policy on both frontier and more settled regions as a means of providing land to smallholders.

This book is primarily concerned with the demand for property rights to land on the frontier and the supply of those property rights, first through informal means and then through the political process. Land reform policies complicate the provision of formal property rights because they affect demand and supply. That is, demand for formal property rights through title is reduced if property rights are attenuated through beneficial-use requirements to maintain ownership, and through the threat of expropriation. The advantages of secure title in promoting land exchange, investment, and in reducing enforcement costs may be diminished. Further, aggressive land reform affects the political supply of titles.

As we show, some legal institutions, such as the courts, are charged with enforcing titles and contracts. Other institutions, such as INCRA, are charged with both providing titles to small claimants to federal government frontier lands and with implementing land redistribution policies. These two mandates are not always reinforcing, so that the agency often has a schizophrenic mission—providing titles on the one hand and contesting ownership on the other. Land reform injects destabilizing factors and additional elements of risk into the demand for land and provision of secure property rights to it. This institutional confusion contributes to broader splits between civil and constitutional law regarding the sanctity of property rights on the Brazilian Amazon frontier.

This said, however, given the skewed land and wealth distributions in Brazil and the social tensions that they engender, arguments can be made for land reform. A more equal distribution of landholdings indeed may make property rights more secure by making the allocation of property rights appear more just and legitimate. The key point is that distributional concerns should be addressed in a manner that maintains the sanctity of property rights and title if they are to play their beneficial roles in promoting wise land use and economic development. We return now to issues of the initial assignment of property rights on the frontier, rights that subsequently may be at risk due to land reform.

In this chapter we expand the framework outlined in chapter 1 for sequential development and the demand for titles. Sequential development characterizes much of the development of the Amazon and is relatively conflict-free. Our framework enables us to predict the characteristics of settlers and the process of turnover as the frontier develops. We will discuss the factors that underlie the demand for titles and the impact of title on land investment and land values. We conclude with discussion of the institutional environment underlying land conflicts.

Settlement and Property Rights

The Brazilian Amazon is still a frontier: population densities are low; the majority of the land is forested; transportation costs from rural to urban areas are high; many of the land claimants do not have title; and conflicts over land, while not ubiquitous, are frequent and at times deadly. In this chapter we develop an analytical framework to help us understand and test hypotheses concerning settlement of the frontier, the demand and supply for property rights, and the causes and consequences of land conflicts.

One defining characteristic of frontier regions is that most people engage in either producing agricultural goods or extracting resources such as timber or minerals. The result is that land is the most important asset in frontier areas. Another feature of frontiers is that transportation costs to developed markets are high. As such, distance to markets will be a primary determinant of the net profitability of economic activities and hence, settlement. We capture this feature in figure 4, panel A by plotting the value of (homogeneous) land—net of private enforcement costs—and distance from market.

In panel A, the value of land (titled or untitled) declines with distance to markets. At any given distance from a market the value of land varies depending on its innate characteristics, such as the fertility of the soil, the richness of its minerals, or the quality of its timber. The fact that land values decline with distance from markets has some implications for settlement. First, at a sufficiently remote distance from markets, transportation costs are so high that economic activity is not feasible. Second, settlers who migrate to the frontier will be endowed with relatively little human and physical capital. In short, migrants to the frontier will have low opportunity costs, though settlers need some wealth to cover moving expenses and living expenses until crops come in. The prediction is thus that settlers further from the market will be younger and have less education and less wealth than settlers closer to markets.

In addition to the innate characteristics of land, the value of land to individuals also depends on the security of the rights that individuals have to it. As long as there are potential claimants to land, the value of land to individual claimants will increase with more secure formal property rights as provided by a title to the land. As explained in chapter 1, titles increase land values by promoting site-specific investment, which is dependent on long-term security of ownership; by serving as collateral to access formal credit markets; by reducing the costs of defending one's land; and by broadening the market for land.

We graph the differential values of titled and nontitled land with line

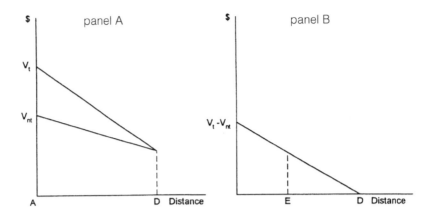

Fig. 4. Distance to market, land value, and the demand for property rights

V_t and line V_{nt}. At point A (the market center, such as Belém), the relative contribution of having a title is greatest. Potentially high-valued, but untitled, land at the market center is subject to more intense competition, raising private enforcement costs and increasing uncertainty of control. These conditions reduce site-specific investment, exchange, and production possibilities that in turn lower land values below what would exist with secure titles to land. By contrast, with titled land, the state assumes most of the enforcement costs, guarantees ownership, and thereby promotes investment, exchange and production. These activities raise land values and shift the value from V_{nt} to $V_{t.}$

Moving from the market center at point A toward the frontier, the contribution of title declines. Though titles also convey value, they are costly to provide. In particular, when population densities are low, the enforcement costs of having a police force to defend property rights will not warrant its existence. Low rental streams from land further from the market implies that there will be less competition over land and therefore lower costs of privately enforcing claims. Indeed, at some point D, the value of land with and without title will be the same. That is, having title adds no additional value to the land.

In the absence of government titles, claimants (by definition called squatters because they have no formal title) still have an incentive to minimize the dissipation of the rental stream that would occur with no rights. In these situations squatters develop a set of informal rights that are generally respected among the squatters, who will band together to defend their rights against outside intrusions. For squatter rights to be recognized, squatters must, in general, mark boundaries, reside on the land, cultivate it or extract minerals, and defend the rights of other claimants if necessary. Among homogeneous claimants, informal rights support limited investment and enable squatters to sell their claims in local markets. Sales transpire with the buyer receiving a receipt from the seller and the transaction witnessed by others.

So far we have discussed settlement across space, but settlement occurs over time as well. With economic development the rental streams from land increase. This could be the result of increases in the prices of the output of land or lowered transportation costs from road building. The higher rental streams will cause in-migration of squatters who have higher opportunity costs and who will buy out the informal rights of the initial settlers. Sales will involve an exchange from lower-valued users to higher-valued users, but markets do not clear instantaneously. As a result, we expect to see more heterogeneity among squatters as one moves closer to markets from the economic frontier.

The initial settlers may opt to sell because, as rental values increase, so too does the value from having a title, and the initial squatters may be at a relative disadvantage in acquiring title compared to the newly arrived squatters. The same low human and physical capital endowments that induced the initial squatters to move to the frontier—illiteracy, limited wealth and political experience—reduce their capabilities to secure formal titles. In addition, new arrivals with more human and physical capital can not only better access capital markets but may also be more aware of the highest-valued use of the land. This pattern of sequential settlement of squatters, with settlers with low opportunity costs selling out to more affluent arrivals, is smooth as long as rental values change slowly, and informal claims are recognized by the new arrivals. The continual settlement of the economic frontier by those with the lowest opportunity costs suggests that there is a life-cycle component to settlement. As squatters acquire assets over their lifetimes, both experience and wealth, they should be increasingly less likely to continue to sell out. This implies that, although there will be "specialists in settlement," they will be life-cycle specific. We will test this hypothesis in the next chapter.

With more market integration—either across space or over time—the demand by squatters for title increases. In figure 4, panel B, we illustrate the individual demand for title. The vertical axis is the difference between the values of titled and nontitled land, that is $V_t - V_{nt}$. This difference reflects the added value of title to the individual claimant at different distances from the market center. Importantly, the position of the curve may differ across individuals. As discussed above, those with more education, farming experience, and wealth likely receive higher added values from title at any distance because of their knowledge or ability to access capital markets.

In addition to the value of titled land declining with distance, most likely the costs to individuals of obtaining title increase with distance from markets. Securing a title entails travel to the administrative center, generally the market town, where individuals record land claims and petition and lobby for titles. Although we do not have information on the exact nature of the individual cost function, there will be a distance at which the expected added benefits from having title are equal to the private expected costs of obtaining title. Beyond that point, individuals will hold their claims as squatters, whereas at distances closer to the market/administrative center, claimants will seek formal title. We represent this threshold distance as point E. The testable hypotheses that emerge are that we should observe a greater likelihood of titles closer to market, and that these are held by individuals whose endowments either increase the benefit from a title or lower their costs of securing title. We present evidence on these hypotheses in chapter 5.

Governments assign and enforce titles. Hence, property rights are political institutions and subject to political and bureaucratic factors that may lead governments to supply titles too soon (before land values warrant) or too late (delay the provision of title even though the added land value offsets the costs of defining property rights). Further, as land reform pressures reveal, political factors affect the enforcement of property rights.

The criteria that governments choose to assign titles and their enforcement of titles influence the demand for title by individuals, shifting the position of the demand curve in panel B. For example, requiring that land be put into beneficial use by squatters, and that squatters reside on the land before titles are assigned, reduces the demand for a title. Similarly, if titles are weakly enforced by the police or courts, the demand for title is less. Alternatively, governments can lower the private costs of obtaining a title. For example, during electoral campaigns politicians have traveled to remote sites and promised titles in exchange for electoral support.

As described in chapter 2, the titling situation in Brazil is complex because state and federal agencies have jurisdiction in different areas. Federal and state agencies face varying budget environments and serve different constituencies. The result is that the cost of acquiring title may differ under federal and state jurisdictions. We expect that state agencies will be more responsive to local demands, but this too may vary with budgets. The governments may also "privatize" part of the titling process by selling large blocks of land to private settlement companies who in turn will subdivide, provide infrastructure, and sell parcels to settlers. Because private companies have a less complex objective function than governments and are direct residual claimants in the added value provided by title, we expect that private companies will title more quickly and effectively than will governments.

Up until now we have discussed primarily the demand for title. But it is important to stress that the demand for titles emanates from the expected effects that title has on investment and land values. Titles decrease the uncertainty about the security of land in the future. Therefore, claimants with title have an incentive to make land-specific investments predicated on the assumption that they will be able to reap the rewards of their investment. In the Brazilian Amazon, land-specific investments include most notably clearing, planting permanent crops, and planting improved pasture. Investments require not only the incentive for investment but the necessary capital. Titles allow those with the incentive to invest the collateral to access formal capital markets and thereby the ability to invest.

Increased investment on land enhances land values, but titles even without investment increase land values. A secure title enforced by government lowers the enforcement costs that individuals otherwise may have to bear. Further, the assurance of government enforcement broadens the market for land and allows potentially higher-valued users to compete for the land and thereby increase land values. We will test for the direct effect of titles on investment and the effect of investment and titles on land values in chapters 6 and 7.

Property Rights and Land Conflict

Titles have value because they are a governmental guarantee of security. This guarantee is not absolute. If it were, there would be no conflict over land once it is titled. Yet, as we have noted, both the assignment and the enforcement of title are political actions. That is, the legal endorsement of a particular allocation of property rights is a political decision, subject to the changing pressures of key interest groups and to court interpretations of property law. Hence the assignment and security of property rights can change over time as political and judicial variables change. These political factors complicate the provision of property rights beyond the resource costs of definition and enforcement.

In principle, the legal rights from having a title in Brazil are similar to the legal rights to title under common law in the United States. That is, subject to paying taxes, title holders have the right "to use, enjoy and dispose of the goods, and *to receive them back from the power of those who unjustly possess them.*[1] Despite these legal guarantees, the politics of land reform that we described in chapters 2 and 3 have resulted in a less secure property rights structure than property law within the Brazilian Civil Code would suggest. As part of land reform, various Brazilian constitutions, including the constitution of 1988, have abrogated the rights of title holders by qualifying their ownership and giving squatters rights through expropriation if the land is not placed in beneficial use.[2] The notion of beneficial use itself is vague and subject to shifting interpretations, depending on political conditions.

In addition to the possibility of obtaining land through squatting, squatters have the right to be compensated for improvements they have made, should they be evicted from private land that they have invaded and occupied. The rationale for these provisions is the reassignment of land that is not being used to landless farmers, thereby changing the skewed land distribution and increasing overall production. These possible benefits aside, there are costs, especially to title holders who lose their land or must compensate those who invade it. These invasions and the rights of squatters weaken the security of property and potentially reduce the incentive to invest and land values.

The constitutional provisions requiring land be placed in the "social interest" (production) as a condition for property rights security encourages squatter invasion and occupancy of private land when the criteria appear not to be met. As noted in chapter 3, by means of invasion, squatters can receive title through adverse possession. Typically, forested land is prima facie evidence of a lack of beneficial ("adequate and rational") use, but any definition will be arbitrary and invite disputes. As a squatter in the município of Conceição do Araguaia in Pará stated: "Here the best title is the biggest ax."

Our analytical discussion provides an explanation for sequential settlement without conflict. Untitled land would be settled by squatters with the lowest opportunity costs, who, in turn, would develop the land. Subsequently those first on the frontier may sell to later arrivals, who have higher-valued uses. Such exchanges may be possible without formal title through informal or locally observed arrangements. To extend the size of the land market and to access credit facilities, frontier farmers, at some point, will demand title.

This pattern of settlement, however, may be complicated if the land occupied by the initial settlers is already privately owned. This may happen if remote frontier land has been granted or purchased in large tracts for later development. Development, such as large-scale farming or ranching, requires access to capital and transportation. If transportation costs are too high or commodity prices too low, then development may be delayed by the title holder. Small-scale clearing and farming by squatters who occupy vacant but titled land may still occur.

In most cases, squatters have lower opportunity costs than do larger title holders, who are waiting for external conditions to change before developing their holdings. At early stages of settlement, land use is labor intensive, and under such conditions squatters will be specialists in clearing and early land use. This would not necessarily be the case if landowners could hire and monitor labor at low cost. But monitoring costs are likely to be high in remote frontier areas, which in turn prompts use by the squatter. The fact that squatters settle on titled land does not necessarily lead to conflict. Indeed, it is still quite common for title holders, at some point in the development process, to pay squatters for improvements and ask them to leave. Conflicts arise in situations where squatters refuse to leave titled land when asked to vacate. Squatters also may invade property that they know to be owned because the property does not meet the beneficial-use requirement of the constitution, and there is the possibility that the invasion will lead to an expropriation. In either case, conflicts over land can result.

Conflicts are costly to both squatters and title holders. If participants knew the outcome, they could save resources by not engaging in conflict and, on net, be better off. Consequently, there must be some uncertainty in the outcome that contributes to conflict.[3] In the Brazilian Amazon, the uncertainty arises over what prompts INCRA to intervene on behalf of the squatters.

Before there can be potential for conflict there must be two parties competing for the same land. As we show in chapter 8, violent conflict over land is not widespread, but concentrated in certain specific areas. This situation suggests that much of the land in the Amazon is not contested either because title holders do not attempt to enforce their property rights or because squatters do not resist eviction when it occurs. Title holders will not attempt to evict squatters on low-valued land that is far from markets; they would dissipate more resources in trying to hold the land than the land is worth. Alternatively, squatters will not attempt to squat on land that is clearly put to beneficial use, land that is close to markets and cultivated or used for pasture. Developed lands satisfy the beneficial-use provisions of the Constitution, and hence, the demands of squatters for expropriation would be rejected. Accordingly, on either land close to markets or far from markets, there will not be competing claimants. It is in the intermediate zone where competition and conflict is likely to occur.

Returning to the notion of sequential settlement, squatters in most cases precede title holders in putting land into use. As regional development proceeds, as roads are extended, and as land values rise, title holders have an incentive to use their "vacant" land. But to do so may mean evicting squatters. Squatters may decide to leave when asked or opt to stay. The decision by title holders to seek an eviction and the decision by squatters to resist an eviction takes place within an institutional environment that is set by INCRA and the courts.

The Courts

In Brazil judges are chosen based on a public examination open to all suitably qualified citizens. Because judges are not elected or appointed by politicians, they may be less subject to political pressures from the competing interest groups in land reform. Both local and federal courts play an important role in land conflicts. As the institutional organizations that uphold statutory law, the courts can be seen as the advocates of the title holders. Title holders go to the local court if they believe that their property rights are violated by squatters. Farmers request a *reintegração de posse* (reintegration of possession) following a squatter invasion, and if the court agrees, the document authorizes the use of the police to evict the squatters.[4] Generally, Brazilian judges treat a land invasion as they would any other taking of private property as interpreted in the Civil Code.[5] As such, there is little uncertainty generated over the eviction processes of the local courts. Additionally, the local courts can influence the costs to squatters and farmers in a land conflict through assessment of criminal charges against either party, although in practice this has been relatively rare.

The federal courts enter the picture once INCRA has determined that a farm should be expropriated. Through an appeal to the courts, a title holder can challenge an expropriation decision on two grounds: the land is being put to productive use and therefore should not be subject to expropriation; or the compensation offered by INCRA is too low. Such suits are common, and they can delay the transfer of the property to INCRA for several years, or in some cases, even reverse the expropriation.

INCRA

Unlike with the courts, there is more uncertainty surrounding the actions of INCRA when an invasion occurs. But this does not mean that the actions of INCRA are completely unpredictable. INCRA's land-reform actions are determined primarily by three factors: (1) the president's commitment to land reform; (2) the strength of a farmer's property rights, which depends in part on the beneficial-use criteria adopted by INCRA; and (3) the amount of violence involved in the land conflict and associated media attention to the dispute. In Brazil the president is responsible for land reform, and his reputation is harmed by violent land conflicts. For example, an article in the February 5, 1997, *Veja,* the largest weekly magazine in Brazil, linked a sharp drop in President Cardoso's approval ratings to the April 1996 land conflict in which 19 squatters were killed. A criterion frequently used by the press and politicians for determining whether a president has been an advocate of land reform is the total area of expropriations he has signed. The current program of settling 280 thousand families from 1995 to 1998 was a campaign promise by President Fernando Henrique Cardoso.[6]

The president has several ways to influence the actions of INCRA.

1. Through adjustments in INCRA's budget and staff. For example, in 1991 INCRA lost half its staff in President Collor's attempt to reduce the size of the civil service.
2. Through replacing the administrative head of the agency. This practice is frequent; between 1990 to 1996 there were 19 different agency heads.
3. Through promoting legislation that makes INCRA's task harder or easier. In 1996, several laws facilitating the expropriation procedure were passed with the help of the president's majority in Congress. Such laws had consistently been blocked by landowner interest groups in previous years.
4. Through changes in INCRA's position in the government's hierarchy. INCRA is currently under the jurisdiction of a newly created Ministry of Land Reform. Previously, INCRA was under the jurisdiction of the Ministry of Agriculture, which was more partial to the interest of landowners.[7]

The second factor influencing the likelihood of INCRA's expropriating a farm is the quality of the farmer's property rights to the land. The strength of a landowner's property rights vary. For property rights to be relatively secure, a farm must have an undisputed, registered title and be productive according to criteria established by INCRA. Both of these conditions may be satisfied to a greater or lesser degree. Titles may be clear, fraudulent, overlapping, or simply nonexistent.[8] Productivity is a difficult criterion to define and may be interpreted in many different ways (for example, only part of a farm may be productive while the rest is untouched). The criteria for determining productivity vary from region to region.[9] In the Amazon, simply clearing the land is generally considered productive use, whereas in São Paulo a fenced pasture may be considered unproductive if it is not sufficiently stocked with cattle.

The third factor influencing the decision making of INCRA is the amount of violence or perceived likelihood of violence. Violence is used strategically by squatters to force INCRA to expropriate a farm.[10] Violent conflict over land is politically costly to INCRA and prompts its action because violence attracts media attention. This attention, in turn, embarrasses federal politicians, particularly the president, who can punish INCRA with reduced agency budgets. This notion is supported by the fact that 85 percent of the farms expropriated by INCRA in Pará between 1986 and 1992 followed violent conflict between squatters and farmers.[11]

To judge more systematically how the quality of property rights and violence by squatters influences the decision by INCRA to expropriate, we present a statistical test of expropriation by INCRA based on a sample of 69 farms we surveyed in contested regions of the state of Pará in 1996. The sample of farms was chosen based on local information that we obtained regarding which properties were subject to conflict. Table 7 lists the descriptive statistics of the survey data.[12]

The following equation is estimated with a multiple probit regression:

(1) Expropriation $[0,1] = B_0 + B_1$Clear $+ B_2$Title $+ B_3$Squatter Organization $+ B_4$Deaths $+ B_5$Families $+ B_6$Area $+ e$.

The dependent variable equals 1 if INCRA expropriated the farm. The variables Clear, Title, and Area capture the effect of the strength of the property rights variable. Clear measures the percent of the farm cleared of forest. Because in the Amazon, clearing is considered a productive use of

TABLE 7. Descriptive Statistics for the Farm Expropriation Survey

Variable	Mean	Standard Deviation	Minimum	Maximum
Percentage of farms expropriated	39	49	0	1
Farm area (hectares)	15,112	58,015	150	411,000
Percentage of farm cleared	52	28	0	100
Whether invasion was organized (1,0)	48%	50%	0	1
Invaded farm titled (1,0)	49%	50%	0	1
Number of squatter families	101	200	0	1,500
Number of fatalities	1.46	3.81	0	22

Note: Number of observations is 69

the land, higher levels of clearing strengthen the property rights of the farmer according to the Brazilian Constitution. We expect that the level of clearing will reduce the likelihood of expropriation.

Title equals 1 if the farm had a definitive title or a long-term nut extraction lease (*aforamento*). Like title, these leases are recognized in Brazilian law as conveying property rights to land. Having clear title should strengthen property rights to land and thereby reduce the probability of expropriation. But the beneficial-use requirement of the constitution suggests that the effect of title on expropriation may be ambiguous. Title, alone, is not sufficient to prevent invasion of "unused" farms. Further, having title may facilitate expropriation if the property is not in beneficial use because INCRA has an "owner" with whom to negotiate. Unused lands that have no official, titled owner may be considered government land (*terra devoluta*) and assigned to squatters, rather than expropriated. The variable Area measures the size of the farm in hectares.

Because invasions typically do not take place on small farms, the sample includes mainly large farms and has a mean of 15,112 hectares. To place these farms into perspective, the mean farm size as indicated in the 1985 agricultural census for the municípios of Paragominas, Marabá, and Conceição do Araguaia was 554, 2,001, and 179 hectares respectively. We expect that larger farms are more likely to be invaded and at least portions expropriated because large farms are more apt to have sections that remain in forest and hence are not in productive use. Further, the boundaries of such large farms are more costly to monitor for intrusion by squatters.

The variables Deaths, Families, and Organization capture the effect of squatter violence on the probability of expropriation. Deaths is the number of people killed in a conflict. Although violence comes in many forms other than deaths, the number of deaths is more uniformly measurable and should be correlated with the amount of violence in a conflict. Fatalities in a conflict increase the likelihood that the media will be attracted to the contested area, which in turn leads to greater political pressure on INCRA to expropriate. Accordingly, we anticipate that this variable will have a positive coefficient. Organization equals One if the squatters were organized by the peasants' union, MST, or a local syndicate of squatters, STR (a rural *sindicato*), in the invasion. Successful invasions and expropriations require planning, selection of vulnerable farms, and media attention. The MST is careful in organizing invasions. Spontaneous invasions are predicted to be comparatively less successful in leading to an expropriation.[13] The variable Families is the number of families involved in an invasion. The number of families involved is generally high, with 101 as the mean number of families. This variable is included to determine whether INCRA was more likely to expropriate farms where large numbers of squatters were involved. Larger groups of squatters may spark more media and political pressure on INCRA to expropriate.

In the estimation reported in table 8, the percentage of correct predictions is 81 percent. Of the 27 expropriations we correctly predict 22 cases, and of the 42 farms not expropriated, we correctly predict 34 cases. As indicated in the table, the variables Clear and Organization have the greatest explanatory power in determining whether or not INCRA will expropriate a property. The performance of the Organization variable is consistent with the notion that INCRA expropriates only those farms where the invasion is well organized, which leads to the selection of farms with little clearing and considerable media attention.

Evaluated at mean values for all other variables, a titled farm invaded by organized squatters has a 57 percent chance of expropriation. By contrast, an unorganized invasion of a titled farm has only a 9 percent chance of expropriation. The MST has a justified reputation for identifying vulnerable farms and drawing media attention to an invasion. Similarly, the strength of the Clear variable in reducing expropriations of contested farms is consistent with the notion that INCRA views clearing as a mea-

TABLE 8. Determinants of INCRA Expropriation

Dependent Variable	Expected Sign	Coefficient (*t*-statistics)
Constant		0.08
		(0.11)
Clear	Negative	−0.02
		−(2.01)
Title	?	−0.05
		−(0.13)
Area	Positive	−0.00002
		−(0.95)
Organization	Positive	1.53
		(3.70)
Families	Positive	−0.001
		−(0.58)
Deaths	Positive	0.03
		(0.55)

Note: Log – Likelihood Ratio = 32.49 with 6 Degrees of Freedom; *t*-statistics in parentheses; $N = 69$; Chow $R^2 = 0.41$. The coefficients presented are the effect of a change in the independent variable on $F^{-1}(P_i)$, where F is the cumulative density function of a standard normal variable and P_i is the probability that Expropriations equals 1. The effect of a change in the independent variable on the probability of an expropriation depends on the values of all independent variables (see Judge et al. 1988, 791).

sure of productive use. Evaluated at the mean values for all variables, a one-half standard deviation increase in the percentage of a titled farm that is cleared reduces the chance of expropriation following an organized invasion to 47 percent from 57 percent.

The results from this exercise indicate that (1) INCRA is considerably more likely to expropriate a farm in which the invasion was organized by an outside group, in most instances the MST; and (2) INCRA is considerably less likely to expropriate a farm that has stronger property rights, which in the Amazon we proxied by the amount of land cleared of forest.

In the next three chapters, we focus more on INCRA's role in providing title to small claimants to government lands in the Amazon state of Pará. In chapter 8 we return to issues of violent conflict, how INCRA implements land reform policies, and how those actions in turn affect title security, land values, and the incentive to invest.

Conclusion

In this chapter we have described a framework for analyzing the demand for, and supply of, property rights on the Brazilian Amazon frontier that yields implications we will test in subsequent chapters. We stress that the provision, maintenance, and redistribution of property rights to land are complex political processes in Brazil. The most straightforward is the assignment of rights to settlers as part of the sequential settlement of the frontier. The process is confounded when there are competing government (state and federal) agencies for the provision of titles; when jurisdictional issues are unresolved so that claimants do not know which government or agency to which to apply for title; when budget and staffing cuts lead agencies to title too slowly; when electoral pressures lead agencies to title too quickly (in terms of social benefits and costs) as a means of winning votes; and when land redistribution pressures lead to the invasion, expropriation, and reassignment of ownership. Although serious land conflicts virtually always involve competition between large owners and squatters, the weakening of title security for large owners affects the security of title for smallholders as well and contributes to broader declines in land values. Hence, frontier settlement and titling policies are intricately tied to land reform efforts.

The framework developed in this chapter motivates the empirical work that follows in the remaining chapters. In chapter 5 we utilize information from household surveys that we conducted in 1992 and 1993 in Pará to analyze aspects of the settlement process. We assess the characteristics of settlers and see how their attributes affect their decision to move or stay as the frontier process develops. We also present evidence on the costs of solidifying informal property rights and subsequently securing a title from federal and state land agencies. In chapter 6 we formally analyze the determinants of property rights and their impact on investment and land values with household data from our surveys of five settlement areas in Pará. These data also enable us to explore the differing motivations of state and federal governments in the provision of titles. In chapter 7 we use data from Brazilian censuses to compare the determinants and impact of property rights on an earlier frontier in the southern Brazilian state of Paraná with the more recent frontier settlement of Pará. In chapter 8 we further develop a theory of land conflict and test hypotheses of land conflict using município-level data on deaths from land conflicts across municípios in Pará.

NOTES

1. Article 524 of the civil code, translated from Fachin 1991. The emphasis is ours.

2. The constitution of 1946 and the 1964 Federal Law 4504 provided similar privileges for squatters.

3. In chapter 8 we test hypotheses regarding conflict over land.

4. A reintegration of possession states that private property was taken from its rightful owner and should be returned immediately. In most cases farmers will first try to evict the squatters by their own means before appealing to the courts because the cost of obtaining a *reintegração de posse* is high, around U.S.$5,000 in the state of Pará in 1996. The estimate of the cost comes from our field survey in 1996.

5. For discussion of the courts' role in land conflicts, see Fachin 1991.

6. The current government's program is called Mãos à Obra Brasil (Hands to Work Brazil).

7. President Cardoso changed the status of INCRA following the bloody land conflict in April 1996 mentioned above.

8. Ironically, as we discuss below, having title may facilitate an expropriation by INCRA if the farm is not placed in beneficial use. On titled land, INCRA has an owner with whom to negotiate compensation for the transfer of property back to the state. When a farmer does not have title to land that is being contested by squatters, INCRA tends to allow the farmer to purchase and title an area proportional to the area he made productive (in Pará this has been 1.5 times the area made productive). The remainder of the original farm is then used to settle the squatters. Thus squatters have incentives to invade both titled and untitled land; however, they know they will only receive land that is not being put to use. The current criteria of INCRA in Pará were determined during our field survey in Pará in December 1996.

9. For discussion of political economy of the productive-use requirement in the 1988 constitution, see Mueller 1994.

10. One of the first indications of the use of invasions as a premeditated strategy to pressure INCRA can be found in Abramovay 1985b.

11. Between 1986 and 1992, 60 farms were expropriated, and 51 of them involved violent conflict. The remaining nine expropriated farms may also have originated from a conflict, but no data could be found on those farms. The list of expropriated farms is from IDESP 1992. Data on conflicts in Pará are from personal correspondence with the Pastoral Land Commission in Goiania and from IDESP 1990.

12. The number of farms and município in which they were located are as follows: 10 in Paragominas, 13 in Marabá, 12 in Rio Maria, 6 in Conceição do Araguaia, 22 in Parauapebas, 4 in Curionópolis, and 2 in Eldorado dos Carajás.

13. This information was conveyed to us by several different interviewees during the survey in Pará in 1996.

CHAPTER 5

Settlement by Smallholders and Property Rights on the Amazon Frontier

The analytical framework developed in chapter 4 yields testable hypotheses concerning the settlement of the Brazilian Amazon: land further from the market should be of lower value and be less likely to be titled; settlers closer to the economic frontier should have less human and physical capital than settlers closer to the market center; as land values increase and the frontier moves on, settlers with less human and physical capital should sell out to settlers with more human and physical capital; settlers who stay in an area should have more human and physical capital than those who sold out; settlers should perceive titled land as more valuable than nontitled land, and they should be willing to expend resources to acquire titles because titles provide security to investments, allow settlers to access capital markets, reduce enforcement costs, and increase the extent of the market. We are able to test these hypotheses with household level data collected in surveys performed in 1992 and 1993 in the state of Pará.[1]

We interviewed settlers at various distances along major roads and feeder roads from the communities of Altamira, Tucumã, Colônia, Reunidas, and Nova Aliança in 1992. Because of the importance of distance in our model, we selected farms sequentially, with each site more remote than the previous location. In 1993 we resurveyed our earlier sites and added settlers near the communities of São Felix and Tailândia. We selected this mix so as to examine the effects of different government agency and land company jurisdictions—INCRA, ITERPA, and private—on the settlement process. This data set is an important component of this study, so we will discuss the characteristics of the communities before discussing the characteristics of the households.

Characteristics of the Frontier Communities That We Surveyed

Altamira

Altamira is a town of approximately 72,000 people bordering the Xingu River and Transamazon Highway. Under the auspices of early land devel-

opment policies, INCRA developed lands near Altamira as a model of settlement projects in 1971 (see Moran 1984, 287; Fearnside 1986; Schmink
and Wood 1992, 70). INCRA initially recruited settlers, many of whom
were from southern Brazil, and settled them on 100-hectare plots. INCRA
constructed transverse roads 12 km long every 5 km. Plots were 400 m ×
2,500 m arranged so that the 400-meter side was on the road. Despite this
planning, by the late 1970s INCRA had brought fewer settlers to Altamira
than had been the original goal.[2] Nevertheless, settlement continued by
migrants from nearby states and elsewhere in Pará. These settlers were not
recruited by INCRA, and the stereotype is that they had fewer assets than
did the earlier migrants. These "spontaneous" (nonrecruited) migrants
pushed the transverse roads further from the Transamazon Highway, generally 30 to 60 km, but sometimes as far as 120 km. The new settlers tended
to continue the pattern of 100-hectare plots, although there is considerable
variation in plot size now.

Our sample consists of 79 settlers east of Altamira along the
Transamazon Highway and side roads at intervals of approximately 3, 18,
27, 55, 105, and 160 km. Interviewees extended up side roads as far as 45
km. Mean farm size for our Altamira sample is 142 hectares (standard
deviation 150) with a minimum of 3 and a maximum of 714 hectares. On
average 50 percent of the farm area is cleared of forest. The mean head of
family in the sample is 44 years old, has three years of schooling, arrived in
1978, moved 1.6 times before arriving, and has 5.4 people in the family.
The mean farm is 61 kilometers from Altamira; 53 along the Transamazon
Highway and 8 along the side road. Of the 79 farms in the sample 65 percent have a definitive title, 14 percent a provisional title, 2 percent a sales
receipt that proxies for proof of ownership, and 19 percent have no title at
all. The mean price of a hectare is U.S.$60.[3]

Colônia Reunidas

Colônia Reunidas is located 25 km from the market town of Paragominas.
Paragominas is a thriving frontier town of approximately 67,000 people,
located on the Belém-Brasília Highway. It reputedly has more sawmills
than any city in Brazil. Colônia Reunidas was settled through invasion of
a large, privately owned tract of land by 115 families in 1982. The settlement was adopted by INCRA in 1986 amid conflict between the squatters
and the titled owner. INCRA eventually expropriated approximately
4,300 ha from the title holder and began to settle the squatters on plots.
INCRA was supposed to issue titles to the claimants, but by 1993 still had
not done so. Some of the settlers have a *declaração do procera* from

INCRA. This is an acknowledgment from INCRA that the title is being processed and enables the settler the potential to receive credit from the Banco do Brasil through PROCERA (Special Program for Credit to Agrarian Reform). Some help in the form of credit, tractor services, pepper plants, and corn seeds was given by various government agencies to some of the settlers in this project from 1989 to 1992.

Our sample of Colônia Reunidas includes 34 settlers. The mean plot size is 52 hectares (standard deviation 15.5) with a maximum of 100 and minimum of 30 hectares. The average area cleared was 44 percent. The mean head of family is 43 years old, has two years of schooling, arrived in 1985, moved 1.9 times previously, and has five people in the family. Given that the plots were all carved from the expropriated land and are all part of the same "colony," our surveys at this site are all considered as the same distance from the market, approximately 25 kilometers. The mean price of a hectare is U.S.$100.

Nova Aliança

Nova Aliança is a relatively remote colony 70 km from Paragominas—35 km of the distance to Paragominas are along a dirt road that is not always passable.[4] Like Colônia Reunidas, Nova Aliança was settled through invasion of private land, in this instance land that was titled to a palm oil company. The land is under the jurisdiction of INCRA, but INCRA has not expropriated the land despite requests from the colonists. Neither INCRA nor any other federal agency has provided any credit or services.

The sample of Nova Aliança has 33 observations. The mean plot size is 50 hectares (standard deviation 34.6) with a maximum of 150 and a minimum of 3 hectares. On average only 37 percent of the farm area was cleared. The mean head of family is 42 years old, has 1.4 years of schooling, arrived in 1989, moved 2.5 times before arriving, and has five people in the family. The mean price of a hectare is U.S.$34.

Tucumã

The settlement of Tucumã originated from a private settlement project of CONSAG (Gutierrez de Andrade Construction Company).[5] At the time of our survey the population of Tucumã was approximately 35,000. In 1980 CONSAG bought from the federal government 400,000 ha of forest land in southeastern Pará (about 800 km from Belém and 350 km from the market town of Marabá) with the objective of selling parcels to settlers, primarily from southern Brazil. Although the company demarcated 1,771 plots, it sold only about 200.[6] The discovery of gold in the region, coupled with the sparse settlement and relatively good road network built by CONSAG, attracted numerous squatters. Despite CONSAG's attempts at evicting the squatters, it was overwhelmed and eventually sold the land back to federal government in 1988. Since that time, the land has been under the jurisdiction of INCRA, although for a brief period it was under the jurisdiction of GETAT (Executive Group for the Land of the Araguaia-Tocantins Region).

We surveyed settlers along side roads in two different locales near Tucumã, one area southwest of town opened in 1982 by CONSAG and the other region northwest of Tucumã and originally occupied by squatters along roads opened by illegal logging operations beginning in 1984. Settlers in the original CONSAG plots came mainly from southern Brazil, while those in the invaded area came principally from the states of Goiás and Minas Gerais.

There are 74 settlers in our sample of Tucumã. The mean plot size is 98 (standard deviation 157.4) with a maximum size of 1,165 and a minimum of 5 hectares. The average area cleared is 47 percent. The mean head of family is 41 years old, has 2.9 years of schooling, arrived in 1987, moved 2.6 times before arriving, and has five people in the family. The average distance from Tucumã to the farms is 24 kilometers. There are four types of tenure: definitive title originally received from CONSAG (24 percent); an authority to occupy issued by GETAT (8 percent); a receipt of purchase (34 percent); and informal squatters' rights (34 percent). On average the value of a hectare in our sample of Tucumã is U.S.$237.

São Felix do Xingu

São Felix do Xingu is an old town along the Xingu River in southern Pará, 1,300 km from Belém. The population is approximately 24,000. Despite being on the Xingu, the town is fairly isolated because the river is not navigable due to rapids, and the road from São Felix do Xingu to Xinguara, passing through Tucumã, is a stretch of 300 km of dirt road. São Felix do Xingu has always been under the jurisdiction of ITERPA, the Pará state land agency, although there is no office in town. Prior to elections, ITERPA hands out titles in exchange for political support.[7] We conducted our surveys in two separate colonies that border the Xingu River: Colônia Santa Rosa, 20 km downriver from São Felix do Xingu; and Colônia Xadazinho, 100 km upriver from São Felix do Xingu.

There are 52 observations in our sample of São Felix do Xingu. The mean plot size is 181 hectares (standard deviation 469.2) with a maximum of 3,500 and a minimum of 50 hectares. The average area cleared of forest is only 18 percent. The mean head of family is 44 years old, has 1.1 years of schooling, arrived in 1987, moved three times previously, and has five people in the family. The average distance from plot to the town of São Felix do Xingu is 150 kilometers: 65 along the river, 80 along the main road, and 5 up the side road. Tenure of our settlers includes definitive title (60 percent), sales receipt as proof of ownership (2 percent), and squatters' right of occupancy issued by ITERPA (38 percent). The average price of a hectare of land in the sample is U.S.$16.

Tailândia

Tailândia is a relatively new town that came to life as a result of Highway PA-150 built in the mid-1970s (the road was asphalted in 1985). Tailândia is 200 km south of Belém and contains approximately 17,000 people. The major activity in the area is logging. The area is under the jurisdiction of ITERPA, who founded the settlement in 1978 by giving and selling plots located 3 to 8 km on each side of PA-150 along a 100 km distance from Tailândia. There is an ITERPA office in town, and settlement has proceeded along the main road as well as side roads developed by logging trucks.

We surveyed 59 settlers along the main road as well as up side roads. The mean plot size is 77.51 hectares (standard deviation 61.34) with a maximum of 350 and a minimum of 45 hectares. On average, 42 percent of the area of each farm had been cleared. The mean head of family is 44 years old, has 1.1 years of schooling, arrived in 1984, moved 3.2 times before arriving, and has six people in the family. The average distance from Tailândia of settlers is 45 kilometers: 41 along the main road and 4 along the side roads. Tenure of our settlers includes definitive title (53 percent), provisional title from the land agency (19 percent), sales receipt (8 percent), and squatters' rights of occupancy (20 percent). The average price of a hectare of land in the sample is U.S.$24.

Table 9 presents descriptive statistics from the survey.

The Frontier Settlement Process

Our framework in chapter 4 allows us to predict that land should decrease in value the further it is from the market. As shown in table 10, which presents correlation coefficients between distance and land/squatter characteristics, land value and distance are negatively correlated for Altamira, Paragominas, and Tucumã.[8] The correlations for São Felix and Tailândia are positive, but the coefficients are relatively small, and for Tailândia the correlation is not statistically significant at conventional levels. Recall that Tailândia and São Felix are our most remote sites and that land values are the lowest of our sample. In both sites our surveyor indicated that much of production is for home consumption and that barter is prevalent for exchanges. At every location except Paragominas, where no settlers have a definitive title, titles are less prevalent the further settlers are from the market town, and all of the correlations are significant at the 95 percent confidence level or greater.[9] This result reflects both the fact that there are greater administrative costs in lobbying and securing a title as distance to an administrative center increases, and there is less added value from having a title the further a settler is from the market.

In columns 4 and 6 we present correlation coefficients between two proxies for human capital—age and education—and distance from the market. Nine of the ten coefficients are negative, indicating that settlers on the frontier tend to be younger and have less education. However, one should not read too much into this result, as the coefficients are small and in general not statistically significant at conventional levels. In column 5 we present the correlation coefficients between distance and wealth, our proxy for physical capital. All the coefficients are negative, suggesting that physical capital has greater value as one moves closer to markets. Again,

TABLE 9. Descriptive Statistics for the Survey Sample (249 observations)

Variable	Mean	Standard Deviation	Minimum	Maximum
Proportion with title[a]	.56	.50		
Proportion with sales receipt	.12	.32		
Proportion with no document	.32	.47		
Value per hectare	$84.83	$188.71	$2.72	$1901.80
Total distance to market (km)	64.81	54.27	4.00	190.00
Area (hectares)	109.19	241.86	3.00	3,500.00
Percentage of farm cleared	40	23	0.00	100.00
Percentage in pasture	38	31	0.00	99.00
Percentage in permanent crop	07	13	0.00	100.00
Education	1.95	2.27	0.00	12.00
Time on plot	8.22	6.9	0.00	58.00
Number of migrations	2.68	1.78	0.00	13.00
Age	43.33	12.73	16.00	78.00
Wealth	$3,269.40	$9,934.60	0.00	$114,300.00

[a]Title or provisional title

one should be cautious in interpretation because three of the coefficients are not significantly different from zero at conventional levels.

Overall, our correlation results indicate that land further from the market declines in value and is less likely to be titled. Our mixed results for our human and physical capital measures may be due to the dynamics of the settlement process itself. An equilibrium has not yet been established whereby the settlers are homogeneous in their attributes. It is to this issue that we now turn.

Land Markets, Turnover, and the Characteristics of Settlers

By definition frontiers are dynamic. As such we would expect that there would be considerable turnover as development proceeds. The initial settlers should be specialists in clearing and making rudimentary investments. As development proceeds, population densities increase, transportation improves, land values increase, and market transactions for land emerge. Because settlers far from market do not generally have a title, the exchange of land will entail the issuance of a witnessed receipt for the squatted claim. The exchange of informal claims—squatters' rights for a witnessed receipt—represents the initial extension of the market to the frontier. During the transition, lower-valued users of land should sell out

TABLE 10. Correlation Coefficients between Distance and Land/Squatter Characteristics

Site	Per Hectare Land Value	Land is Titled	Age of Claimant	Wealth of Claimant	Education of Claimant
Altamira	−0.50***	−0.26**	−0.07	−0.15	−0.08
	(50)	(79)	(79)	(79)	(76)
Paragominas	−0.41***	N.A.	−0.05	−0.33***	−0.13
(Reunidas, Nova	(38)		(67)	(67)	(67)
Aliança)					
Tucumã	−0.39***	−0.32***	−0.05	−0.14	−0.07
	(55)	(73)	(74)	(74)	(74)
Tailândia	0.13	−0.32**	−0.04*	−0.02	−0.22*
	(59)	(59)	(59)	(59)	(59)
São Felix	0.25*	−0.34**	0.31**	−0.39***	−0.19
	(46)	(52)	(52)	(52)	(52)

Note: The number of observations for each site is in parentheses.
*Significant at 90%
**Significant at 95%
***Significant at 99%

to higher-valued users. Typically, this means that those who sell have less human and physical capital than those who stay, and in-migrants should have the greatest asset endowments. Whether initial settlers stay or opt to move on to another frontier depends on their accumulation of assets— wealth and experience—since their arrival. As long as settlement is wealth enhancing, that is, settlers acquire wealth and experience, at some point in their life cycle former specialists in clearing will choose to stay rather than move to a new frontier.

The scenario that we describe is one where turnover improves the welfare of both in- and out-migrants. To this extent, high turnover should be associated with increases in land value rather than land degradation and abandonment.

We interviewed settlers near the communities of Altamira, Paragominas, and Tucumã in 1992 and 1993, and therefore we are able to compare the characteristics of those settlers who stayed with those who sold their plots and migrated. Unfortunately, we do not have systematic data on the in-migrants. We have 54 observations for both Altamira and Paragominas, and 62 observations for Tucumã. To capture the impact on whether to stay or move, we collected data on the following variables: age of the settler, years of education, wealth (value in U.S. dollars of chickens, pigs, cattle, and horses) and previous number of migrations. Age and education are proxies for human capital, and wealth is a proxy for physical capital. The number of prior moves is an additional measure of human and physical capital. Our hypothesis is that each move represents a sale where the seller improves his stock of assets. Our measures of physical capital— wealth, and number of moves—most likely increase with age, as does experience. As such, our framework has a life-cycle component. This is in contrast to a view that a class of settlers remains landless, drifting from frontier to frontier.

In table 11 we present the mean characteristics of settlers who stayed or left in the year between our two surveys—May and June 1992 to May 1993. Measured differences between the two groups will provide strong support for our life-cycle view of settlement because our data are biased against finding such differences. We have data on those who left the settlement and those who remained. But because of the short time period between the two surveys, those who stayed in one year may not differ significantly from those who moved. The former may be in the process of selling and migrating. Even so, the data in table 11 reveal important differences between the two groups.

The first point to draw from the data in table 11 is the large turnover in just one year. The percentage of our sample who sold land between 1992 and 1993 ranged from 9 percent in Altamira to 20 percent in Nova Aliança and Colônia Reunidas (the communities near Paragominas) to 34 percent in Tucumã.

Overall, the raw data is consistent with the view that human and physical capital are determinants of migration. In each sample, those who stayed are older, wealthier, and had more prior moves than those who moved between our sample periods. Interestingly, education does not appear to influence the migration decision. This suggests that formal education may not add much to the productivity of settlers; at least the variation around the low levels of education in our sample does not matter for the migration decision. Furthermore, land values are highest in Tucumã, which is consistent with land being put into higher-valued uses over time, rather than a view that turnover was high because of land degradation.

Further evidence of the life-cycle view of turnover and its positive effect on settlers is given in Schneider 1994 and Ozório de Almeida 1992.[10] In a comparison of settlement projects across the North region, Schneider concludes, "These data show the same pattern as among regions—higher farm incomes associated with higher farm turnovers" (1994, 16). Ozório de Almeida also finds that migrants were younger and significantly wealthier than those who remained in high turnover locations.

To systematically test for the importance of age, wealth, education, and previous migration on the sell/stay decision, we performed a probit estimation of the coefficients of the following variables: Sell (1) or Stay (0) = f(age, age^2, wealth, $wealth^2$, education, number of previous moves, and site dummies). Table 12 contains the results.

The major conclusion to be drawn from the estimation is that physical capital, in the form of livestock wealth, is an important determinant in the decision to sell or stay, whereas age and education do not matter much, though the coefficients are positive. The marginal effect of (logged) wealth on the probability to sell, with all variables at their mean value, is a decrease of 12 percent in Tucumã, 9 percent in Altamira, and 8 percent in

TABLE 11.   Mean Characteristics of Settlers Who Stay or Leave

	Altamira		Paragominas[a]		Tucuma	
	Sold	Stay	Sold	Stay	Sold	Stay
N	5	49	11	43	21	41
Mean age	35	43	37	43	39	43
Mean education (years)	3.0	2.9	1.5	1.8	3.3	2.9
Mean wealth	$3,262	$5,595	$9	$1,256	$2,342	$6,011
Number of prior moves	1.4	1.8	1.9	2.4	2.2	2.8

Note: Differences in the means are significant at 99%; differences in the means are significant at 95%.
[a]Nova Aliança, Reunitas

Paragominas. Transforming these results into dollars, an increase of wealth from the mean of approximately U.S.$3000 to $3,500 leads to a decrease in the probability of the settler selling the land of 1.13 percent, 0.9 percent, and 0.79 percent in Tucumã, Altamira, and Paragominas respectively.

The coefficient on the moves variable further reinforces the view that physical and human capital reduces the likelihood of moving, if, as seems reasonable, settlers accumulate net wealth by selling. At the mean values of all variables an additional move decreases the probability of selling by 4.4 percent in Tucumã, 3.6 percent in Altamira, and 3.3 percent in Paragominas. The coefficients on our site dummies indicate that turnover was less in Altamira and Paragominas, which is consistent with our view that in-migrants bid up the price of land because they have attributes that better enable them to acquire titles and make site-specific investments.

To test more directly for our life-cycle view of migration, we estimated the coefficients of the determinants of total moves of our migrants. For this estimation, we can add the sites of São Felix and Tailândia to the independent variables included in our sell/stay regression. It is important to keep in mind the characteristics of the sites: São Felix, Tailândia, and Tucumã (after the demise of the private settlement project) were settled through spontaneous migration, whereas Colônia Reunidas, one of the colonies near Paragominas, and Altamira were directed settlement projects. As such, we expect that settlers arriving on their own initiative might have to move more often before they settle (more or less) permanently.

TABLE 12.   Determinants of Sell or Stay
(sell = 1; stay = 0)

Variable	Coefficient	t-ratio
Age	1.02	0.11
Age^2	−0.21	−0.17
Wealth	−0.32	−2.15
Wealth^2	0.0009	0.61
Education	0.23	1.15
Moves	−0.49	−1.55
Altamira	−1.22	−3.65
Paragominas[a]	−1.33	−3.44
Constant	0.78	0.05

Note: $N = 170$; left out site is Tucumã; right-hand side variables are in logs. The substantive results are the same whether or not the variables are in logs, although the Maddala R^2 increases from 0.14 for the nonlog specification to 0.22 for the log specification.

[a]Includes colonies of Reunidas and Nova Aliança

Age should increase the number of total moves but at a decreasing rate. Age brings experience (human capital), and wealth (physical capital) and thereby will reduce the likelihood of continually moving. Wealth should reduce the number of moves at a decreasing rate. Education, to the extent that it increases human capital relevant to settlement, should decrease the number of moves. We present the results in table 13.

There is considerable variation across our sample sites in the number of moves of our settlers. The results indicate that the settlers in the directed settlements of Altamira and Paragominas had fewer moves than settlers in sites of self-initiated migration, Tucumã, São Felix, and Tailândia. Age and wealth play a role in determining migrations. Though people have more total moves with age, they do so at a decreasing rate. For a settler in Tucumã of age 20, for example, with all other variables at their mean values, an additional year adds 0.035 moves, while for a settler of age 50 the additional year leads to an increment of only 0.011. This result is consistent with our life-cycle view of migration. The evidence suggests that over time people acquire experience that helps to secure titles and credit and thereby reduce the likelihood of future moves.

The effect of wealth on the decision to move is negative, and its impact increases with greater wealth. For a mean settler in Tucumã, a one-half standard deviation increase in wealth, from approximately U.S.$3,000 to $8,000, leads to 0.23 fewer moves. Education does not influence the number of moves, which is the same result that we got with our probit regression of the sell/stay decision.

There is a clear pattern for jurisdictional effects. The baseline site is Tucumã, which was originally a private settlement project whose owners

TABLE 13. Determinants of the Total Number of Moves by Settlers

Variable	Coefficient	t-ratio
Age	0.03	1.62
Age^2	–0.0002	–1.26
Wealth	–0.00002	–2.34
Wealth^2	0.17E-9	1.83
Education	0.018	1.00
Altamira	–0.45	–3.82
Paragominas[a]	–0.34	–2.80
São Felix	0.02	0.18
Tailândia	0.09	0.75
Constant	0.21	0.51

Note: $N = 246$; specification semi-log; $R^2 = 0.20$.

[a]Includes colonies of Reunidas and Nova Aliança

could not suppress invasions by squatters. As a result, CONSAG, the owner, sold the land back to the government and the land came under the jurisdiction of INCRA at a time of declining budgets for INCRA. Relative to settlers in Tucumã, the settlers in Altamira and Paragominas have moved less, while the settlers in São Felix and Tailândia have the same migration patterns as those of Tucumã. These results make sense. Altamira was an early showcase colonization site in Pará, and the settlers recruited by INCRA, many of whom were from southern Brazil, came with the intention of staying. Paragominas consists of two colonies: Colônia Reunidas and Nova Aliança. The site of Colônia Reunidas was given special treatment by INCRA in an attempt to quell a violent invasion. Credit and crop subsidies, though eventually not very substantial, were promised, along with titles. The provision of subsidies may account for fewer moves. In contrast, in the ITERPA sites of São Felix and Tailândia there were not promises of support, and the settlers typically moved from poorer regions of Brazil than the settlers of Altamira, and as such they needed more moves before accumulating sufficient wealth to stop moving.

The results presented in tables 11 through 13 indicate that in the dynamic frontier of the Amazon, individual migration from one frontier site to another falls with the accumulation of assets or wealth. From the perspective of the individual settler, movement is not indicative of failure but rather is a means by which poor settlers can assemble sufficient wealth to eventually develop permanency. The early market exchanges of squatter claims are the mechanism for economic advancement, and they occur in the absence of formal property rights to land. But, as development proceeds, formal titles provide the guarantee for permanent investments and broader exchanges, which can further raise land values and increase the wealth of the settlers. To this issue we turn in the next chapter.

The Value of Titled Land and the Costs of Establishing Property Rights

It is important to summarize the role of title to land in Brazil and the process by which individuals can claim land and receive title to it. Title is a formal document, issued by the Brazilian federal government or the state government, depending on jurisdiction, that signifies government recognition of an individual's property rights to land. Having a title not only gives legal standing to the landowner, but the recording of the title in the local land registry (*cartório*) includes survey descriptions (*memorial descritivo*), the location of boundary markers, and the date of recording to establish precedent for the land claim. Land exchanges are recorded by the cartório in a document that includes a *cadeia dominal,* a list of previous owners. This record can be valuable if there are disputes over land transfers. With title, the police power of the state is used to enforce private property rights to land, according to surveyed and recorded individual property boundaries. The courts issue eviction notices or arbitrate boundary disputes, and law-enforcement officials implement court orders.

As the most visible form of ownership recognition by the government, having title reduces private enforcement costs, provides security and collateral for long-term investment in land improvements, and promotes the development of land markets. All of these activities are wealth enhancing. The role of title in Brazilian law is recognized throughout Brazil, and for the most part, titles function well and are respected.

Although frontiers are remote by definition, there are strong reasons to believe that title on the frontier plays at least some of the roles described above. First, consider the collateral argument. Even though credit may be quite limited on a frontier, that is not the case for the rest of Brazil, where agricultural credit has been commonplace and requires title. Migrants to the frontier, mostly from rural areas, likely carry this understanding with them. Settlers are aware that as financial markets extend to the frontier, credit will become more available and that having title will assist them in obtaining funds. Moreover, practically every small urban center in Brazil has a branch of Banco do Brasil, which historically has provided credit to agriculture. Further, living under inflationary conditions of up to 50 percent a month has resulted in a population that is accustomed to dealing with banks and other financial institutions in efforts to respond to inflation.

The arguments also apply to the role of title in promoting land exchanges. Throughout Brazil, title is a recognized institutional device for designating private property rights and facilitating land transfer agreements. Formal titles are exchanged with land to document the transfer of ownership of land. Land exchange contracts and titles are recognized throughout the country and are defendable in court. Hence, they provide security for those more remote potential purchasers (say from more settled areas) who might be interested in purchasing frontier land. Absent titles, individual holdings are based on squatter claims and subject to local agreements and practices. Potential purchasers, who are not part of such arrangements, may have little understanding of local conditions or confidence in the property rights they provide. Although there is a market for land without title, having title is perceived as an advantage by settlers for broadening the range of potential purchasers. Finally, consider the ability of title to reduce private enforcement costs. With state-recognized title, landowners can appeal to the police to patrol property boundaries and to evict trespassers. Further, the judicial system can be used to issue injunctions against squatters who invade private property. A review of land-conflict records held by ITERPA, the Pastoral Land Commission, and other federal and state government agencies shows that having title facilitates the introduction of the rule of law in resolving land disputes.

To initiate the titling process, claimants generally must organize collectively, travel to a local agency office, and formally request surveys and documentation of their land claims. Group organization is necessary because land agencies usually wait until a threshold number of requests are made before traveling to the site. When they respond, agency officials take a census of settlers in the area, survey and mark claims, and grant claimants an authorization to occupy or *authorização do ocupação* or a *licensa de ocupação*. The authorizations are forwarded to the state or federal government, depending on the government unit involved, for final recording. Normally, title applications can be processed within two to five years, but if the initial claimant moves to a different site and sells the claim, the title application must be reprocessed, extending the titling time.

The survey data from Tucumã allows for an examination of the perceived value of land titles. In Tucumã, farmers had four types of property rights: (1) a formal title issued either by INCRA or CONSAG, the private company that initially developed Tucumã; (2) a provisional title of sorts issued by a temporary emergency agency, GETAT (GETAT was a federal agency created in the late 1980s to halt violent confrontation over land in some areas. GETAT mediated disputes and granted titles, though these titles are not widely recognized nor are they the basis for collateral); (3) a sales receipt, which connotes that the settler purchased the informal rights of a squatter and had the transaction documented and generally witnessed; (4) squatter rights.

As part of the Tucumã survey, a subset of farmers without title were asked the questions "How much is your land worth now?" and "How much would it be worth if you had a definitive title?" In table 14 we summarize their responses. Based on the evidence in the table, on average, settlers perceived that having a title would increase the value of their land by U.S.$35 per hectare, or by 36 percent. There is considerable variation in the perceived value of a title. This is not surprising, as some settlers are secure without a title and others value a title because they hope that it would enable credit.

If titles are valuable, we would expect that settlers would expend resources to strengthen their property rights and attempt to secure titles to their claims. In Tucumã, Nova Aliança, and Colônia Reunidas, we asked settlers what activities they undertook regularly to maintain their claims. We have responses from 43 settlers in Tucumã, and 45 settlers in the sites of Nova Aliança and Colônia Reunidas. Clearing the boundaries of a claim was the most frequent response. In Nova Aliança and Colônia Reunidas, 40 settlers indicated that they keep the boundaries to their claim clear, and they expended considerable effort in doing so. On average, six days a year are spent clearing boundaries. In Tucumã, 31 settlers indicated that they spent an average of five and a half days a year clearing their boundaries. Additionally, eight Tucumã settlers solidified their informal rights by having their sales receipts notarized, and one settler paid land taxes, an uncommon practice in the Amazon. In Colônia Reunidas, some settlers hired a topographer to map their borders, while other settlers built markers on their boundaries.

In all three sites, settlers went to INCRA offices to petition for titles. In Tucumã, 24 settlers went to the local office at least once in the previous year, and most made multiple trips; at the extreme, one settler made 20 trips to the INCRA office. These trips cost at least a day's work for each settler. Settlers in Nova Aliança elected an emissary from their colony who spent 15 days traveling to Belém and Brasília to try and hasten the titling process. Settlers within the community paid for this trip, as well as attended meetings to discuss titles and other issues of collective interest. Some settlers also paid the community organization for membership cards that signaled that a claim was recognized by the community. Others in Nova Aliança traveled to the INCRA office in Paragominas to petition for titles. In Colônia Reunidas, 15 of the 26 settlers traveled to the INCRA

TABLE 14. Perceptions of the Value of Title (in U.S. dollars)

Current Tenure Condition	Current Estimated Value per Hectare	Estimated Value with Formal Title	Percentage Increase
Getat title	$200	$200	0
Getat title	$100	$150	50
Sales receipt	$60	$100	67
Sales receipt	$200	$240	20
Sales receipt	$60	$100	67
Sales receipt	$40	$80	100
Squatter	$100	$150	50
Squatter	$40	$40	0
Squatter	$60	$80	33
Squatter	$40	$70	75
Squatter	$100	$200	100
Squatter	$60	$100	67
Squatter	$200	$200	0
Average	$97	$132	36

office to request more expeditious titling, and most settlers attended community meetings to discuss how to obtain titles.

These activities to strengthen property rights to land represent investments by settlers to raise the rental stream from the land they occupy. These investments involve time and resources. In table 15 we present crude estimates of the dollar value of the costs incurred by seven settlers in Tucumã in 1992 in efforts to maintain or strengthen their informal claims, or acquire formal titles. We also present the settlers' estimates of how much their land would increase with a formal title. We derived the increase in value by multiplying the estimated per hectare values contained in table 14 by the number of hectares of their claim. We estimated the costs by assuming that a day of labor was worth two U.S. dollars, since during the surveys this was the lowest rate at which we observed unskilled labor being hired.

The results are startling at first glance. Collectively, these settlers expended U.S.$188 in 1992 to firm their property rights, and, if they succeeded, the perceived collective return in increased land value was $10,800. Although these figures are only suggestive, they indicate that, even if it takes years to secure a title, the payoff is high.

Conclusion

In this chapter we presented evidence on settlement and the role of titles on the frontier. We found that sequential settlement of the frontier induces those with lower opportunity costs to move to the frontier and, over time, sell to those with higher opportunity costs. But this does not imply that there exists a class of permanently landless. Our evidence indicates that there is a life-cycle component to settlement. With each successive move and sale of land, settlers acquire more human and physical capital. This

TABLE 15. Expenditures on Property Rights and the Perceived Value of a Formal Title (in U.S. dollars)

Tenure Condition	Expenditure to Obtain Title	Perceived Increase in Value
GETAT title	12	0
GETAT title	12	800
Sales receipt	28	2,000
Sales receipt	24	2,000
Sales receipt	60	4,000
Squatter	20	2,000
Squatter	32	0

capital eventually enables settlers to stay more permanently on a squatted piece of land and become infra-frontier settlers. The settlement process also generates a demand for secure property rights. We found that settlers perceived titles as increasing land values and that they were willing to expend resources to acquire a title. When land is abundant and resource values are low, informal norms are sufficient to protect the claims of squatters on the frontier. As land values increase due to population pressure or lower transportation costs, settlers need more than informal norms to solidify their claims. Moreover, to increase the value of their claim, settlers need secure property rights in order to give them the incentive to invest in site specific improvements, and the collateral to access capital markets for investment. In the next two chapters, we investigate more rigorously the relationships among property rights, land values, and investment.

NOTES

1. This chapter draws from the work presented in Alston, Libecap, and Schneider 1995a.

2. For discussion of early settlement policies, see Butler 1985.

3. The mean land price presented for each of our sampled communities is based on the values claimed by each of the interviewed settlers. To judge their reasonableness we compared these stated prices with those recorded in newspapers and other written sources where available.

4. In surveying the site, Ricardo Tarifa, our surveyor, got stuck five times on the road to Nova Aliança. At the conclusion of his interviews he wrote: "I really understand now the transport difficulties the colony faces and why everybody complains about it. They [the colonists] are quite worried because, if someone gets sick, this can mean a life or death situation. The only means of transport they have is a monthly truck from the local government, or walking 10 km and hopefully getting a lift on the top of logging trucks. But, this is unpredictable and also difficult because the road is bad and the drivers are forbidden to stop; fifteen days ago a colonist fell down and died under the truck tires."

5. For a detailed account of the settlement of Tucumã and São Felix do Xingu, see Schmink and Wood 1992.

6. See Butler 1985 for discussion.

7. For discussion, see Schmink and Wood 1992, 303.

8. The z-statistics for Altamira, Paragominas, Tucumã, Tailândia, and São Felix are -3.77, -2.58, -2.97, 0.98, and 1.68 respectively. In subsequent chapters we will test more formally the relationships among these variables with simultaneous multivariate analysis.

9. The z-statistics for Altamira, Tucumã, Tailândia, and São Felix are –2.32, –2.78,– 2.48, and –2.48 respectively.

10. Schneider 1994 provides an analytical framework similar to ours to discuss turnover. He also provides the best overview of the literature on turnover in the Amazon.

CHAPTER 6

The Determinants and Impact of Property Rights: Evidence from Household Surveys

In this chapter we provide empirical results from our household surveys regarding the demand and supply of title, its impact on land value, and its effects on agricultural investment on the Amazon frontier. We utilize data on 206 smallholders from the sites of Altamira, Tucumã, São Felix, and Tailândia.[1] We have data on the characteristics of the settlers, the nature of their land tenure, the identity of the land agencies involved, land values, and investment. In our analyses, the frontier is defined with respect to distance from a market center. By examining the frontier, we can follow the rise in land values with movement toward a market center, the associated increase in demand for title, the response of government to those demands, and the impact of titles on site-specific investment and land values.[2]

A Model of Property Rights, Land Value, and Investment

In chapter 4 we presented the analytical framework that underlies our empirical work. We argued that higher potential rental streams from a resource with secure property rights generates a demand for titles. In turn, titles promote land specific investment and thereby increase land values indirectly. Titles also increase land values directly by broadening the market for land and reducing private enforcement costs. It is this simultaneous relationship among titles, investments and land values that we will test in this chapter. To do so, we specify the following relationships:

(1) Value $= a_1 + a_2$Distance $+ a_3$Distance·Title $+ a_4$Clear $+ a_5$Investment $+ a_6$Title $+ a_7$Jurisdiction $+ e$.

(2) Title $= b_1 + b_2$Change in Value $+ b_3$Jurisdiction $+ b_4$Distance $+ b_5$Human Capital $+ b_6$Physical Capital $+ e$.

(3) Investment $= d_1 + d_2$Distance $+ d_3$Title $+ d_4$Human Capital $+ d_5$Physical Capital $+ d_6$Jurisdiction $+ e$.

The rationale for equation (1) is as follows: Land is an input to agricultural production. Its derived value is a function of supply factors, primarily the amount and quality of available land, and demand factors that include population density, the net prices of agricultural output (gross agricultural prices less transportation costs), and the nature of property rights to land. Productivity is determined by soil quality (inherent land productivity), past investment in improvements, and other characteristics, such as land contours, access to water or irrigation, and the degree to which the land has been cleared of forest, which is a precondition for most agricultural activity. The effect of clearing on land value depends upon whether forests were considered valuable or an impediment to farming.

Having title should increase demand for land and, hence, land values by reducing private enforcement costs, promoting investment, and expanding market exchange. Distance from the market center toward the frontier should reduce demand and land values per hectare because of increased transportation costs and lower net returns to farming. As illustrated in chapter 4, the effect of distance is different for titled and untitled land. Up to some remote point, distance should have a greater negative effect on the value of titled land than on the value of untitled land because of the declining contribution of title to value with greater distance.

From our survey we use various proxies for the theoretical variables in the above equations. Value is the reported per hectare value of a settler's farm.[3] Site dummies for São Felix, Tailândia, and Tucumã with respect to Altamira are included to account for the impact of differences in soil quality or other site-specific variables, such as agency jurisdiction, on land value that would affect the demand for land. We do not have information about differences in soil quality along the roads within each of the four sites where we interviewed. There are no indications, however, that soil quality differs importantly within each site. We include other demand variables—the extent of forest clearing, land-specific investment, the existence of title, and distance from the market center.

Distance is reflected in two variables. The Distance variable accounts for the expected negative effect that distance from the market center has on land values. The Distance·Title interaction variable reveals the effect having title has on land value with respect to distance. The Distance variable reflects the additional effect of distance on the value of untitled land. Hence, we expect both coefficients to be negative; this is consistent with the value of title being greater as one moves from the economic frontier to the market center.

Clear is the percentage of the farm that is cleared of forest. Investment is the percentage of the farm that is placed in pasture or permanent crops. This variable should capture the effect of past improvements on land value, leaving the exchange and enforcement effects on land value to be captured by the Title variable.[4]

Equation (2) contains both demand and cost variables for title as suggested by the analytical framework in chapter 4. The dependent variable is a dichotomous variable, taking the value one if the farmer had title and zero otherwise. In general, the demand for title should be a function of expected private net returns, which in turn are due to the increase in land value from having title, less the private costs of obtaining title. Land values will increase with title because of a greater opportunity for investment in land improvements, greater exchange opportunities for land sales, and reduced private enforcement costs.

The private costs of securing title, and hence demand, also will be affected by the requirements of the land laws, such as beneficial use, occupation, boundary marking, and documentation. Unfortunately, we do not have systematic data on these factors. Additionally, costs will be an increasing function of distance due to the higher costs of traveling to and from remote farm sites to the administrative center, and of surveying and recording claims. We have the distance in kilometers from each farm to the local community and land office site, which is the city of Altamira for the Altamira site, the city of Tucumã for the Tucumã and São Felix sites, and the city of Tailândia for the Tailândia colony.

The characteristics of farmers may also affect their demand for title or the costs associated with acquiring titles. In the previous chapter we argued that more human and physical capital should increase the likelihood that a farmer could secure a title. Our measures for human and physical capital are age, education, time on plot, and wealth. Lastly, as described in chapter 4, the greater the expected change in land value from securing a title, the greater will be the demand for a title.

Because private enforcement costs are likely to be higher for large farms or ranches, we expect that larger average farm sizes would increase the demand for title. Although we test for the effects of farm size in the estimation using census data in chapter 7, we do not include farm size in the demand for title in the estimation in this chapter because our sample consists of smallholders. Both formal colonization projects for small farmers and invasions by squatters of a particular area lead to a clustering of small farms in the Amazon with few neighboring large farms or ranches.[5]

For example, the four sites we sampled are almost totally made up of smallholders. 80 percent of the 206 farmers in the survey had under 100 hectares, and 93 percent had under 200 hectares. Among smallholders in the Amazon there is comparatively little conflict. In our survey, small farmers repeatedly stated that their claims were "safe," indicating that there were few private enforcement costs that would differ by farm size.

There are several reasons why there are few disputes over land claims among smallholders. One is that the land is in beneficial use. Smallholders with 200 hectares or less use much of their land to earn a nearly subsistence living for their families. Their plots are either in full production or are gradually being cleared at a rate of three to five hectares per year.[6] Further, since small farmers typically occupy the land, they can observe intrusion by neighbors or other squatters on their small holdings. Land claims are marked with cleared boundaries and planted trees, often cashews. Finally, as discussed in chapter 5, smallholders in an area organize groups to lobby the local land offices to provide formal titles.[7] These collective actions create a sense of cohesion or community among smallholders that promotes recognition of individual land claims.[8] There are occasional disputes between adjacent smallholders over the location of boundary lines or the drift of cattle and between smallholders and loggers, who trespass to harvest valuable timber species. Both our survey responses and the land dispute records of ITERPA and the Pastoral Land Commission in Brasília, however, clearly indicate that disagreements among smallholders over property rights are resolved routinely.

The costs of obtaining title will be affected by jurisdictional issues. The jurisdictional effects are represented with site dummy variables to capture agency and other site-specific factors that might affect the private cost of title. The intercepts are with respect to Altamira, the baseline. We chose Altamira as the baseline because it was a showcase INCRA settlement. Because Altamira was an early colonization site along the Transamazon Highway, established when INCRA had large budgets to provide title at low private cost, we expect that settlers close to the market will have title in that colony. Tucumã is another INCRA site; however, it was placed under the agency's jurisdiction late, after budgets had declined, reducing its capability to process titles. This factor may have raised the private costs of obtaining title in that colony. The ITERPA areas of Tailândia and São Felix may be more likely to have titles than at Altamira, because of the aggressive actions of ITERPA to subsidize the provision of titles to smallholders in exchange for political support and the closer proximity of ITERPA headquarters in Belém.

The rationale for equation (3) is as follows: Investments in land improvements will be made on the basis of expected returns, which in turn are a function of the private costs of investment and the increase in farm revenue that results from the investment. Investment is measured as the portion of the farm placed in improved pasture and permanent crops.

Preparing pasture and planting permanent crops, such as cacao, pepper, and citrus, represent the most important investments made by the small-holders in our sample. Most costs are labor devoted to improving pasture—building fences, chopping brush and weeds—and planting and tending permanent crops.

Expected returns from investment depend upon transportation costs and land quality. Distance from the market should reduce the expected returns from investment by raising transportation costs. Distance is measured in kilometers from the market center to the farm. Site dummies with respect to Altamira are used to control for soil quality and jurisdictional effects from INCRA and ITERPA administrations. The private costs of investment include the costs of capital plus the costs of the actual investment. Access to and the cost of funds to purchase inputs for investment depend in part on whether the farmer has title, and hence can use the farm as collateral.

Having title also will provide more security for long-term investments. Title should provide greater security for long-term investment in pasture and permanent crops and assist in accessing credit. Human-capital variables, such as age, education, wealth, and time on the farm, outlined in the survey, also should raise the expected returns from investment. Those with greater education may be more aware of market conditions and how to respond to them. Personal wealth may increase an individual's ability to obtain additional funds for investment. Age and time on the farm may reflect greater farming experience.

Empirical Results

Table 16 provides descriptive statistics for the pooled survey sample. We estimated the determinants of land value, title, and investment in the following ways. For the land value equation (1), we used a log-linear specification and OLS. For the title equation (2), we used a probit because Title is a binary variable. For the investment equation (3), where the dependent variable is a percentage, we used a tobit. These equations make use of the variables available to us in our survey.

As shown in equation (1), having title increases land value and, hence, should affect the demand for title, as reflected in equation (2) through the Change in Value variable. This variable, however, is not directly observable in our data set. Accordingly, we introduce an instrument for the expected change in value from having title, calculated from equation (1). We take the difference in the antilogs of the value equation when title equals one and zero, and this expression contains both exogenous variables and investment. Because of simultaneity between title and investment, we use a two-stage procedure to estimate those variables. Predicted investment is used to calculate the Change in Value variable, and predicted title is used in estimating investment in equation (3).

The two-stage procedure addresses possible correlation of the errors in the investment and title equations. Because title and investment are in the value equation, there is the possibility of correlated shocks across the equations; accordingly, we performed the Breusch and Pagan (1980) test for correlation in the error terms in all three equations and found none.[9] Based on these tests, estimating the land value equation with OLS yields consistent results.

Table 17 contains the estimated coefficients and t-statistics for the estimations of equations (1), (2), and (3). Column 2 of table 17 provides the estimation of the determinants of land value. The site dummies in the equation account for the differences within each region that might affect land value, such as soil quality. Hence, the intercepts can be different across the sites. The results indicate that land values are higher at Tucumã than at the baseline of Altamira, and soil conditions are known to be relatively good at Tucumã (Butler 1985). The estimated values per hectare are U.S.\$34.12, \$28.22, \$21.76, and \$148.41 for Altamira, São Felix, Tailândia, and Tucumã, respectively.[10] As predicted, the effect of title on land value is positive and significant. Because we have controlled for the impact

TABLE 16.   Descriptive Statistics for the Survey Sample (206 observations)

Variable	Mean	S.D.	Minimum	Maximum
Percentage of farmers with title	61	49		
Value per hectare	\$86.78	\$200.95	\$2.72	\$1,902.00
Total distance to market (km)	68.14	57.70	4.00	190.00
Area (hectares)	119.70	261.82	5.00	3,500.00
Percent of farm cleared	40.00	24.00	0.00	100.00
Percent of farm in pasture and permanent crops	19.00	19.00	0.00	100.00
Education (years)	1.99	2.21	0.00	10.00
Time on plot (years)	8.60	7.32	0.00	58.00
Age (years)	43.67	13.01	16.00	78.00
Wealth (value of livestock)	\$3,651.20	\$10,734.00	0.00	\$114,300.00

of investment, as in the census estimations in chapter 7, the Title variable largely reflects the gain in value due to increased exchange opportunities and lower private enforcement costs.

The log specification of the model implies that the percentage increase in land value due to having title will be the same across all of the sites, holding distance constant. If distance is zero so that the farm is at the market center, where values and competition for control are potentially the greatest, the estimated coefficient suggests that title would raise values by 189 percent.[11] Similarly, at a distance of 40 kilometers, land values would

TABLE 17.   Determinants of Land Value, Title, and Investment: Survey Data for Smallholders (*t*-statistics in parenthesis)

	Land Value per Hectare	Title	Investment
Constant	3.53	0.51	– 0.23
	(6.00)	(0.82)	–(1.43)
Tucumã	1.47	–2.28	0.22
	(8.87)	–(3.32)	(4.08)
São Felix	–0.19	0.33	–0.09
	–(1.06)	(0.78)	–(2.75)
Tailândia	–0.45	–0.07	–0.07
	–(3.12)	–(0.21)	–(2.31)
Title	1.06		0.36
	(2.14)		(3.50)
Distance	–0.23	–0.006	0.003
	–(1.75)	–(1.74)	(0.19)
Distance title	–0.14		
	–(1.14)		
Clear	0.58		
	(1.33)		
Investment	0.97		
	(2.14)		
Time on plot (years)		0.04	–0.02
		(2.38)	–(1.09)
Education		0.08	–0.01
		(1.59)	–(0.92)
Wealth		0.00002	0.01
		(1.18)	(2.33)
Age		–0.007	0.03
		–(0.83)	(0.95)
Change in value		0.01	
		(1.35)	
Calculated log–likelihood ratio		59.61 $(C^2_{9,.05} = 16.92)$	119.54 $(C^2_{9,.05} = 16.92)$
R^2	.69		

be increased by 72 percent.[12] This estimated increase in value is consistent for the actual observations. For instance, for farms in the range of 20–39 kilometers from the market, actual land values per hectare are 71 percent higher for titled land than for untitled land.[13] The regression predicts that at a distance of 140 kilometers, land values would be 45 percent higher for titled land. Actual observations for all farms 140 kilometers or greater from market reveal a 35 percent difference in land value between titled and untitled land.

Title also affects the slope of the estimated relationship between land value and distance. The estimated coefficients for the Distance and title-distance interaction variables indicate that a 1 percent increase in distance from the market leads to a 0.37 percent decline in the value of titled land.[14] The estimated impact of distance on untitled land is negative, with a 1 percent increase in distance reducing land value by 0.23 percent. As distance from the market center increases, values fall for titled and untitled land. As predicted, the results suggest that the decline in value with distance is greatest for titled land. Hence at some point the two estimated relationships meet. Using the estimated coefficients for title and the title-distance interaction, we can solve for the distance where land values with title equal those without title. In the case at hand, the distance is 1,942 kilometers, which is beyond any of our sampled locations.[15] Hence, having title provides some value to all of our sampled smallholders.

Agricultural investment in permanent crops and pasture has the predicted positive effect on land values with a 1 percent increase in the percentage of farmland in pasture and permanent crops resulting in a 0.97 percent increase in value per hectare. Clearing also has a statistically weak, positive effect on land value, with a 1 percent increase in the percentage of the farm that is cleared yielding a 0.58 percent increase in value per hectare.

Column 3 of table 17 provides the probit estimation for the determinants of title equation (2). Title is a binary variable, one if the individual had a definite or provisional title, and zero otherwise.[16] The estimation is reasonably accurate as a predictor, correctly predicting the existence of title in 84 percent of the cases and correctly predicting no title in 53 percent of the cases.[17] The lower prediction success for the absence of title is consistent with our qualitative evidence of aggressive titling practices of the state land agency, ITERPA in São Felix and Tailândia, where low-valued, remote land claims are granted title for political reasons.

The regression also tends to overpredict title; that is, we predict a title for 144 settlers while only 127 have title. This result suggests that the government titling agencies may not be assigning titles strictly in accordance with the economic costs and benefits of titling, that is, providing title when the individual private net benefit calculations lead claimants to demand formal recognition of their claims. This outcome is no surprise, as political and bureaucratic factors, such as constituent lobbying, election pressures, budget allocations, and staffing levels, affect the government response. How the government responds influences the private costs of obtaining title and, hence, shifts the cost curve. We do not have sufficient information about agency titling to effectively model the process or to include political variables in the regressions.

We attempt to control for political differences associated with federal and state jurisdictions and land agencies, INCRA or ITERPA, through the site dummy variables. But the results indicate that the problem of undertitling claimants who have comparatively high-value land close to markets exists across the sites, at least to some degree. For example, there are plots in both Altamira and Tailândia with reasonably high values and short distances that are not titled.[18] This problem is most pronounced in the INCRA community of Tucumã. INCRA's budget and staffing for processing claims have declined as the federal government has allocated budgets to other national issues (Yokota 1981, 33; Schneider 1994, 8). The undertitling in Tucumã is reflected by the intercept, which indicates that settlers are less likely to have title there than in the baseline, Altamira, or in the ITERPA colonies of São Felix and Tailândia. In the latter colonies, there are no significant differences in the probability of having title from that found in Altamira, where titling by INCRA initially was aggressive, but now also is lagging (Moran 1984, 291). Mean distances from the market are 26 km in Tucumã, 63 km in Altamira, 153 km in São Felix, and 45 km in Tailândia. Further, mean land values in Tucumã are U.S.$237.34 per hectare, while in Altamira they are $59.66, and $16.64 and $24.10 in São Felix and Tailândia, respectively.

To examine this issue further, using the estimated coefficients evaluated at the means for each site and the cumulative normal density function, the predicted probability of having title in each area is 89 percent at Altamira, 59 percent at São Felix, 73 percent at Tailândia, and 32 percent at Tucumã. Alternatively, if settlers with the mean characteristics for each site were located in the baseline colony of Altamira, then the predicted probability of having title is 75 percent for Tailândia, only 46 percent for São Felix, and a much greater 96 percent for Tucumã.[19]

The role of political and bureaucratic variables in influencing agency response to demands for title also is indicted in the apparent overtitling in São Felix by the state agency ITERPA, whose agents in some cases have handed out titles prior to local elections. The agency thereby appears to have lowered the private costs of obtaining title, even though the social costs of providing title in these areas to low-valued sites may be quite high—but those costs are not completely internalized by the agency.[20]

For the human-capital variables, only time on the farm has a statistically significant contribution to having title, although education comes close. Those who have been on their claim longer are more likely to understand the requirements of the land agencies and meet their requirements. For instance, evaluated at the means, the marginal increase in the probability of having title, given a one-year increase in time on the farm, is 0.8 percentage points in Altamira, 1.6 percentage points in Tucumã, 1.7 percentage points in São Felix, and 1.5 percentage points in Tailândia. A half-standard-deviation move from the mean number of years raises the probability of having title by 4.3 percentage points in Altamira, 2.0 percentage points in Tucumã, 4.6 percentage points in São Felix, and 3.8 percentage points in Tailândia.[21] Similarly, evaluated at the means, the marginal increase in the probability of having title, given a one-year increase in education is 1.6 percentage points in Altamira, 3.0 percentage points in Tucumã, 3.2 percentage points in São Felix and 2.8 percentage points in Tailândia. A half-standard deviation move from the mean number of years of education raises the probability of having title by 1.6 percentage points in Altamira, 4.1 percentage points in Tucumã, 2.3 percentage points in São Felix, and 2.3 percentage points in Tailândia.[22]

Distance has the predicted negative effect on the incidence of title, which is consistent with costs of obtaining increasing with distance from an administrative center. Evaluated at the means, the marginal effects on the probability of having title, given a one kilometer increase in distance is –0.1 percentage points in Altamira, –0.2 percentage points in Tucumã, –0.2 percentage points in São Felix, and –0.2 percentage points in Tailândia. A half-standard-deviation move from the mean distance lowers the probability of having title by 2.7 percentage points in Altamira, 0.9 percentage points in Tucumã, 4.2 percentage points in São Felix, and 2.7 percentage points in Tailândia.[23]

The expected change in land value from having title has the predicted effect on the incidence of title, although the significance level is low. The regression suggests that, evaluated at the means, the marginal increase in the probability of having title, given a U.S.$1 increase in the expected change in value due to title, is 0.2 percentage points in Altamira, 0.3 percentage points in Tucumã, 0.4 percentage points in São Felix, and 0.3 percentage points in Tailândia. A half-standard-deviation move from the mean change in value raises the probability of having title by 1.3 percentage points in Altamira, 5.2 percentage points in Tucumã, 0.2 percentage points in São Felix, and 0.8 percentage points in Tailândia.[24]

Column 4 of table 17 provides the tobit estimation of the determinants of agricultural investment—equation (3). Investment is the portion of farmland placed in improved pasture or permanent crops. The regression results show that site characteristics influence investment considerably. Everything else equal, settlers in Tucumã have more investments than do those in Altamira, and settlers in São Felix and Tailândia have the least investment. In addition to good soil, Tucumã has the shortest mean distance to market of the four sites, and it is a relatively prosperous market town.

The existence of title has a positive effect on investment. The effect of title on the percentage of farmland in pasture and permanent crops can be estimated, using the mean values for settlers at each of the four sites. The results suggest that the ownership assurance provided by title provides support for investment in costly fencing, other pasture development activities, and in cultivating permanent crops. For Altamira, having title adds 29 percentage points to the proportion of farmland in pasture and permanent crops. The mean proportion of land so devoted in Altamira is 25.5 percent. Similarly, for São Felix and Tailândia, having title raises the share of farmland in pasture and permanent crops by 21 percentage points at each site, and for Tucumã, the increase is 48 percentage points.[25] The mean proportion of land in pasture and permanent crops in those sites is 7.3 percent, 12.1 percent, and 31.6 percent, respectively. Of those who have pasture, the mean level of fencing is 1,181 meters, which represents an investment of approximately U.S.$550.[26] Accordingly, title plays a very important role in promoting investment in land improvements. In comparison, the human-capital characteristics do not appear to have an impact on the private returns to investment.[27]

Overall, the statistical tests using our survey data support the analytical framework described in chapter 4. Land value per hectare is a positive function of title. Moreover, for titled and untitled land, distance differentially reduces value. The contribution of title to land value is greatest at the market center, where competition and private enforcement costs would otherwise be the highest. The role of title, however, appears to decline with distance as competition for control declines and production and exchange opportunities diminish. The estimations suggest that for all of our sampled smallholders, title always offers some added value. Whether or not it pays for a settler to seek title depends upon the corresponding private costs of obtaining it. Land agencies influence those costs, with the state agency, ITERPA, appearing to provide title liberally, whereas the federal agency, INCRA, appears to be very slow in titling in the colony of Tucumã, where land values are relatively high and distances comparatively short. ITERPA is as likely to provide title to settlers in its remote colonies, as is INCRA in its showcase and more accessible Transamazon colony of

Altamira. We find strong empirical support for the notion that formal property rights to land promote farm-specific investments, which, in turn, raise land values directly.

Conclusion

In this chapter, we examined the determinants and impact of the most basic institutions for markets, secure property rights in the form of title to land. For our empirical analysis we used individual observations drawn from surveys that we conducted in 1992 and 1993 in four frontier sites in Pará. Two of the sites—Altamira and Tucumã—are under the jurisdiction of INCRA, and the remaining sites of São Felix and Tailândia are under the jurisdiction of ITERPA. These jurisdictional variables allow us to examine the effect of political variables on the provision of title on the frontier.

The empirical results support the framework presented in chapter 4. Title and investment contribute to land value, and title, in turn, promotes farm-specific investment. Additionally, the expected change in value from having title appears to increase the incidence of title. In other words, the expectation of increased land value with title motivates settlers on the Brazilian Amazon frontier to demand title. This response is consistent with the predictions of economic theory. Although we estimated the Change in Value variable, the results reported here are consistent with actual survey evidence for a subsample of the surveyed group discussed in chapter 5. We asked 13 of the sampled farmers in Tucumã to give estimates of the change in land value attributable to title. Of those, 11 replied that title would raise their land values by at least 20 percent, and eight reported that title would increase their land values by 50 percent or more.

The demand for titles has produced a response by government agencies. But in this case, the political and bureaucratic reactions are less straightforward. There is a differential response by state and federal titling agencies to the economic demands of settlers. ITERPA, the state land agency, has titled more aggressively than has the federal counterpart, INCRA. Our econometric results support the observation by us and by others that, at times, ITERPA has issued titles for political support prior to elections. INCRA's lack of titling reflects other bureaucratic factors, such as a cutback in budgets and staffing in the late 1980s and early 1990s. These results underscore the importance of examining political and bureaucratic factors in the institutional response to the demand for property rights.

The strength of our empirical tests in this chapter rests in our ability to control for individual characteristics. A potential criticism of our results is that they are not generalizable across time or space. We confront this criticism in the next chapter by examining the simultaneous relationship among titles, land values, and site-specific investment using Brazilian census data from two states over a period of frontier development: in Paraná for 1940 to 1960; and in Pará for 1970 to 1985.

NOTES

1. Data limitations do not allow us to use the information from our two sites near Paragominas.

2. The analysis in this chapter draws from Alston, Libecap, and Schneider 1996b. Although not extensive, there is an empirical literature that addresses property rights institutions in contemporary developing areas and in an historical context. See Feder and Feeny 1991; Besley 1995; Ostrom 1990; Place and Hazell 1993; Migot-Adholla et al. 1991; and Ensminger 1995 for analyses in contemporary development. Besley (1995) provides an analysis with respect to tenure and investment in Ghana. Feder and Onchan (1987) and Feder et al. (1988) compare the performance of farmers and land values on titled and untitled land in Thailand. These studies examine the nature and impact of tenure in more or less settled regions. For more historical studies and contemporary natural-resource problems, see Libecap 1989. Our analysis is of frontiers, allowing us to examine the development of property institutions as land values rise. Furthermore, none of the above-cited analyses examine the simultaneous relationship among titles, land values, and site-specific investments.

3. Although the land prices are those reported by individual farmers and are not actual transactions, as noted above, there are active land markets in all four sites. Hence, individuals would have opportunities to observe actual sales prices of nearby farms.

4. We considered whether clearing was an explanatory variable affecting the costs of obtaining title. The smallholders that we surveyed in Pará indicated that having title had little impact on their clearing activity. Additionally, they claimed that clearing did not promote title. According to them, in a densely forested region such as the Amazon, everyone cleared as a precondition to engaging in any agricultural activity. As an empirical check we included Clear in a regression run and found that it had no statistically significant impact, nor did title have a significant impact on clearing. In contested regions of the Amazon, the relationship between title and clearing may be different. We examine this issue in more detail in chapter 8.

5. Although this is the general case in Pará, there are a few municípios where federal subsidies for ranching under SUDAM were also attractive for squatting. These areas are claimed by both large ranchers and smallholders, and these counties, not surprisingly, are where violence occurs. We address violent conflict in chapter 8.

6. Field notes by Ricardo Tarifa, May 18, 1993, for Tucumã.

7. The role of *sindicatos* and church groups in squatter efforts in the Amazon is well known. We attended a meeting of a rural *sindicato* in Altamira in 1992.

8. A discussion of local "networks" and corresponding recognition of individual land claims is provided in Ricardo Tarifa's field notes, May 18, 1993, for Tucumã. For a discussion of local enforcement of property rights in a different context, see Ellickson 1991.

9. The Breusch and Pagan (1980) technique involves a Lagrange multiplier test for correlation between the error terms of the model equations.

10. The estimated values are drawn directly from the site dummy coefficients: $e^{3.53} = 34.12$, $e^{3.53-.19} = 28.22$, $e^{3.53-.45} = 21.76$, and $e^{3.53+1.47} = 148.41$.

11. The change in land value is $e^{1.06} - 1$, or 189 percent. Although the coefficient 1.06 represents an approximation of the percentage change in the land value due to having title, the magnitude of the coefficient makes it a less accurate approximation. Accordingly, it is preferable to directly calculate the percentage change in value due to having title.

12. The change in land value with title is $e^{1.060-.14\text{lndist}} - 1$, or at 40 km, 72 percent.

13. In chapter 5 we presented the responses of 14 settlers in Tucumã who reported increases in land value with title ranging from 0 percent to 100 percent. All of these settlers are somewhat remote from the market center in Tucumã. Hence, a 189 percent increase in value is conceivable when distances are zero.

14. This result is obtained by adding the coefficient for the title-distance interaction to the estimated coefficient for the Distance variable, $-0.14 + 0.23 = -0.37$.

15. We solve for the distance by setting the two estimated lines equal to each other. Dividing the estimated coefficient for title by the estimated coefficient for the title-distance interaction (1.06/0.14) gives 7.57, and $e^{7.57} = 1,942$ km.

16. Some farmers have a provisional title, rather than a final or definitive title. A provisional title may be issued while final processing of the title application takes place. The survey of settlers and discussion with land agency officials indicated that provisional and definitive titles were viewed as essentially the same, and we treat them as equals in the analysis. We estimated the equation reported in the text using only definitive title, and the results essentially are the same.

17. The regression correctly predicts 42 farms without title and 107 with title when 79 did not have title and 127 had title. Overall, the regression correctly predicts 149 out of the sample of 206, or 72 percent.

18. Examination of the data reveals at least two plots without title in Altamira that are only 12 and 13 km from the market, and both are reasonably high valued, although somewhat below the mean price per hectare. Similarly, there are two plots in Tailândia with values above the mean price per hectare that are not titled.

19. For the alternative probabilities of having title, each site was estimated as if the settlers were in Altamira. The dummy variables for the sites other than the baseline were set to zero (Greene 1993, 696–98).

20. In chapter 5 we discussed the titling practices of ITERPA as reported by Schmink and Wood (1992, 303); our field surveyor, Ricardo Tarifa, described the assignment of titles by ITERPA prior to state elections.

21. The standard deviations from the mean time on farm are 10.35, 5.38, 5.13, 2.51 for Altamira, São Felix, Tailândia, and Tucumã, respectively.

22. The standard deviations from the mean years of education are 2.06, 1.39, 1.68, 2.72 for Altamira, São Felix, Tailândia, and Tucumã, respectively.

23. The standard deviations from the mean distances are 50.27, 37.76, 28.52, and 9.00 for Altamira, São Felix, Tailândia, and Tucumã, respectively.

24. The standard deviations from the mean change in value are U.S.$15.36, $1.26, $5.12, and $32.05 for Altamira, São Felix, Tailândia, and Tucumã, respectively.

25. Following Greene 1993, 696–98, and McDonald and Moffit 1980, the effect of having title on investment was estimated by calculating the cumulative density at the means of each site. The result is used to scale the estimated coefficients.

26. Our field surveyor, Ricardo Tarifa, reported that 1,000 meters of fence cost approximately U.S.$500, including labor and wire, with poles coming from the farm.

27. There may a spurious relationship between investment (pasture) and our wealth measure, which is value of livestock. Hence, we do not draw strong conclusions about the variable.

CHAPTER 7

The Determinants and Impact of Property Rights: Census Data from Two Frontiers in the States of Paraná and Pará

In this chapter we continue the analysis of the demand and supply of title, its impact on land value, and its effects on agricultural investment on Brazilian frontiers. We use census data from the Brazilian agricultural census from 1940 through 1985, with observations at the município (county) level to examine the development of property rights to land on two agricultural frontiers. We examine the emergence and impact of land titles in the southern state of Paraná during the agricultural boom between 1940 and 1970 and in the Amazon state of Pará during the period of rapid migration to the region after 1970. With census data across time, we can observe much greater variation in land value, tenure, and investment than is possible with household survey data, which do not exist over such a long time period or for comparable frontier regions. As such, we can determine whether the development of property rights to land changed over time as relative prices changed. If the results are similar for both data sets, we can have greater confidence in the robustness of the tests of the theory.[1]

The Frontier States of Paraná and Pará

Settlement data from the states of Paraná and Pará provide an opportunity to examine land titling on the frontier at different points in time. There was rapid settlement of unoccupied government land in the state of Paraná after 1940 due to high coffee prices and declining yields in the neighboring state of São Paulo. The population of the state rose from approximately 1.2 million in 1940 to nearly 7 million by 1970 (FIBGE 1990a, 183). Between 1940 and 1960, the amount of agricultural land almost doubled, and the number of farms increased more than fourfold. On the western and northern frontiers of the state, cropland increased by over seven times (Nicholls and Paiva 1969, 8). Average per hectare farmland values in constant 1970 cruzeiros rose from Cr$98 in 1940 to Cr$674 in 1970.[2]

In contrast to Paraná, where migration was gradual and spontaneous, except for recruitment by private land companies, settlers were attracted to Pará through directed colonization projects and other subsidies initiated by the federal government, beginning in the late 1960s. The population of Pará grew from 2,167,018 in 1970 to 4,318,400 in 1985 (FIBGE 1990a, 180–83). The land in farms doubled in the 1960s and again in the 1970s, and the number of farms rose sharply. Vast tracts of new lands were opened to private claiming through construction of regional road systems, such as the Transamazon and Belém-Brasília Highways. Yet, Pará is sparsely settled. In 1980 only 5 percent of the land in Pará had been cleared of forest and placed into agriculture, whereas in Paraná, 65 percent of the land was cleared and in agriculture.[3] These additions of new lands, as well as the isolation of the region from the rest of Brazil, kept land values comparatively low. Census data indicate that per hectare farmland values in constant 1970 cruzeiros grew from Cr$41 in 1970 to Cr$153 in 1980 in Pará.[4] Even so, Pará real land values in 1970 were less than half those in Paraná in 1940 (in constant 1970 prices) and 1980 Pará land prices remained less than half of Paraná land prices in 1950.[5]

Figures 5 and 6 describe the settlement processes in Paraná and Pará from 1940 to 1985. As shown in figure 5, the total hectares in farms grew steadily in Paraná, and the total number of farms jumped sharply after 1950. The total number of farms shown in figure 6 remains higher in Paraná than Pará throughout the period, indicating denser and smaller farms in the southern state. In Pará, the total hectares in farms declined between 1940 and 1960 with a shift out of Brazil nut and natural rubber production after the end of World War II. Both Brazil nuts and natural rubber were collected from lands that otherwise were not farmed or heavily settled. When the census stopped considering these areas as farm properties, total farm area fell. With the adoption of new settlement policies in the late 1960s, farm area rose once again, although as figure 6 reveals, the total number of farms remains well below that found in Paraná. Population densities on the frontier remain low in Pará relative to those in Paraná.

With the exception of western municípios, land distribution policies appear to have been relatively straightforward in Paraná. Squatting, the occupation of land without title, was limited at the aggregate state level. As indicated in figures 7 and 8, census data for the state level show that the proportion of farmland held by squatters peaked at 9.3 percent in the late 1950s, and the proportion of farms operated by squatters peaked at 13.5 percent somewhat earlier, in the late 1940s (FIBGE 1950, 154; 1960a, 27).

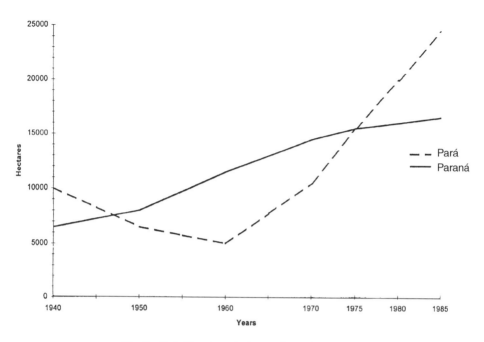

Fig. 5.   Total hectares in farms: Paraná and Pará

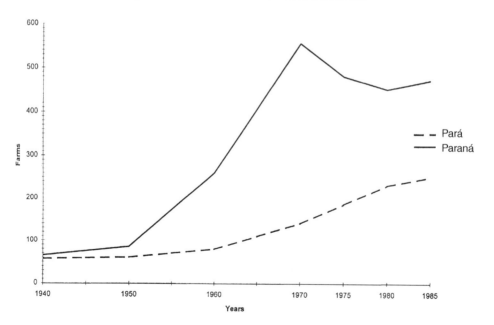

Fig. 6.   Total number of farms: Paraná and Pará

Within Paraná the state government had sole jurisdiction over land settlement, except in the western municípios, where there was dispute over jurisdiction between the federal and state governments (Foweraker 1981, 88–92). This dispute was not resolved until the mid-1960s, and it delayed the assignment of clear property rights to land and encouraged conflict among settlers over claims (Westphalen, Machado, and Balhana 1968).

The effect of confused jurisdiction between the governments is reflected in squatting data. In 1950, the average percentage of land operated by squatters in the nine western municípios was 21 percent, but in the northern frontier, where there was no jurisdictional conflict, the level of squatting was low. In those 26 municípios, only an average of 2 percent of the land was occupied by squatters. In 1950, the western region accounted for 66 percent of Paraná's squatters and 84 percent of all squatted land, while the northern region had 16 percent of total squatters and 8 percent of squatted land (Nicholls and Paiva 1969, 60). By the 1970 census, there was much less variation in squatting across the state, and overall, only 5.1 percent of the farmland was occupied by squatters, and 9.0 percent of the farms were operated by squatters. Those proportions continued to decline through 1985.[6]

In the northern region, the state government sold much of the land to private land development companies that recruited settlers and provided titles. The Companhia de Terras do Norte do Paraná obtained 12,463 sq. km of land in the north and sold urban and rural lots to settlers and extended railways and roads. The municípios included accounted for over 12 percent of the size of Paraná in 1960.[7] Because it first gained clear legal title to its land before attracting colonists, the company appears to have been able to transfer titles quickly and to avoid conflict and legal disputes that would have resulted in tenure uncertainty (Nicholls and Paiva 1969, 27–30; Foweraker 1981, 130).

As indicated in figures 7 and 8, squatting has been more prevalent and has lasted longer in Pará than in Paraná. In 1975, 23.3 percent of the agricultural land in Pará was occupied by squatters, and 49.2 percent of the farms were operated by squatters (FIBGE 1975b, 150). Moreover, the shares of farmland and farms operated by squatters have remained high, 11.2 percent and 34.0 percent, respectively, in 1985 (FIBGE 1985, 166). Further, the statewide data in the figures mask even more squatting on the frontier. The data in table 18 indicate not only higher average levels of squatting, but even in frontier counties, squatting was more extensive in Pará, suggesting that the tenuring process has moved more slowly and less completely in that state.

In Pará, the frontier has been quite different in a number of ways from that in Paraná, ways that might affect the titling process, leading to more

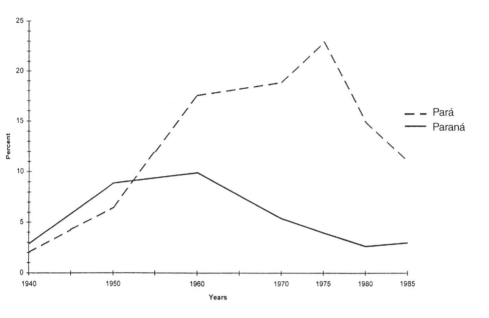

Fig. 7. Percentage of total farmland held by squatters: Paraná and Pará

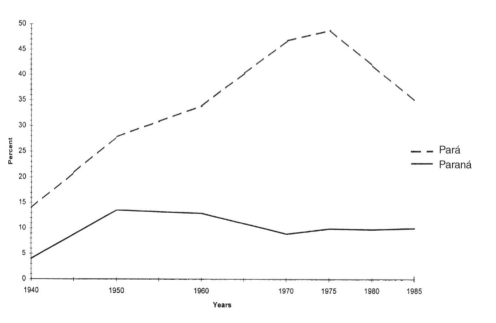

Fig. 8. Percentage of all farms operated by squatters: Paraná and Pará

squatting. First, more than one land agency has been involved, often with no clear demarcation of authority. In Pará, both the federal government and the state have had jurisdiction over land. As described in chapter 2, in 1965 the federal government initiated Operation Amazônia to settle the region and to secure Brazil's claim to the Amazon. Under the constitution of 1969, the federal government claimed all lands essential to national security. This action was followed by Decree Law 1164 in 1971, by which the federal government took control of all land up to 100 km on either side of all roads constructed, under construction, or projected. These areas subsequently were placed under the federal land colonization agency, INCRA, for administration. Municípios where INCRA processed most claims included nearly 75 percent of Pará, leaving the rest of the state for the state land agency, ITERPA. The government of Pará contested the usurpation of its jurisdiction of public land, bringing confusion to claimants and additional delays in the titling process (Schmink and Wood 1992, 62–64).

A second difference between Paraná and Pará is that the directed colonization programs of the federal government and promises of infrastructure investment encouraged early migration to the Amazon, before land rents had risen to a level that otherwise would have attracted migrants. Beginning in 1966 and continuing into the 1970s, the military government provided tax and credit incentives to private firms for investment in the Amazon. These initiatives were joined in the early 1970s with road-building programs, pledges of other infrastructure investment, and directed (subsidized) colonization efforts. INCRA organized colonization projects, especially along the Transamazon Highway, bringing colonists from southern Brazil with pledges of infrastructure and credit.

In 1971, the Program for National Integration (PIN) was launched to bring colonists to the Amazon. In Pará, INCRA established three colonization areas: Marabá, Altamira, and Itaituba. Although the goal of placing 100,000 families, each with 100-hectare plots, in organized colonies and planned urban centers was not met (only 7,800 families were

TABLE 18.   Mean and Maximum Share of Farmers Who Were Squatters by Município in Paraná and Pará

Paraná Year	Mean Share	Maximum Share	Pará Year	Mean Share	Maximum Share
1940	3	55	1970	46	99
1950	8	84	1975	48	92
1960	7	97	1980	39	96
1970	8	55	1985	33	89

Source: Brazilian Agricultural Census

actually settled along the Transamazon Highway), settlers were attracted from other areas, especially the northeast, to Pará.[8] As discussed in chapter 2, there were other formal projects for colonization in Pará.

The claims of the many settlers who rushed to the region, or who were brought there by official colonization projects, flooded the federal agency, INCRA, beyond its capabilities to process them. INCRA, established to administer orderly settlement colonies, was forced to respond to spontaneous migration and informal land claims (Mueller 1992, 6). As INCRA and the state land agency, ITERPA, competed for jurisdiction, they focused more on directing settlers to particular areas, and less on assigning title. Indeed, settlers were to remain on the land with licenses to occupy before the agencies would return to process title applications. This practice led to a lag between settlement and the assignment of title.

With a growing influx of migrants and fluctuating budget appropriations the agencies were severely limited in their ability to provide titles. Although there was considerable migration to the Amazon in the 1970s, most title applications were not processed until after 1980 (Yokota 1981, 33). ITERPA processed title applications according to state election cycles, with officials promising titles in exchange for electoral support.[9] Recently, however, the pressure on both agencies has subsided as the flow of migration to the Amazon has slowed with the end of federal highway building and maintenance, subsidies, and colonization projects.

A third difference between settlement and titling in the two states is violent conflict among competing claimants. Although there was confusion over property rights to land in the western municípios in Paraná, where the federal and state governments competed for jurisdiction, in Pará there has been violence between smallholders and ranchers, particularly in southeastern Pará along the Belém-Brasília Highway in the município of Conceição do Araguaia and others near Marabá. We address this issue in more detail in the following chapter. Ranchers have been subsidized by the Superintendency for the Development of Amazonia (SUDAM), a federal agency that administered a series of credit benefits and fiscal incentives, and settlement by smallholders has been encouraged by investment in infrastructure by the federal government and by colonization projects organized by INCRA (Schneider 1994, 2–6).

Characteristics of the Census Data Set for the Two States

Our comparative empirical analysis of the determinants and impact of land titles on the frontier uses census data by município (county). In our data set, there are 79 municípios in Pará in the four census periods, whereas in Paraná the number of municípios grows from 49 in 1940 to 288 by 1970 through subdivision of existing municípios.[10] In general, the data are averages for each município, and they include average land value per hectare, distance from the município capital to the state capital (Curitiba and Belém) as a measure of remoteness from the market and administrative center, the proportion of farmers with title, average farm size, average soil quality, population density, and average investment per hectare.[11] Analysis of these census data allows us to test for the broad determinants of property rights to land as they emerge over time.

An Analytical Model and Estimation of Titling, Land Values, and Investment on the Frontier

We return to the framework estimated in chapter 6 for the survey data to estimate the determinants and impact of land titles with census data in Paraná and Pará. We use a log-linear specification and OLS for the land value and investment equations and OLS for the title equation.[12]

(1). $\text{LnValue} = a_1 + a_2\text{LnDistance} + a_3\text{LnDistance·Title} + a_4\text{LnSoil} + a_5\text{LnClear} + a_6\text{LnInvestment} + a_7\text{LnDensity} + a_8\text{Title} + a_9\text{Jurisdiction} + a_{10}\text{Conflict} + e.$

(2). $\text{Title} = b_1 + b_2\text{Change in Value} + b_3\text{Size} + b_4\text{Jurisdiction} + b_5\text{Conflict} + b_6\text{Distance} + b_7\text{Human-Capital Characteristics} + e.$

(3). $\text{LnInvestment} = d_1 + d_2\text{LnDistance} + d_3\text{Title} + d_4\text{LnSoil} + d_5\text{LnCharacteristics} + d_6\text{Jurisdiction} + d_7\text{Conflict} + e.$

As shown in equation (1), having title increases land value and hence should affect the demand for title, as reflected in equation (2) through the Change in Value variable. As described in the previous chapter, this variable is not directly observable in our data. The technique for estimating instruments for the change in value from having title is described in chapter 6. Predicted investment is used to calculate the Change in Value variable, and predicted title is used in estimating investment in equation (3). The two-stage procedure that we use addresses possible correlation of the errors in the investment and title equations. As noted earlier, because title and investment are in the value equation, there is the possibility of correlated shocks across the equations; accordingly, we performed the Breusch and Pagan (1980) test for correlation in the error terms in all three equations and found none.[13] Based on these results, estimating the land value equation with OLS yields consistent results.

The motivation for each of the three equations also was described in the previous chapter. Because there are somewhat different variables in the census data from those collected in the survey, we briefly summarize the motivation for each of the estimated equations modified from those presented in chapter 6.

Land Value

The value of land is a function of supply and demand factors. For our estimation we have population density; distance to market centers; soil quality, past investment, and clearing (proxies for agricultural productivity); title (property rights to land); government jurisdiction (affecting the supply of titles); and evidence of conflicts over land.

The effect of clearing on land value depends upon whether forests were considered valuable (Paraná) or an impediment to farming (Pará). Having title should increase demand and, hence, land values by reducing private enforcement costs, promoting investment, and expanding market exchange. Distance from the market center toward the frontier should reduce demand and land values per hectare because of increased transportation costs and lower net returns to farming. As noted earlier, the effect of distance is different for titled and untitled land. Up to some remote point, distance should have a greater negative effect on the value of titled land than on the value of untitled land because of the declining contribution of title to value with greater distance.

In the estimation of equation (1) the value of agricultural land per hectare in the município is the dependent variable.[14] Among the independent variables, title is represented by the percentage of município farmers with title to their land.[15] Land-specific investment per hectare in the município as of the census year is calculated from county-level census data as described in the text below. Distance is the distance from the município capital to the state market center, Curitiba and Belém.[16] The measure is used to indicate relative remoteness of a município's farms to a major market. Indexes of average soil quality in the município also are created from county-level data provided by the Brazilian census agency Fundação Instituto Brasileiro de Geographia e Estatístico (FIBGE).[17] The Clear variable is the percentage of município agricultural land that is cleared of forest.[18] Other variables likely affecting the value of agricultural land on the frontier include município population density taken from the census, whether the município was administered by a private land company or whether it was one of the municípios contested between the state and federal governments (Paraná), whether the município was administered by INCRA or whether the município was the site of conflict over land (Pará), and the differential effects of distance from the market center on titled and untitled land values, introduced through an interaction term for distance and title.

We include the variable for private land companies in Paraná to test whether the most important private land company, Companhia de Terras do Norte do Paraná, was granted the most valuable land or whether it added extra infrastructure. To capture this effect, we introduce a dummy variable for the northern municípios under its jurisdiction.[19] Additionally, we test whether conflict over land lowered values in those western municípios in Paraná characterized by jurisdictional disputes between the state and federal governments.[20] We test for similar jurisdictional and conflict effects in Pará. Private land companies were much less important in the settlement of Pará, but the federal government may have claimed the best land along major highways and assigned it to INCRA. We assign a dummy variable for those municípios under INCRA's jurisdiction.[21] As in Paraná, we expect that conflict over land will reduce land values. In the late 1970s and 1980s there was conflict in 44 of the 79 municípios in our data set (Pará Pastoral Land Commission), especially in the southeastern part of Pará. For those municípios we assign a dummy variable the value of 1. We do not have data on conflict for this estimation for 1970 and 1975, although disputes likely were more limited at that time because of the early stage of settlement.

Title

Equation (2) contains both demand and cost variables for title. We expect that the change in value from having title will be a major factor in determining the demand for title. As discussed earlier, this variable is created from the estimation of land value. We expect that distance from the município capital to the main administrative center, which is the state capital (Curitiba, Paraná or Belém, Pará) will raise the costs of obtaining title because individuals may have to travel to the administrative center to lobby land agencies. Further, the costs of providing title should be higher for more remote municípios. Other demand variables for which we have census data include the size of the farm (average farm size in the município) and the characteristics of the individual farmer. Because private enforcement costs are likely to be higher for large farms or ranches, we expect that larger average farm sizes increase the demand for title, hence the sign of the coefficient is anticipated to be positive. With regard to individual characteristics, we have data for average age, income, and education in the município only for the 1980 census year.[22] Age as a proxy for experience, education, and income or wealth could increase the demand for title and reduce the private costs of obtaining title. Individuals with greater experience, education, and income or wealth may be better able to take advantage of having title and realize the extra returns made possible by it, and they may understand the political process and bureaucratic requirements better to secure title at lower private cost. Hence, the estimated coefficients on these characteristics variables should be positive.

In chapter 6 we saw that the costs of obtaining title were affected by jurisdictional issues. We examine those effects more broadly with the census data by including dummy variables for the western municípios in Paraná where there were conflicts between the state and federal governments over which had authority to grant title. This factor likely raises the private costs of obtaining title. These effects should lead to a negative estimated coefficient. In addition, in Paraná, private land companies played an important role in settlement and the provision of title. Because the private land companies were residual claimants for increases in land value from providing title, we anticipate that they would provide title at lower cost to claimants. Hence, those municípios under private jurisdiction would have more titles, on average, giving a predicted positive coefficient to the Jurisdiction variable in Paraná. In the estimation, the northern municípios under the jurisdiction of the private land company, Companhia de Terras do Norte do Paraná, are indicated with dummy variables.

In Pará, we use two different jurisdictional variables. One is also a jurisdictional dummy variable. Private land companies have been less important in that state, but the federal and state land agencies, INCRA and ITERPA, had separate jurisdictions. We expect that ITERPA, with local constituencies and headquarters in nearby Belém, would be more responsive to local demands for title and provide title at comparatively lower private cost. Accordingly, those municípios under its jurisdiction would be titled more extensively than would those under the federal agency, INCRA, which had national constituencies and was headquartered in more distant Brasília.

In the estimation, INCRA municípios are represented with a dummy variable with a value of one, otherwise zero. As a result, the estimated coefficient on the INCRA variable is predicted to be negative. The conflict variable is used to identify those municípios in Pará characterized by violent conflict over land between ranchers and squatters as described above. We view this conflict as a demand variable since the returns to secure title would be particularly large in areas where ownership was uncertain. Accordingly we anticipate a positive coefficient on the violence variable.

Land-Specific Investment

The dependent variable for equation (3) is average land-specific investment per hectare in the município. We calculate the variable from a broad census investment measure by deleting livestock and other mobile agricultural investments. The agricultural census provides a combined variable that includes the value of land and investment in buildings, fences, corrals, equipment, and animals. Since the census separately provides land value and livestock data, we can remove livestock values to get an overall land-specific investment variable.[23]

Distance from the market should reduce the expected returns from land investment by raising transportation costs. Although livestock and commodity prices generally will not vary across municípios for any census period, transportation costs will be different across the sample. As above, distance is the distance between the município capital and the major state market center, which is Curitiba in Paraná and Belém in Pará. Average soil quality in the município as described above also is included because soil quality would affect the returns to investment.

We add dummy variables for those municípios where conflict occurred in Paraná and Pará and property rights were uncertain, even with title, to determine whether investment was reduced. Moreover, private land companies in Paraná and the federal land agency, INCRA, in Pará provided some subsidies for permanent crops, fertilizers, and other infrastructure that may have raised the net private returns from investment, and we control for these effects with dummy variables for the municípios involved. Access to and the cost of funds to purchase inputs for investment depend in part on whether the farmer has title, and hence can use the farm as collateral. Having title also will provide more security for long-term investments. Title is represented by the percentage of farmers in a município with title.

Empirical Results

Tables 19 through 21 present the estimation results for equations (1) through (3).[24] In general, the estimations perform better for the state of Paraná than for Pará, perhaps because of much lower land values in Pará and the other differences in frontier settlement between the two states described above.

As indicated in table 19, title and investment have the predicted positive effects on land value for seven of the eight census periods in the case of title and for all eight census years for investment, where the estimated

TABLE 19. Determinants of Land Value on the Frontier: Census Data

					Dependent Variable: Land Value per Hectare						
	Constant	Title	Title distance	Invest	Population Density	Cleared Area	Soil Quality	Distance	Private Company	Govt. Dispute	R^2	N
Paraná												
1940	-9.70	8.88	-1.41	0.52	0.14	-0.27	0.18	1.47	0.17	-0.27	.73	49
	-(1.75)	(1.63)	-(1.59)	(3.72)	(0.77)	-(0.96)	(1.21)	(1.65)	(0.42)	-(0.88)		
1950	-6.17	5.93	-0.87	1.05	0.04	-0.93	-0.07	1.14	0.68	-0.38	.86	80
	-(1.58)	(1.40)	-(1.18)	(8.69)	(0.22)	-(2.70)	-(0.64)	(1.68)	(3.93)	-(0.72)		
1960	-4.09	3.45	-0.35	0.68	0.44	-0.19	-0.06	0.66	0.16	0.21	.87	162
	-(1.68)	(1.39)	-(0.88)	(9.21)	(5.80)	-(1.28)	-(0.67)	(1.69)	(2.22)	(1.13)		
1970	-8.21	7.66	-1.31	0.46	0.30	0.46	0.07	1.46	-0.05	-0.15	.75	288
	-(5.39)	(4.56)	-(4.29)	(9.16)	(3.88)	(2.46)	(1.42)	(5.25)	-(0.67)	-(2.59)		

	Constant	Title	Title distance	Invest	Population Density	Cleared Area	Soil Quality	Distance	INCRA Area	Violent Conflict	R^2	N
Pará												
1970	-0.36	0.21	-0.03	0.37	0.20	0.07	0.04	-0.07	N.A.	N.A.	.51	78
	-(0.29)	(0.18)	-(0.12)	(3.59)	(1.97)	(0.48)	(0.16)	-(0.45)				
1975	0.39	0.70	-0.24	0.27	0.11	0.03	0.02	-0.06	-0.18	N.A.	.44	79
	(0.34)	(0.43)	-(0.82)	(2.59)	(1.62)	(0.29)	(0.10)	-(0.31)	-(1.42)			
1980	0.87	-1.07	0.25	0.41	-0.15	-0.02	-0.10	-0.32	0.51	-0.06	.51	79
	(0.55)	-(0.50)	(0.68)	(4.11)	-(2.26)	-(0.13)	-(0.44)	-(1.26)	(3.00)	-(0.39)		
1985	0.28	1.42	-0.13	0.07	0.14	0.16	-0.31	-0.16	0.26	0.24	.37	79
	(0.15)	(0.55)	-(0.29)	(0.94)	(1.90)	(1.24)	-(1.38)	-(0.49)	(1.39)	(1.17)		

Note: *t*-statistics in parentheses. N.A. = not available.

coefficient is statistically significant in all periods, except 1985 for Pará. Title has a significant impact at the 90 percent level or better in two of the four runs for Paraná, but the variable never has that statistical punch for Pará. The impact of title on land value is captured partially by the investment variable, so that the Title variable in equation (1) reflects the gain in value due to increased exchange opportunities and lower private enforcement costs. These results are consistent with the findings for the relationship between land value and title and investment with the survey data presented in chapter 6.

The effect of title on land value tends to decline with distance from the market center, with a negative coefficient for the title-distance interaction variable for seven of the eight census periods. The effect is weak, however, particularly for Pará. For nontitled land, the effect of distance always is negative, as expected for Pará (although not significant), but positive for Paraná. The other explanatory variables for land value tend to have the predicted signs and generally have greater statistical significance for Paraná, where the overall regressions explain more of the variation. Greater population density, reflecting demand for land, leads to higher land values in at least five of the eight census periods. Municípios under the jurisdiction of private land companies in Paraná, at least in 1950 and 1960, and under INCRA in Pará in 1980 tend to have higher land values, likely due to greater infrastructure and investment. Confused property rights due to conflict between the state and federal government in parts of Paraná appear to lower land values, particularly in 1970.

With regard to the determinants of private property rights to land as reported in table 20, jurisdictional conflict in Paraná in the western municípios over whether the federal or state government had authorization to issue titles reduced the portion of farmers with title, particularly in the last three census periods. In Pará, however, there is no observed difference between the proportion of farmers with title in those municípios characterized by violent conflict over land from elsewhere in the state. INCRA municípios may have had a smaller percentage of farms with title than elsewhere, but the census estimations reveal no significant effect. Recall that in the survey data analyzed in the previous chapter, the INCRA colony of Altamira in Pará had extensive titling, whereas the INCRA colony of Tucumã, also in Pará, appeared to be undertitled, given land values and distances to market. In Paraná those municípios under the jurisdiction of the private land company had a greater percentage of titled farms only by the 1970 census. This result suggests that the state of Paraná responded well to its constituents' demands for title.

As hypothesized, distance from the market/administrative center tends to reduce the portion of farmers with title, a finding consistent with

TABLE 20. Determinants of Property Rights on the Frontier: Census Data

				Dependent Variable: Proportion of Farmers with Title				
	Constant	Distance	Farm Size	Private Company	Govt. Conflict	Change in Value	R^2	N
Paraná								
1940	1.03	-0.0002	0.0001	0.02	-0.15	-0.24	.25	49
	(22.71)	(2.02)	(0.70)	(0.90)	(0.99)	(0.68)		
1950	0.93	-0.0002	0.0001	-0.02	-0.29	0.10	.25	80
	(33.83)	(1.00)	(1.80)	(0.31)	(1.63)	(1.54)		
1960	0.95	-0.0001	0.0002	0.02	-0.35	0.07	.37	162
	(45.26)	(1.50)	(1.83)	(0.91)	(3.37)	(1.54)		
1970	0.91	0.00002	-0.0003	0.05	-0.03	-0.02	.10	288
	(40.68)	(0.31)	(2.33)	(4.85)	(1.95)	(1.12)		

	Constant	Distance	Farm Size	INCRA Area	Violent Conflict	Change in Value	Age	Income	Education	R^2	N
Pará											
1970	0.53	-0.0003	0.0001	N.A.	N.A.	8.43	N.A.	N.A.	N.A.	.48	78
	(6.67)	(3.95)	(1.50)			(2.90)					
1975	0.60	-0.0003	0.0001	-0.05	N.A.	-0.17	N.A.	N.A.	N.A.	.20	79
	(5.31)	(3.95)	(1.06)	(0.88)		(0.50)					
1980	-0.66	-0.0002	-0.0002	-0.03	0.04	0.09	0.05	0.12	0.06	.20	79
	(1.13)	(1.79)	(2.01)	(0.52)	(0.60)	(0.28)	(2.02)	(1.37)	(0.74)		
1985	0.48	0.0001	0.0001	-0.02	-0.001	0.46	N.A.	N.A.	N.A.	.09	79
	(5.36)	(0.91)	(1.22)	(0.30)	(0.01)	(2.21)					

Note: t-statistics in parentheses; N.A. = not available.

the notion that administrative costs rise with remoteness. This result also is consistent with the survey estimation in chapter 6. The Distance variable is significant at the 95 percent level in four of the eight census runs. The relationship between farm size and title is mixed in both states. The estimated coefficient generally is positive as predicted, but there is a census period in each state where the effect is negative and significant. We had hypothesized that private enforcement costs would rise with farm size, increasing the demand for title by large farmers.

For the 1980 census in Pará, we have socioeconomic measures by município for age, income, and education. All three have a positive impact, but only age leads to greater titling statistically. Finally, the expected change in value from having title has a positive effect on the incidence of title in five of the eight census periods, with the greatest statistical significance in Pará in two of the census periods.

Table 21 provides the estimates for agricultural investment per hectare. Having title has the predicted positive impact in seven of the eight census periods and is statistically significant six of those periods. This result underscores the role of title in promoting investment found with the survey data. With regard to distance from the market, in the two cases where the coefficient is significant at the 95 percent level, the effect is to reduce investment. In most cases the variable is not significant, a result also identified with the survey data examined earlier.

Confused property rights associated with conflicting government jurisdictions over land in Paraná appears to reduce investment in that state, especially in the 1940 census period. There is a similar weak effect for violent conflict in Pará. The private land development companies that sold land to farmers in Paraná and the federal agency, INCRA, which established colonies of settlers in Pará, provided infrastructure and some subsidies for investment. These practices are reflected in the regression results.[25] Soil quality plays a positive and generally significant role in investment in Paraná.

Over time, the factors identified in equation (3) contributed to the growth in investment in land in Paraná (in constant 1970 cruzeiros) from Cr$31 per hectare in 1940 to Cr$453 in 1970.[26] Although the same forces appear to have been active in Pará, the amount of investment in that state is considerably less than in Paraná. For example, in 1980 per hectare investment in Pará was Cr$79 (1970 cruzeiros), which was less than one-fifth the level in Paraná in 1970 (FIBGE 1970a, 252; 1980b, 282).

All in all, the predictions of the theory outlined in chapter 4 are supported by the empirical evidence drawn from the census between 1940 and 1985, and the results are similar to those reported in chapter 6 for estimations using household survey data. In general, title and/or investment

TABLE 21. Determinants of Agricultural Investment on the Frontier: Census Data

				Dependent Variable: Agricultural Investment Per Hectare				
	Constant	Title	Distance	Private Company	Government Conflict	Soil Quality	R^2	N
Paraná								
1940	2.44	-5.16	-0.21	0.05	-2.13	0.37	.36	49
	(0.94)	(-2.07)	(-2.24)	(0.07)	(-3.66)	(1.47)		
1950	-5.50	2.67	-0.03	0.80	-0.27	0.50	.28	80
	(-3.69)	(1.88)	(-0.35)	(3.01)	(-0.51)	(2.35)		
1960	-5.47	3.07	0.01	0.68	0.74	0.42	.26	162
	(-3.13)	(1.82)	(0.12)	(4.30)	(1.05)	(2.04)		
1970	-10.47	9.80	0.05	0.38	-0.04	0.27	.42	288
	(-9.56)	(7.06)	(0.58)	(2.88)	(-0.37)	(2.52)		
	Constant	Title	Distance	INCRA Area	Violent Conflict	Soil Quality	R^2	N
Pará								
1970	-6.70	4.55	0.49	N.A.	N.A.	-0.19	.27	78
	(-2.73)	(3.58)	(1.65)			(-0.54)		
1975	-4.07	3.93	0.02	0.71	N.A.	0.34	.24	79
	(-0.70)	(0.91)	(0.05)	(2.67)		(0.50)		
1980	-0.94	2.54	-0.31	0.67	-0.32	-0.16	.44	79
	(-0.77)	(2.65)	(-2.41)	(3.34)	(-1.50)	(-0.63)		
1985	-4.71	6.78	-0.10	0.27	-0.28	-0.31	.28	79
	(-2.48)	(3.71)	(0.59)	(0.99)	(-0.90)	(-0.91)		

Note: *t*-statistics in parentheses; N.A. = not available.

raised land values on both Brazilian frontiers across time. The independent effect of title on land value, however, tended to decline with distance from major market centers in Paraná, while the distance effect on the value of titled land was not significant in Pará. Higher costs associated with greater distance from administrative centers tended to reduce the proportion of farmers in a município with title in both states, with the strongest results in Pará. Jurisdictional confusion as to which government had authority to issue titles also lowered titling on the frontier in Paraná. Except for one census period, neither the private land company in Paraná nor the federal agency, INCRA, in Pará provided significantly different titling services from elsewhere in the two states. The expected change in value from having title also generally had the predicted positive effect on the incidence of title in both states. As predicted in most cases, title led to more land-specific investment in both states across the census periods.

Concluding Remarks

This chapter continued the analysis in chapter 6 by examining the development and impact of property rights to land on agricultural frontiers in two Brazilian states, Paraná and Pará, at different times in this century. The estimations used aggregate census data with observations at the município level for earlier frontiers in the state of Paraná between 1940 and 1970 and for more recent frontiers in the Amazon state of Pará between 1970 and 1985. For both the survey data presented in chapter 6 and the census data presented in this chapter, the predictions of the theory generally are supported by the empirical analyses using the two data sets: Title and investment contribute to land value, and title promotes farm-specific investment. Additionally, the expected change in value from having title appears to increase the incidence of title.

The general consistency of the econometric results for both the census and survey data sets underscores the robustness of the theoretical predictions about the role of property rights in influencing investment and raising land values. Additionally, this case study of Brazilian frontiers provides evidence regarding the political and economic processes that underlie the demand and supply of title. These empirical results provide insights into the contribution of property rights for economic behavior and the development of markets.

The results are all the more important given the general lack of titling in Pará. As we have pointed out in tables 3 and 18 and in figures 7 and 8, squatting is far more prevalent in Pará (and the Amazon in general) than in other regions of Brazil. Although in part the absence of titles reflects lower land values, more generally this condition reflects a lack of a clear policy by INCRA to follow through in settlement projects with the assignment of clear title to small farmers. Our empirical results indicate that titling provides important economic and social benefits to farmers. Hence, the timely provision of titles at low cost to settlers should be of higher priority.

NOTES

1. The analysis in this chapter draws on the material presented in Alston, Libecap, and Schneider 1996b.

2. Fundação Instituto Brasileiro de Geographia e Estatístico (FIBGE) 1940, 244; 1970a, 77. The index used to deflate prices was the general price index calculated by Fundação Getúlio Vargas. For the period 1940–44, the price index for São Paulo found in FIBGE 1990b, 226–36, 285–86, was used. The values reported in the text are the total value of farmland in Paraná divided by total farm area.

3. The cleared area as reported in the census includes land in permanent crops, temporary crops, planted pasture, natural pasture, planted forest, and unused but usable land. It is divided by the area of each state.

4. FIBGE 1970b, 178; 1980b, 282. The index used to deflate prices was the general price index calculated by Fundação Getúlio Vargas. The values reported in the text are the total value of farmland in Pará divided by total farm area.

5. Paraná land values in 1940 were Cr$98 per hectare in 1970 prices, while those in Pará in 1970 were Cr$41 per hectare. In 1950, Paraná land prices were Cr$312, while in 1980 Pará land prices were Cr$153. These data are from the FIBGE 1940, 244; 1950, 184; 1980b, 282. The following factors were used to convert nominal prices to 1970 prices: 1940–70: 885.133; 1950–70: 230.552; 1970–80: 29.616.

6. FIBGE 1970a, 140. For example, the 1985 census (FIBGE 1985, 238) reported 2.9 percent of farmland operated by squatters.

7. This figure was calculated using the map in Nicholls and Paiva 1969, 28, and the area of the municípios within the company's jurisdiction from FIBGE 1965, 42–43.

8. Fearnside 1986, 19–20; Wood and Wilson 1984, 142; Sawyer 1984, 189. For an assessment of government settlement projects, see Moran 1989b. The leading states in order of number of migrants to Pará for the period 1970 to 1980 were Maranhao, Goias, Ceará, and Minas Gerais (FIBGE 1991a, 190). For discussion of the settlement of the Amazon in general, see Mueller 1992; Sawyer 1984, 189; and Santos 1984. For Pará see Moran 1984, 1989b; Foweraker 1981; and Schmink and Wood 1992.

9. Pinto 1980, 187. Our survey findings reported in the previous chapter support this claim.

10. For 1970 for Pará, we have only 78 municípios because of problems with the census measure of investment in one município.

11. As we describe below, some of the variables, such as investment, are

constructed using census data. In all cases where prices are involved it is necessary to deflate. All values for Paraná are in 1970 cruzeiros and all values for Pará are in 1985 cruzeiros. The index used to deflate prices was the general price index calculated by Fundação Getúlio Vargas. For the period 1940–44, the price index for São Paulo found in FIBGE 1990b, 226–36, 285–86, was used.

12. We performed a test proposed by Davidson and Mackinnon (1981) to decide between a linear and log-linear specification for the value of land and investment equations in the four census periods in each state and for the survey data. Of the eight equations estimated for each state, the test either led to the rejection of the linear specification (nine of the sixteen estimations) or was inconclusive regarding the use of the linear or log specification (five of the sixteen estimations). In only two cases (one in each state) was the log specification rejected. We performed the test outlined by Breusch and Pagan (1979) for heteroskedasticity in the census estimations and corrected for it as necessary. Where heteroskedasticity is found, the estimation is corrected by using White's (1980) consistent estimator of the covariance matrix. The problem was greatest in the Paraná estimations, where 10 of the 12 runs required correction. For the Pará estimations, only 3 of the 12 runs required correction, 2 in the early value runs and 1 in the early investment estimation. We also estimated the title equation for the census data, where the proportion of município farmers with title is the dependent variable, with a probit specification. The results were essentially the same as with OLS, and for ease of coefficient interpretation, we chose the OLS specification. In Pará, the municípios of Belém, Ananindeua, and Benevides were not used in the analysis because they are primarily urban areas.

13. The Breusch and Pagan (1980) technique involves a Lagrange multiplier test for correlation between the error terms of the model equations. The chi-square statistics for Pará and Paraná were all well below the critical value.

14. Land values for 1940–80 are from FIBGE, *Censo Agropecuario—Paraná.* The values are those declared by the proprietor or administrator of the farm to the census interviewer. The agricultural census is done over the universe of agricultural establishments in each state, and the results are presented aggregated at the município or county level. The value of land in 1985 in Pará was not provided in the census. It was estimated by taking the ratio of land value to the value of farms (which included the value of investments, machinery, and animals) for 1970, 1975, and 1980. The growth rates of this ratio were obtained and an average growth rate calculated. The 1980 ratio was then multiplied by this average growth rate to give the 1985 ratio, which in turn was multiplied times the 1985 agricultural farm value as provided in the census.

15. The census provides the proportion of município farmers who occupy their land without title (squatters). Hence, our measure is 1—the proportion of farmers who are squatters.

16. The distance between the município capital and the state capital was calculated using maps. For Pará the data are provided in a map, *Republica Federativa do Brasil, Estado do Pará, Rodoviario, Politico e Estatistico,* 3d ed., 1988, published by Editora Turistica e Estatistica, Goiania. The data are from DER (Departamento

Estadual de Rodagem) and from DETRAN (Departamento Nacional de Transito), respectively the state and national highway agencies. The distances are to Belém. Because of the importance of river transport in Pará, we used distance by river if this were less than distance by road or if no roads existed. For Paraná, the Distance variable is created from a map prepared by the state of Paraná road department (DER) in 1966. The distances are to Curitiba, the capital of the state, even though some municípios in the north of Paraná probably are more under the influence of the markets in São Paulo, which is closer. Lacking more complete information, we maintained the same market for all of the municípios in Paraná.

17. Soil quality for each município was constructed using the maps in Geografia do Brasil, Região Sul (vol. 2, 33) and Região Norte (vol. 5, 90–91), published by IBGE, Rio de Janeiro, 1990. The maps classify the potentiality of the soil for agriculture in five categories, considering fertility and topography. Each município was assigned a number ranging from 1 to 5, increasing with the quality of the soil's potential.

18. The cleared variable was constructed by dividing the number of hectares of agricultural land cleared by the total amount of agricultural land in the município. The area cleared was defined as the sum of the land in permanent crops, temporary (annual) crops, planted pasture, natural pasture, planted forest, and unused, but usable, land. These variables are defined by the agricultural census.

19. The dummy variable for the municípios in which the private land company, Companhia de Terras do Norte do Paraná, allocated land was created using the map in Nicholls and Paiva 1969, 28. By examining maps by FIBGE (DT-SUEGE DEGEO/DIATA) that designate municípios, it is possible to identify those municípios included in the company's holdings. These areas then can be projected to 1970 and extended back to 1950 and 1940 to identify the municípios involved.

20. Determination of whether a município was involved in government jurisdictional disputes is based on discussion of Paraná settlement in Westphalen, Machado, and Balhana 1968. These authors clearly define 11 municípios where there were disputes in the 1950s between the federal and state governments. They also indicate that such conflicts were long-standing and not settled until the mid-1960s, although they do not identify the contested municípios in earlier or later years. Due to subdivision, the number of municípios grew in Paraná over time. In the estimation, we traced the municípios as identified in the 1960 census back to 1950 and 1940 and extended them forward to 1970. Of the 49 municípios that existed in 1940, 1 was classified as private and 3 with jurisdictional conflict. In 1950, of 80 municípios, 8 were private and 4 were in the disputed area. In 1960, there were 162 municípios in Paraná, with 29 having private land company holdings and 11 in the disputed area. By 1970, there were 288 municípios, with 49 having large private company holdings and 61 within the area of jurisdiction confusion.

21. Municípios were considered as being under INCRA's jurisdiction if the capital of the município was within 100 km of a federal highway, following Brazilian law.

22. Before 1980, socioeconomic data are at the state level only.

23. For 1985, livestock values are not provided, but were estimated by multiplying the number of animals (as given) by estimated prices. The prices were calculated by dividing the value of sales for each category as provided in the census by the number sold. All values for Paraná were converted to 1970 cruzeiros and for Pará to 1985 cruzeiros. The price index used for this was the general price index as described by Fundação Getúlio Vargas, Rio de Janeiro. The investment amount then was divided by the amount of agricultural land in the county as provided in the census.

24. We did not pool the census data for two reasons. One was that we wanted to examine changes across time, which can be best illustrated with the individual census year runs. Further, there are problems with pooling Paraná data in particular since the number of municípios and hence, observations, changes across time from 49 to 288. This increase in the number of municípios is through subdivision of municípios so that the observation base is not the same across time. Additionally, for Pará we do not have information on all of the variables across time. On another point, in the estimations for 1970, for Pará one record is lost due to a negative value for investment, giving 78 observations.

25. For example, after its creation in 1971, INCRA provided a variety of subsidies, including housing, other infrastructure, and seeds to Amazon settlers in its colonies (Moran 1981, 79–83). Regarding the performance of the soil quality variable, as noted earlier the LnSoil variable appears to be especially weak, giving expected results for Paraná, but negative results for Pará.

26. FIBGE 1970a, 252. The values reported in the text are total farm investment in each state, as we define it, divided by total farm area.

CHAPTER 8

The Determinants and Impact of Violent Conflict over Land on the Amazon Frontier

Our purpose in this volume is to describe the development of land tenure institutions on the frontier. As we have seen, property rights arrangements have been molded by changing land polices and land reform efforts. Even though the land settlement and distribution policies described in chapters 2 and 3 have not always been consistent over time, property rights have evolved in a manner close to that predicted by the analytical framework. Nevertheless, conflicting governmental jurisdictions in Paraná earlier in the twentieth century and competition between large and small claimants in Pará in recent years have led to violent land conflicts on the frontier. In this chapter we assemble data on rural land conflicts to estimate the determinants of violence and speculate on its impact on land values, investment, and tenure institutions.

We begin with data for all of Brazil to analyze the aggregate evolution of land conflicts and to relate that evolution to land policy. Next, we use state-level data to examine the distribution of land conflicts within Brazil. Following this, we utilize município-level evidence to analyze the distribution of violence throughout the state of Pará, which is the Brazilian state with the highest incidence of rural conflicts. Finally, we use município-level data on deaths in rural conflicts in Pará from 1978 to 1985, together with other data from the Brazilian agricultural census, to statistically test for the determinants and economic impact of violence over land.

Rural Conflicts: The Decision Making of Titleholders and Squatters

With the institutional environment for land settlement and reform as background we can develop a model to help us to better analyze the behavior of the antagonists in land conflicts. As described in chapter 4, much of the hostility is between large and small land claimants. Indeed,

153

most violence on the frontier occurs as squatters invade land held by large ranchers or farmers. Squatters hope to elicit the assistance of the federal land reform agency, INCRA, in expropriating the farm and dividing it among the invaders. Landowners, naturally, seek to evict the invaders privately or obtain the assistance of the courts and police in removing them from the property. The appendix to this chapter outlines a model of land conflict.[1]

Violence typically involves physical conflicts. Squatters may actively and tenaciously resist the private efforts of landowners to force them off the land. Squatters may also oppose the actions of the police. Shootings, torture, whippings, knife battles, and mob disturbances may occur. Men, women, and children may be affected. Property—farm buildings, fences, crops—may be destroyed, livestock killed, and nearby roadways blocked. It is clear that violence can be costly for both sides. It can result in deaths or injuries, incarceration, and lost production as property is destroyed and as the parties divert scarce resources (typically their labor) from farming to occupying someone else's land or evicting trespassers.

Other costs to squatters include organizational and lobbying costs, as well as the opportunity costs incurred in camping before an invasion, and the forgone income associated with an invasion. Other costs to landowners include hiring gunmen, obtaining warrants of eviction, paying police, and lobbying politicians. Because of these costs, both large farmers and squatters use violence in a calculated manner, applied strategically so as to maximize the value of their respective expected outcomes.

For squatters, violence will increase the likelihood of INCRA intervening in their behalf. But as described in chapter 4, the likelihood of INCRA intervening will also depend on the strength of the farmer's property rights to the land and the presidential political commitment to land reform. Furthermore, squatters need to consider the role of the courts that enforce property law.

Landowners engage in violence as means of intimidating squatters to abandon the invaded farm. And, like squatters, they make their decision with an understanding of the position of the courts and INCRA. There are three possible outcomes to an invasion: (a) if squatters are evicted and the land remains with the farmer, the squatters get nothing; (b) if squatters are not evicted, but there is no expropriation, then squatters remain on the land with title held by the farmer; and (c) if there is an expropriation, squatters receive the land, and the farmer is compensated in some manner by INCRA.

Because historically compensation has been below land values, landowners have challenged the payments proposed by INCRA. More recently, as land values have fallen, INCRA compensation has become relatively more attractive in some instances. For our analysis, however, we presume that landowners would prefer to retain their land as compared to receiving compensation for expropriation from INCRA. Accordingly, for landowners, the first outcome is preferred to the second and third, with the reverse ordering preferable to squatters.

We begin by examining the decision to use violence by squatters and farmers as a means of obtaining or maintaining frontier lands when conditions change. These exogenous shifts include (1) changes in the strength of property rights to land; (2) changes in the value of land; (3) changes in the cost of violence; and (4) changes in the position of the courts.[2] The discussion abstracts from the details provided in the appendix to this chapter. The comparative statics of variable changes are outlined in table A.1.

An increase in the level of the farmer's property rights security, such as the availability of a well-defined and uncontested title, will give the farmer an incentive to be less violent in part because the court system can enforce the title. As described in the appendix, the impact of more secure property rights for farmers on the behavior of squatters is ambiguous. Hence, the interaction between the two antagonists is more complex than might be perceived initially. To better understand their behavioral responses, we focus on how changes in property rights to land might affect the decision of INCRA to expropriate and on how these changes might affect the actors' responses to the use of violence by each other.[3]

More secure tenure reduces the likelihood of an INCRA expropriation. This situation is understood by both parties, and it encourages them to refrain from violence because the payoff to its use has declined. Farmers have less to fear from an invasion when they have more secure tenure. INCRA will be less responsive to the actions of squatters, and farmers can rely on the courts to order the removal of the invaders. At one level, squatters too may reduce the use of violence because they anticipate less support from INCRA. At another level, however, squatters may engage in more violent confrontations to resist eviction in response to the farmer's relaxation or reduced use of violence in enforcement of his land claims. Because of the mixed incentives on squatters, the overall impact of stronger property rights remains an empirical question that we investigate in the statistical analysis below.[4]

Similarly, as described in the appendix, an overall increase in land values will lead to mixed incentives for squatters to engage in violent activity and ambiguity as to their actions as land values rise. For landowners, however, the reaction is clear. Both the direct and indirect effects of rising land values are for them to be more violent in protecting their (now more valuable) holdings. As land values rise, the direct payoffs to squatters from the use of violence to obtain land increase. But these payoffs may be countered by the actions of landowners, who are sure to strongly resist invasion and occupation of their lands. Knowing this, squatters may be intimidated and choose not to invade and resist evictions. Which factor dominates—the attraction of higher land values or the desire to avoid the likely response of the landowner—requires empirical investigation.

The third factor affecting the use of violence by the two parties is change in the costs of violent conflict. If the costs to squatters of engaging in violence fall, the incentive for both parties would be to engage in more violence. For example, more effective organizational efforts to plan and execute invasions and more concerted actions by INCRA to implement land reform lower squatter costs. As costs to squatters fall, both the direct and indirect effects of violent activity increase. In response to more violence by squatters, farmers have an incentive to engage in more hostility in order to secure their land claims. As farmers take more direct actions to forcibly remove squatters, squatters will resist even more tenaciously because the costs of doing so have fallen.

This implication casts doubt on the wisdom of the current land reform policy in reducing land conflicts. Greater squatter access to INCRA and more responsiveness by INCRA to violent outbreaks following an invasion may lead instead to even more hostilities. Squatters see that violence becomes a means by which INCRA's agenda can be forced. Its efforts to quell conflicts through greater land redistribution only encourage more violence in order to force the agency to intervene again and again.

If the costs to landowners of using violence rise—an increased fear of negative press or political reaction, for example—the overall impact on the incidence of hostilities also is ambiguous. For landowners, the direct and indirect effects of higher costs will be to reduce violence. But for squatters the benefit to more violence may increase as landowners become more reticent to resort to hostility.

Finally, if the courts become more favorable to land reform, the direct and indirect incentives for squatters are to be more violent because for any level of violence they are less likely to be evicted. Alternatively, the incentives to landowners are mixed. The courts being less sympathetic to landowners reduces the direct benefit of their use of violence to retain their lands, but they may still increase their actions to evict squatters in response to the more aggressive efforts by squatters. This possibility also raises questions as to the ultimate consequences of current proposals (see chap. 3) for the courts to be more responsive to squatters as a means of ameliorating land conflict.

This discussion points out the pivotal role played by INCRA in affecting the decision making of squatters and landowners in choosing whether to engage in violent confrontation on the frontier. Particularly important are the factors that make INCRA more responsive or more accessible to squatters. The goal of squatters is to prompt INCRA to expropriate an invaded farm. The goal of landowners is to prevent expropriations by intimidating squatters to abandon the invaded land. Intimidation comes through the courts, which act consistently to enforce titles, and through the use of police and hired gunmen. The empirical question that we will address is the following: What prompts INCRA to intervene in a land conflict and, hence, increases the incentive for violence?

We can summarize some of the factors that we believe affect INCRA actions. Presumably, one criterion by which INCRA decides to intervene will be whether the land is placed in beneficial use by the title holder. Large holdings are more likely to contain significant areas that are forested that may not be considered in beneficial use. Hence, large forested farms that are invaded are more likely to be investigated by INCRA for possible expropriation.

Another factor that may influence INCRA's intervention is the accessibility of an agency office for squatters involved in a particular land conflict. INCRA has limited budgets and more requests to intervene than can be accommodated. Squatters must contact an office and lobby the agency to step into a land dispute based on inadequate use. Very remote conflicts involve high travel costs for squatters, whereas squatters close to an INCRA office can take advantage of relatively lower travel costs to urge agency officials to intervene.

Moreover, INCRA is likely to be particularly responsive to larger groups of squatters that are well organized to present their case to the agency, politicians, and the press. In addition, squatters banded together will be better able to resist attempts at forcible eviction by the title holder. Further, organized squatting efforts may include those individuals with contacts and knowledge of government behavior that is beyond the expertise of most squatters, who have limited education. Rural unions, such as the MST provide the organization and lobbying that individual squatters may lack.

This discussion of landowner and squatter decision making and of INCRA reaction illustrates how complex the issue of land violence can be on Brazilian frontiers. If violence is used strategically by squatters as a means to prompt INCRA to act on their behalf, and if landowners are cognizant of the objectives of squatters, the role for policy is complicated. More support for land reform adopted in an effort to diffuse explosive competition over land may have the unanticipated result of leading to even more conflict. The empirical analysis in this chapter helps to identify some possible outcomes of policy change. The following chapter draws some policy conclusions.

Country-, State-, and Município-Level Data on Rural Conflicts, 1987 to 1995

The most complete data on rural conflicts in Brazil are collected by the Pastoral Land Commission (PLC), which is sponsored by the Catholic Church. The PLC has been monitoring rural violence since 1974, although their data has only been collected systematically since 1987, the year in which it also started publishing its yearly reports. The PLC collects data from a variety of sources: the regional PLC offices, newspapers of national circulation, publications of other entities, unions, churches, signed letters, and police reports. Table 22 shows the evolution of land conflicts in Brazil from 1987 to 1995, and the pattern is made clearer with figure 9. The number of conflicts peaked at 621 in 1988 and then declined to 361 in 1992 and 1993. Thereafter, conflicts rose as the peasants' union, MST, increased the pace of its land invasions. Although the data for 1996 are not yet available, 1996 was marked by intense activity by squatters and the number of conflicts is sure to be high.

It is possible to relate the number of conflicts to land policy. Recall that in chapter 2 we discussed the initiation in 1985 of the PNRA (National Program for Land Reform), which initiated land reform through expropriation and settlement projects. Although the actual program was a shadow of the announced plan, in the years following 1985 the government did expropriate some land and create settlement projects. By the end of 1988 it had expropriated 4,034,455 hectares and settled 42,995 families (Comissão Pastoral da Terra 1989, 78). These expropriations demonstrated that the government might expropriate even more land and create even more settlement projects. It is reasonable to infer that this observation encouraged landless peasants to compete to become the next to be settled. The high number of conflicts in 1987 and 1988 likely reflects the response of squatters and farmers to the new land reform policies adopted at that time.

The drop in land conflicts following 1988 as shown in figure 9 may be related to difficulties imposed on land reform by the new Constitution of 1988, which exempted productive land from being expropriated. This provision provided a loophole for landowners to use in court. Further, there was a shift away from land reform by the government as landowners organized to change policies (chap. 2).

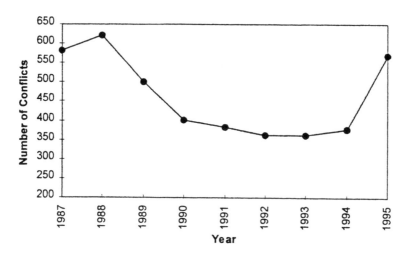

Fig. 9. Rural conflicts in Brazil, 1987–95

TABLE 22. Number of Land Conflicts in Brazil

Year	Conflicts
1987	582
1988	621
1989	500
1990	401
1991	383
1992	361
1993	361
1994	379
1995	569

Source: Comissão Pastoral da Terra. *Conflitos no Campo,* Goiania, yearly reports 1987–95. This data includes only conflict over land and not conflict over other issues such as worker's rights or politics.

In 1988, President Sarney abolished INCRA, the agency that had been in charge of land reform since 1970, and replaced it with a small secretariat. One year later the president resurrected INCRA on a smaller scale, and the agency was disorganized by the experience. Further testimony to the decline in the government's support of land reform was the demotion in 1989 of the former Ministry of Land Reform to a lower priority in the political hierarchy. Another blow to INCRA came in 1990 when President Collor reduced the staff of INCRA by more than 50 percent. The final assault on land reform came from a judicial ruling that forced INCRA to stop expropriating private farms because the new rules set by the Constitution had not yet been incorporated into the broader body of law. This condition was exploited by landowners to overturn cases against them, which had been based on lack of beneficial use (INCRA 1992, 7).

Instead of passing the necessary legislation to allow expropriations, the government adopted a more politically palatable purchase plan, but the budget was very limited. In 1992 only 21 farms, covering 199,443 hectares, were acquired by INCRA for land reform (INCRA 1992, 9). Only in 1993 did the government pass Complementary Law no. 76/93, which allowed INCRA to obtain land through expropriation. In 1993 the president signed 86 expropriation decrees, involving 554,039 hectares, enough to settle 13,825 families (INCRA 1993, 19–21). In 1994, the expropriated area increased to 907,958 hectares and in 1995 to 1,169,607 hectares.[5]

This discussion of the time series of expropriations and land conflict is consistent with our view of the interaction between conflict and land reform. When the government was relatively active in expropriating and settling in the wake of the PNRA, from 1985 to 1988, there were many conflicts. As land reform stalled, the number of conflicts fell. It was only after 1993, when the government resumed expropriating and settling squatters on formerly private lands, that the number of conflicts once again grew. From 1995 to 1997, as land reform again became a major political issue, both the number of conflicts and the number of settlements expanded.[6] Given the limited number of observations for the country as a whole, our evidence thus far should be viewed as suggestive. We next turn to a more diseggregate look at conflicts using data at the state level.

Table 23 shows the Pastoral Land Commission data on rural conflicts from 1987 to 1995 in Brazil by state, and figure 10 shows the evolution of those data at the regional level—North, Northeast, Southeast, South, and Center-West. The data reveal that most states and regions follow the same path of the country as a whole, with more conflicts in 1987–88, less in 1989–93, and an increase thereafter. The region with the most conflicts

TABLE 23. Number of Land Conflicts by State 1987–95

State	1987	1988	1989	1990	1991	1992	1993	1994	1995
North	**160**	**163**	**157**	**108**	**104**	**86**	**109**	**99**	**98**
Rondonia	16	7	4	9	10	7	5	9	15
Acre	24	19	40	6	8	3	12	8	7
Amazonas	33	22	6	2	5	3	0	7	5
Roraima	6	5	6	4	1	0	0	0	15
Para	58	88	66	55	47	40	53	35	45
Amapa	2	0	1	0	0	1	1	1	2
Tocantins	21	22	34	32	33	32	38	39	9
Northeast	**197**	**199**	**166**	**174**	**157**	**142**	**125**	**157**	**198**
Maranhão	78	43	26	35	36	44	29	33	23
Piauí	17	8	6	23	15	15	18	18	18
Ceará	14	19	20	20	9	10	5	14	20
Rio Gr. Norte	4	1	1	8	10	9	6	11	6
Paraíba	12	14	11	10	18	16	19	13	22
Pernambuco	16	15	12	12	9	3	19	12	34
Alagoas	4	3	17	1	5	9	3	4	17
Sergipe	15	9	7	3	2	7	5	8	11
Bahia	37	87	66	62	53	29	21	44	47
Southeast	**103**	**78**	**58**	**43**	**24**	**49**	**37**	**32**	**121**
Minas Gerais	30	38	27	22	16	20	16	9	50
Espirito Santo	8	13	8	6	2	7	3	5	5
Rio de Janeiro	16	9	11	7	2	6	8	6	19
São Paulo	49	18	12	8	4	16	10	12	47
South	**41**	**88**	**70**	**36**	**60**	**45**	**40**	**37**	**52**
Paraná	15	50	24	15	31	17	12	17	30
Sta. Catarina	9	18	20	11	10	10	9	11	14
Rio Gr. Sul	17	20	26	10	19	18	19	9	8
Center-West	**81**	**93**	**49**	**40**	**38**	**39**	**50**	**54**	**100**
Mato Gr. Sul	20	26	9	10	15	10	14	18	20
Mato Grosso	37	41	21	20	15	16	23	22	39
Goiás	21	23	19	10	7	10	12	8	34
D.F.	3	3	0	0	1	3	1	6	7
Brazil	**582**	**621**	**500**	**401**	**383**	**361**	**361**	**379**	**569**

Source: Comissão Pastoral da Terra, *Conflitos no Campo,* Goiânia, yearly issues 1987–95.

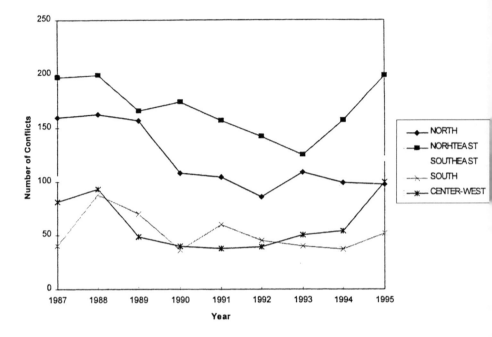

Fig. 10.   Land conflicts by region in Brazil

throughout the entire period is the Northeast, followed by the North, which comprises the Amazon. The state with the most conflicts in the nine-year period is Pará (487), followed by Bahia (446) and Maranhão (347). Maranhão is the eastern neighbor of Pará, so these two states together clearly form the most violent area in terms of rural conflicts. It is noteworthy that the only state that is relatively free from conflicts is Amapá, which is the most sparsely settled state in the Amazon.

In order to explore the relationship between land conflicts and the Brazilian government's land policy, we show the number of settlement projects by state from 1987 to 1995 in table 24. Figure 11 shows the evolution of the number of projects in each of the five regions. Land settlement projects involve placing landless farmers on government land, and they typically follow expropriations. These settlement projects are the main vehicles for land reform. There is a similar pattern between settlement projects (land reform) and land conflicts. As with conflicts, the region with the most settlement projects in the nine-year period is the Northeast (433), fol-

TABLE 24. Number of Settlement Projects by State, 1987–95

State	1987	1988	1989	1990	1991	1992	1993	1994	1995
North	**34**	**42**	**25**	**7**	**16**	**47**	**15**	**8**	**57**
Rondonia	4	4	2	7	0	3	1	1	13
Acre	3	2	4	0	4	3	0	1	3
Amazonas	3	3	2	0	1	10	1	0	0
Roraima	1	0	0	0	0	2	0	0	9
Para	12	19	2	0	6	17	11	3	19
Amapa	3	3	0	0	0	0	0	1	1
Tocantins	8	11	15	0	5	12	2	2	12
Northeast	**93**	**30**	**38**	**15**	**36**	**48**	**13**	**14**	**146**
Maranhão	17	4	5	0	4	15	2	5	43
Piauí	2	2	2	0	2	2	1	2	6
Ceará	19	9	10	2	10	7	1	0	44
Rio Gr. Norte	11	4	3	0	3	5	2	0	15
Paraíba	4	4	4	4	4	4	4	4	10
Pernambuco	9	3	10	5	7	6	0	0	10
Alagoas	2	0	2	0	0	1	0	2	1
Sergipe	2	2	1	1	6	1	1	1	2
Bahia	27	2	1	3	0	7	2	0	15
Southeast	**18**	**10**	**6**	**1**	**8**	**9**	**2**	**1**	**15**
Minas Gerais	3	3	3	0	4	8	0	1	7
Espirito Santo	3	1	0	0	1	0	1	0	1
Rio de Janeiro	8	0	3	0	2	1	1	0	3
São Paulo	4	6	0	1	1	0	0	0	4
South	**40**	**25**	**22**	**1**	**10**	**20**	**6**	**7**	**41**
Paraná	21	7	14	1	4	15	2	2	24
Sta. Catarina	16	15	6	0	5	0	3	0	12
Rio Gr. Sul	3	3	2	0	1	5	1	5	5
Center-West	**39**	**8**	**9**	**1**	**11**	**7**	**1**	**3**	**81**
Mato Gr. Sul	8	2	3	0	1	1	0	1	1
Mato Grosso	27	4	2	1	2	6	1	1	60
Goiás	4	2	4	0	8	0	0	1	20
D.F.	0	0	0	0	0	0	0	0	0
Brazil	**224**	**115**	**100**	**25**	**81**	**131**	**37**	**33**	**340**

Source: Comissão Pastoral da Terra, *Conflitos no Campo,* Goiânia, yearly issues: 1987–95.

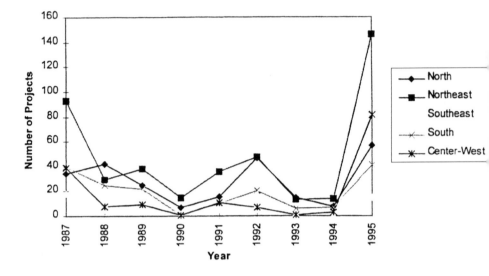

Fig. 11.   Settlement projects by region

lowed the North (251). In addition, the path of settlement projects followed by most states fits loosely with the time path of conflicts, with a high
level in the first years dropping to lower levels in the intermediate years
and a strong climb in the final years of the period covered by the data.

Recall that in chapter 4 we argued that violence increased the probability that INCRA would expropriate an invaded farm. Because expropriations are usually the first step toward a settlement project, this implies
causality from conflicts to settlements. On the other hand, we also argued
that greater policy emphasis on expropriations and settlements would in
turn lead to more conflict.

Using the data from tables 23 and 24, we calculated the correlation
coefficient between conflicts and settlement projects. There is a weak positive relationship of .28. This estimate provides some empirical support for
the view that the net effect of the government's land reform project is to
increase violence.[7]

The first direction of causality between conflicts and settlement projects (following an expropriation) comes through INCRA's reaction to
violence. The agency responds by initiating more expropriations and subsequently creating settlement projects in an effort to forestall further vio-

lence. The second direction comes from the reaction of squatters to the increase in the number of settlements. Settlements that follow a successful invasion and expropriation signal potential squatters that they too can increase the likelihood of an INCRA expropriation by using violence.

In order to investigate more formally the two-way causality between conflicts and settlement projects, we performed a Granger causality test. The definition of causality used in this test is that variable x causes variable y if taking account of past values of x improves the predictions for y.[8] Table 25 shows the results.

In the first column of table 25, conflicts are regressed against lagged conflicts and lagged settlement projects. The test rests on the statistical significance of the lagged settlement project variable. If it is statistically different from zero, then we can infer that settlements "Granger-cause" conflicts. Likewise, in the second column settlement projects are regressed against lagged projects and lagged conflicts, with the significance of the lagged conflicts variable determining whether conflicts "Granger-cause" settlement projects.[9]

The results of the test using both one and two lags shown in table 25 indicate that we cannot reject the existence of Granger causality in both

TABLE 25. Granger Causality Test

Granger Causality Test between Settlement Projects and Conflicts

Dependent Variable	I $Conflict_t$	II $Projects_t$	III $Conflict_t$	IV $Projects_t$
$Conflict_{t-1}$	0.671	0.080	0.606	−0.134
	(16.19)	(4.85)	(9.11)	(1.64)
$Conflict_{t-2}$			0.132	−0.049
			(2.26)	(0.725)
$Projects_{t-1}$	0.546	−0.060	0.261	0.120
	(5.25)	(0.98)	(2.05)	(5.31)
$Projects_{t-2}$			−0.187	−0.023
			(1.86)	(1.12)
Constant	2.889	2.745	3.364	2.984
	(4.38)	(6.76)	(5.16)	(6.29)
N	216	216	189	189
Schwartz Crit.	0.6525	0.6071	0.3133	0.2771
F–stat. for H_0	5.25	4.85	3.03	14.11
H_0	Proj. $\Rightarrow$ Conf.	Conf.$\Rightarrow$ Proj.	Proj. $\Rightarrow$ Conf.	Conf. $\Rightarrow$ Proj.
Decision	Accept**	Accept**	Accept*	Accept**

Note: Estimated as a pooled cross–section time–series of 27 states from 1987 to 1995 (see SHAZAM User's Reference Manual Version 7.0, 1993, 241–50); *t*-ratios in parentheses.

*Significant at 5%

**Significant at 1%

directions between conflicts and settlement projects.[10] This finding is consistent with the predictions of our model of the interaction between violent land conflicts and expropriation-based settlements: Conflicts increase settlements via expropriations, and settlements in turn increase conflicts.

The fact that there seems to be a causal link from conflicts to settlement projects is straightforward and is generally recognized by all parties involved. The existence of a causal link from settlement projects to conflicts is not that obvious. This relationship indicates that greater land reform emphasis (with more expropriations and settlements) contributes to even more land conflicts. Squatter organizations use violent conflicts as a means of forcing INCRA intervention, expropriations, and settlements.

This result is clearly not the outcome intended by the government. Political pressures for land reform in response to conflicts have been motivated by a desire to reduce violence. The problem is that for every conflict resolved by an expropriation and settlement project, several other conflicts arise, spurred by the demonstration effect of the success of earlier invasions. Although the government now seems to be aware of this unintended consequence of its land reform policy, it has been politically constrained to continue in this same track. Halting the current land reform program or substituting it for another program without expropriations could lead to claims that the government was faltering in its resolve to go through with land redistribution.[11]

Before examining the determinants of violence more precisely, it is useful to analyze data on conflicts at an even more disaggregate level than the state-level data used above.

Table 26 shows the number of conflicts per year, from 1987 to 1994, for each município in the state of Pará that suffered at least one conflict. Of the 105 municípios that existed in Pará in 1990, 50 suffered at least one conflict. The total number of conflicts in the state was 344.[12] From these data it is clear that conflicts do not occur randomly throughout the state, but rather are geographically bunched together. Only about half of the municípios had incidents of violent conflicts. Further, 16 municípios in the southeast of Pará accounted for 202 of the conflicts; that is, 59 percent of the conflicts took place in 15 percent of the municípios.

In terms of our analytical framework, the southeast of Pará is neither at the economic frontier nor at the market center. Instead, it is in the intermediate region, where land prices have been rising, fiscal subsidies have been available for land investment, and infrastructure, such as highways, have been built. Where property rights are insecure in this region, due to lack of beneficial use or contested titles, the land is vulnerable to invasion by squatters, with violent conflict a result.

TABLE 26. Conflicts by Município in Pará

Município	Southeast Pará	1987	1988	1989	1990	1991	1992	1993	1994	Total
Abaetetuba		0	1	0	0	0	0	0	0	1
Acara		1	2	0	0	0	0	0	1	4
Afua		4	1	1	1	0	0	1	1	9
Agua Azul		0	0	0	2	2	3	2	1	10
Altamira		0	0	0	1	0	0	0	0	1
Ananindeua		0	1	1	0	0	0	0	0	2
Barcarena		0	0	0	0	0	0	2	1	3
Belem		0	0	0	0	0	1	1	1	3
Benevides		2	3	2	0	0	0	2	0	9
Breu Branco		0	0	0	0	0	0	0	1	1
Breves		0	0	0	0	0	0	0	1	1
Cachoeira do Arari		0	1	1	1	0	0	0	0	3
Castanhal		0	0	0	0	1	1	0	0	2
Conc. do Araguaia	*	10	10	9	10	5	3	7	2	56
Cumaru		0	0	0	0	0	0	1	0	1
Curionopolis		1	1	0	1	4	0	0	0	7
Curuca		0	0	0	0	1	0	0	0	1
Eldorado		0	0	0	0	0	0	1	1	2
Goianesia		0	0	0	0	0	1	1	0	2
Ipixuna		0	0	0	0	0	0	1	0	1
Irituia		1	1	1	0	0	0	0	0	3
Itaituba		0	1	1	0	0	0	0	0	2
Itupiranga	*	0	0	0	0	0	1	0	0	1
Mae do Rio		0	0	0	0	0	1	0	0	1
Maraba	*	2	3	3	3	2	1	4	4	22
Marapanim		0	1	0	0	0	0	0	0	1
Medicilandia		1	0	0	0	0	0	0	0	1
Moju		3	3	5	2	2	1	0	1	17
Monte Alegre		0	0	0	1	1	1	1	1	5
Oeiras do Para		0	0	1	0	0	0	0	0	1
Oriximina		0	0	1	1	1	0	0	0	3
Paragominas		3	4	4	6	2	2	1	0	22
Parauapebas	*	0	1	0	2	2	1	2	1	9
Porto de Moz		0	0	1	1	1	0	0	0	3
Rendencao	*	1	0	1	1	0	0	0	0	3
Repartimento	*	0	1	1	0	0	2	2	2	8
Rio Maria	*	2	2	5	5	2	3	1	0	20
Rondon do Para		1	0	1	0	0	0	1	1	4
Sta. Maria Barreiras	*	0	1	3	2	2	2	1	1	12
Santana do Araguaia	*	1	2	2	1	2	2	2	1	13
Santarem		0	2	3	1	3	0	0	0	3
S. Domingos Capim		0	2	3	1	3	0	0	0	9
Sao Felix do Xingu	*	2	1	1	1	1	1	1	1	9
S. Geraldo Araguaia	*	2	1	1	1	0	1	1	1	8
S. Joao Araguaia	*	2	2	0	1	2	1	0	0	8
Tailandia		0	0	0	1	2	0	2	0	5
Tome-Acu		0	0	1	1	1	1	1	1	6
Tucuma	*	0	0	0	1	0	0	1	0	2
Tucurui	*	0	1	1	1	0	0	2	1	6
Xinguara	*	4	3	4	0	4	1	1	1	18
Total	16 muni.	43	52	58	50	46	31	43	27	344

Source: Comissão Pastoral da Terra.files at their headquarters in Goiânia.
Note: * = municípios in southeast Pará.

The Determinants of Violent Conflict Over Land in the Amazon

In this section we use município-level data to test the determinants of violence in rural conflicts in the state of Pará. We discuss the comparative statics regarding the impact on violence from changes in the security of property rights, the value of land, and the costs of violence to farmers and squatters discussed earlier in this chapter and in the appendix.

Although the conflict data presented above provide a good indicator of rural violence for the period from 1987 to 1995, there are no data for this period that would allow us to test the framework we have outlined; the most recent published agricultural census in Brazil is from 1985.[13] Accordingly, we rely on census and Pastoral Land Commission data for the period 1975 through 1985 for econometric analysis. These data sets, however, do not include information on squatter organization, which we have argued is important in explaining expropriations and the success of invasions. Organization through unions, such as the MST, plays a critical role in the strategic use of violence.

The lack of organization data, however, may not be too critical in the time period for which we have data. During the period 1975 to 1985, landless peasants were not as well organized nationally as they have become more recently. In addition, our econometric analysis is across municípios in Pará, and the strength of the MST should not vary much across our data set. For these reasons, the omission of a variable measuring the impact of the MST may not be serious.

The available data allow us to estimate the following equation:

(1) Deaths/Rural Population = a_0 + a_1Squatting + a_2Increase in Land Values + a_3Land Concentration + a_4INCRA + a_5Clear + e.[14]

The data are at the município-level for the state of Pará. The dependent variable, Deaths/Rural Population, is a proxy for squatter and farmer violence, and it comes from data that we assembled from the Pastoral Land Commission, MIRAD (the Ministry of Land Reform and Development), and the Brazilian census. We use deaths rather than land conflicts, which are presented in the tables and figures earlier in the chapter, because death is a consistent measure across conflicts. Cumulative deaths from 1978 to 1985 are used as the dependent variable because conflicts take time to develop and can be spread over several years. By using cumulative deaths over an eight-year period we avoid the problem of predicting the precise time that deaths will occur without diminishing the ability to examine the important relationships between deaths and the specified independent variables.

The data for the independent variables are from the Brazilian census. The variables Squatting, Land Concentration, and Clear measure various aspects of the security of farmer property rights. These variables are intended to measure the preconditions for land invasion and conflict.

To see how each of these variables might affect property rights security, consider the following:

1. The Squatting variable is the percentage of farms in a município operated by squatters in 1975. This variable places squatters on site, occupying both private and government land. Their presence is a precondition for subsequent conflict with farmers, and where squatters are most numerous, property rights to land will be less secure.

2. Large farms are more likely to have insecure property rights, both because they often have extensive forested areas and because monitoring the boundaries of large farms is more costly. Indeed, large farms, not small ones, are the target of land redistribution efforts. Our measure of the incidence of large farms in a município is a land-concentration variable, which is the sum of the area in farms larger than or equal to 5,000 hectares divided by the total area in farms in the município.

3. As defined by the Constitution, beneficial use is an essential requirement for property rights to be secure, and forest clearing in the Amazon is accepted evidence of beneficial use. More cleared areas in a município would increase property rights security. Our clearing variable is the mean farm area cleared in a município.[15]

Accordingly, municípios with more squatters, highly concentrated farm sizes, and more forest cover are more likely to be characterized by violent conflict between farmers and squatters over land. We have discussed the importance of increases in land value in stimulating greater competition for land, and, hence, greater use of violence by farmers to protect their claims by evicting squatters. Our Increase in Land Values variable is the change in average município land values between 1975 and 1985.[16]

Throughout our discussion, we have pointed to the importance of the presence of the land reform agency, INCRA, as a factor in violent land conflict. The likelihood of INCRA intervention should reduce the cost to squatters of using violence, and at the same time, encourage farmers to resort to more violence to protect their farms. INCRA is a (0,1) measure of the agency's jurisdiction in a particular município in Pará.[17] Although INCRA has general authority over land reform in Brazil, the agency has jurisdiction for settlement only over land bordering federal highways. As such, INCRA does not maintain offices in all municípios. Having INCRA jurisdiction in a município makes expropriation more likely, a factor that should lower the costs of squatter organization and associated use of violence.

It is important to stress that our measure of INCRA is exogenous to our Deaths variable. INCRA established its offices in municípios according to where it had jurisdiction for land settlement based on proximity to federal highways. Hence, INCRA jurisdiction in a município was established prior to subsequent settlement and conflict over land.[18]

Descriptive statistics for the variables used in the estimation of equation (1) are provided in table 27, panel A.[19] The results of the tobit estimation are shown in table 28, panel B. Of the variables capturing the security of property rights, the most explanatory power comes from Squatting, where the coefficient is significant at better than the 90 percent level. We argue that a high incidence of squatting in a município weakens property rights because it means that squatters are occupying private and government lands in the area. This situation is a precondition for the subsequent use of violence by farmers to remove squatters from their lands. The result suggests that high levels of squatting in 1975 reduced property rights security and hence, contributed to violent conflict between squatters and titleholders between 1978 and 1985.

By contrast, those municípios characterized by high levels of forest clearing tended to have fewer violent deaths. The estimated coefficient is negative, but it is significant only at the 85 percent level. Cleared areas are considered in beneficial use and are likely to be occupied by the farmer as well. Hence, cleared farms are not apt to be invaded and subject to violent disputes. This finding supports the prediction that an improvement in property rights security (in this case, compliance with the beneficial-use requirement of the Constitution) would reduce the use of violence by farmers. Moreover, despite the ambiguity of the theoretical prediction of property rights security for squatter violence, the empirical result suggests that squatters also are less likely to invade and resist eviction from farms that are largely cleared of forest. The incentive to invade those farms is reduced because INCRA is less apt to expropriate farms that meet the social-use criteria of the Constitution.

Finally, we argue that large farms are more likely to have insecure property rights than are small ones, with the prediction that owners of large farms are more likely to resort to violence. The coefficient on the Land Concentration variable is positive, although insignificant at the usual levels. The weak positive relationship indicates that municípios characterized by high concentrations of landholdings of 5,000 hectares or more were somewhat more likely to have fatal land conflicts. The weak positive impact may be due to the fact that the most remote municípios often have highly concentrated landholdings, but because of high transportation costs, the land is not worth contesting.

A rise in land value was predicted to result in more farmer violence, though the overall impact was theoretically ambiguous. The coefficient on the land-value-increase variable is positive, but significant only at approximately the 85 percent level.[20] The positive relationship is consistent with the notion that an increase in land values between 1975 and 1985 contributed to fatalities as higher land values encouraged farmers to solidify their property rights through violence. While the predicted effect on squatter violence was unclear, empirically, the rise in land values appears to have encouraged squatters to invade lands and resist farmer evictions.

Finally, a reduction in the costs of violence by squatters should increase the use of violence by both farmers and squatters alike. The

TABLE 27. Determinants of Violent Conflict over Land in the Amazon

	A. Descriptive Statistics			
	Mean	Standard Deviation	Minimum	Maximum
Cumulative deaths/rural population	0.083	0.229	0.000	1.170
1975 squatting	0.482	0.238	0.084	0.921
1975 land value	0.606	0.500	0.057	2.897
1985 land value	0.630	0.432	0.074	2.173
Increase in land value, 1975–85	0.024	0.566	−2.389	1.316
Clearing	0.351	0.165	0.018	0.806
INCRA	0.662	0.476	0.000	1.000
Land concentration	0.134	0.177	0.000	0.770

B. Regression Results: Cumulative Deaths Due to Land Violence		
Variable	Anticipated Sign	Estimated Coefficient
Constant		−0.50
		−(2.28)
Squatting	Positive	0.49
		(1.72)
Land value increase	Positive	0.18
		(1.38)
INCRA	Positive	0.43
		(2.51)
Land concentration	Positive	0.08
		(0.23)
Clear	Negative	−0.68
		−(1.38)

Note: See text for definitions and sources; *t*-statistics in parentheses; $N = 71$; log-likelihood ratio = 13.40 ($X^2_{5,10} = 9.24$).

TABLE 28. Simultaneous Estimation of Frontier Land Conflict, Land Value, Title, and Investment

Variable	Cumulative Deaths	1985 Land Value per Hectare	Title	Investment
Constant	−0.30	0.44	0.47	−3.44
	−(1.22)	(0.23)	(7.87)	−(1.66)
Title	0.35	−0.06		4.40
	(1.31)	−(0.02)		(1.91)
Distance		−0.17	0.00004	−0.05
		−(0.52)	(0.73)	−(0.27)
Distance title		0.08		
		(0.17)		
Average farm size			−0.0004	
			−(1.67)	
Soil quality		−0.02		−0.45
		−(0.10)		−(1.21)
Population density		−0.04		
		−(0.47)		
Clear	−0.95	−0.02		
	−(1.74)	−(0.17)		
INCRA	0.33	0.03	0.04	0.50
	(1.87)	(0.15)	(0.81)	(1.54)
1985 deaths		3.29		
		(0.75)		
Cumulative deaths				−3.07
(1978–85)				−(1.86)
Credit				0.03
				(1.26)
Investment		0.56		
		(3.38)		
Land concentration	0.38			
	(0.95)			
Change in value	0.53		0.90	
	(1.85)		(3.47)	
Log likelihood ratio	14.96			
	($X^2 = 9.24$)			
R^2		.46	.23	.39

Note: t-statistics in parentheses. For discussion of the variables, see the text in this chapter and in Chapter 7.

coefficient on the INCRA variable is positive and significant at the 99 percent level. Municípios with INCRA offices had more fatalities in land conflicts between 1978 and 1985 than did those without INCRA offices. The presence of INCRA is a critical factor in reducing squatters' costs of resisting eviction and of ultimately gaining the land. Given high transportation and information costs on a frontier, squatter lobbying of INCRA is more likely to occur where there is an INCRA office nearby. The greater ability of squatters to secure INCRA intervention in those municípios appears to reduce their costs of organizing and resisting farmer evictions. Ironically, as we have argued, the likelihood of an INCRA expropriation could increase the strategic use of violence by squatters.

Using the estimated coefficients, it is possible to calculate the marginal effects of changes in the independent variables on the dependent fatalities variable and the effects of a one-half standard deviation shift in the independent variables on deaths. In terms of marginal effects, in 1980, the average rural population per município was 20,007. Evaluated at the means for all of the variables, the expected cumulative deaths per 1,000 rural population was 0.074, or 1.48 deaths per município. The marginal effect of each independent variable is interpreted in terms of the impact on expected deaths per município.

The marginal effect of a unit change in squatting is a 0.146 increase in deaths per thousand rural population. Evaluated at the means, a one percentage point increase in the percent of squatters in a município results in a 2.0 percent increase in deaths per average rural population. Similarly, the marginal effect of a unit change in the concentration of landholdings leads to a 0.025 increase in deaths per thousand rural population. Again evaluated at the means, a one percentage point increase in land concentration results in a 0.3 percent increase in deaths per average rural population. For clearing, the marginal impact of a unit change in cleared farm area is a 0.204 decline in deaths.

Evaluated at the means, a one percentage point increase in cleared land leads to a 2.8 percent fall in expected deaths. For the land price change between 1975 and 1985, the marginal effect is 0.054, which evaluated at the means suggests that a 0.01 increase in the change in land value brings a 0.7 percent rise in expected deaths per average rural population. Because we have scaled land prices by dividing by 1,000, a 0.01 unit increase corresponds to 10 cruzados. At an exchange rate of 13.7 cruzados per dollar, the increase would be approximately U.S.$1 per hectare. Finally, INCRA has a marginal effect of 0.128, but since INCRA enters as a dummy variable, it is instructive to see the effect in the cases when INCRA = one and INCRA = zero. The expectation of deaths per average rural population due to land conflicts in the absence of INCRA is 0.019.

Alternatively, the expected deaths in municípios under INCRA jurisdiction is 0.127 per average rural population. Accordingly, the presence of INCRA increases the expectation of deaths during violence over land by 568 percent.

In terms of the larger changes in the independent variables, a one-half standard deviation change in the mean level of squatting leads to a 26 percent increase in deaths per thousand rural population due to land conflict. A one-half standard deviation increase in the mean land value increase results in a 22 percent rise in deaths over land. A one-half standard deviation change in INCRA jurisdiction brings a 48 percent rise in violent deaths, whereas a one-half standard deviation increase in the mean of clearing results in a 21 percent reduction in deaths.

Overall, the estimation of equation (1) indicates that the incidence of fatal disputes across municípios was strongly influenced by INCRA jurisdiction and the level of squatting as of 1975. The rise in land values between 1975 and 1985 had a somewhat weaker positive impact. In contrast, clearing tended to reduce the likelihood of violent conflicts over land.

Land Conflict: The Impact on Investment and Land Values

We are primarily interested in the determinants of land conflict. It is obvious that the potential for injury and death reduce the welfare of individuals directly involved in land conflicts. Additional welfare losses to combatants occur through the costs incurred in defending and invading land. Less obvious are the community-wide losses resulting from land conflict. Land claimants residing in areas undergoing conflict may postpone site-specific investments if they believe that their property rights may be threatened by land conflict in the future. As we demonstrated in chapters 6 and 7, lower investment in turn reduces land values, the primary asset in frontier communities. To address this issue, we place equation (1) into the simultaneous system estimated in chapter 7. Instead of the system of three equations we now estimate the following four-equation system:

(2) Deaths/Rural Population $= a_0 + a_1$Squatting $+ a_2$Increase in Land Values $+ a_3$Land Concentration $+ a_4$INCRA $+ a_5$Clear $+ e$.[21]

(3) LnValue $= b_1 + b_2$LnDistance $+ b_3$LnDistance·Title $+ b_4$LnSoil $+ b_5$LnClear $+ b_6$LnInvestment $+ b_7$LnDensity $+ b_8$Title $+ b_9$INCRA $+ b_{10}$Deaths $+ e$.[22]

(4) Title = c_1 + c_2Change in Value + c_3Size + c_4INCRA + c_5Distance + e.[23]

(5) LnInvestment = d_1 + d_2LnDistance + d_3Title + d_4LnSoil + d_5Credit + d_6INCRA + d_7Cumulative Deaths + e.[24]

As in the earlier estimation of equation (1), we use a tobit procedure to estimate equation (2). For the estimation of equations (3) and (5), we use a log-linear specification, and for the estimation of equation (4) we use OLS.[25]

The estimation results for the system of equations are shown in table 28. Column 2 shows the estimates of cumulative deaths. The estimates are quite similar to those in table 27 for the single-equation estimation of deaths due to violent conflict. The only substantive difference is that the coefficient on land value increase grows in magnitude and statistical significance. This result is as one would expect, since the simultaneous system better controls for the impact of violence on land values. In column 3 the predicted variables contributing to 1985 land values do not reveal significant effects, except for investment, which is significant at the 99 percent level.

This result underscores the important contribution of investment to land values on the frontier. Moreover, it indicates the importance of property rights, because having title encourages investment. Column 4 provides the results of the estimation for the title equation. The most important influence is the expected change in land value from having title, which is positive and significant at the 99 percent level. Column 5 shows the results for the investment equation. The estimation indicates that INCRA jurisdiction and credit availability contributed to greater investment, with the variables significant at approximately the 90 and 80 percent levels respectively. Having title promoted investment, with the variable significant at approximately the 95 percent level. Moreover, title generally was necessary to obtain credit. Investment also tended to occur in areas with poorer land quality. Finally, and most relevant to this chapter, long-standing land disputes as reflected in cumulative deaths between 1978 and 1985 retarded investment, with the variable significant at close to the 95 percent level. Given the importance of investment in land values, it is possible to see the ultimate impact of violence on the value of land. Since land is the most important asset for frontier settlers, the negative effect of violence on welfare may be greater than commonly understood.

As an illustration of the impact of land conflict consider the following: an increase in cumulative fatalities from zero to the expected value of 0.073 deaths per 1,000 rural population reduces estimated investment by

19.6 percent and estimated land values in Pará by 7.8 percent, all else constant. To put this estimate into context, mean estimated land values in Pará rose only 3.9 percent between 1975 and 1985.[26] Accordingly, violent conflict over land can have a serious dampening effect on incentives to make land-specific investments and on agricultural land values.

Conclusion

Violent conflicts over land in the Amazon have attracted considerable international attention. These conflicts have the potential to reduce welfare through the dissipation of rents as well as through the death of the parties involved. Yet violence is not a uniform characteristic of settlement in the Brazilian Amazon. It occurs in specific locations. Determining the characteristics of those regions where violent conflict has taken place provides policy implications for reducing the potential for violence. In this chapter, we have analyzed data on conflicts at the country, state, and município levels from 1987 to 1995, as well as land conflicts in the state of Pará between 1978 and 1985 with census data and data from the Pastoral Land Commission.

The factors that most contribute to conflicts include the presence of INCRA and a high incidence of squatting in a município. Increases in land values also promote violent conflicts. Forest clearing, however, reduces the potential for fatal disputes. This condition suggests that farmers particularly, but perhaps also squatters as well, have incentives to clear in order to firm their claims to Amazon lands. Regarding forested lands as *unused* lands, and therefore subject to invasion and redistribution, raises problems for international efforts to set aside large tracts of rain forest.

The principal antagonists are large farmers and squatters. The basis for their disputes are conflicting aspects of Brazilian law. Title holders have rights through statutory law for government enforcement of their property rights, whereas squatters have rights for land redistribution (land reform) under the Constitution, most recently reaffirmed in 1988. Land must be placed in beneficial use or it is subject to expropriation and reassignment to squatters. Our survey of contested farms discussed in chapter 4 revealed that virtually all lacked productive use. Because large farms in the Amazon often have not developed their properties and left them in forest, they have been vulnerable to invasion by squatters. Squatters organize and lobby INCRA to expropriate titled, but unused, lands.

Our econometric results indicate that areas witnessed greater fatalities where INCRA had jurisdiction, squatting was prevalent, land values had increased, and the land was not cleared of forest. Anticipation of INCRA expropriations appears to have encouraged the strategic use of violence by squatters in land conflicts. In response to increased farm invasions and resistance to eviction by squatters, farmers also have a greater incentive to defend their claims with violent actions. INCRA is charged with land reform by the Brazilian president and Congress, and both the agency and the president are embarrassed politically by highly visible incidents of violent conflict over land. Organized groups of squatters understand this condition and can exploit the use of violence to force INCRA expropriations. As a result, the greater policy emphasis on land reform in Brazil through expropriation to reduce violent conflict is likely to have the unanticipated impact of *increasing* violence.

The conflicting practices of assigning and enforcing title in civil law, but allowing for expropriation and land redistribution if the property is not placed in beneficial use, create a volatile environment for violent conflict over land. The problem extends beyond Brazil to elsewhere in Latin America where there is tension between the efficiency gains from secure property rights and distributional objectives of land reform.

The Brazilian government confronts two inconsistent objectives— maintaining the sanctity of title and promoting land reform. Secure property rights to land, as reflected in enforced titles, contribute to investment and promote the formation of markets and land exchange. At the same time, highly skewed land ownership distribution intensifies social pressures and threatens the sanctity of title and the economic growth it fosters. Responding to both objectives requires careful maneuvering by politicians and bureaucrats under the best of conditions. Given the existing complex and volatile situation, it is unclear how effective the government will be. Indeed, the Minister of Land Reform in July 1996 called for revised popular expectations as to what could be realistically accomplished by the government for land reform.[27] The situation in Brazil underscores the importance of politics and competing objectives in determining how well governments can create and maintain the necessary institutions for sustained economic growth.

APPENDIX

In this appendix we present a formal model of rural conflicts that underlies much of the discussion in the chapter.

The probability that INCRA will expropriate a farm is given by

$$\theta\,(s,P,G)$$

with

$$\theta_s \ge 0, \theta_{ss} < 0 \quad \text{and} \quad \theta_{sv} < 0 \tag{A.1}$$

where s is the amount of violence supplied by the squatters, P is the quality of the landowner's property rights to land, and G is the level of the president's commitment to land reform.

The probability that a landowner's attempt at evicting the squatters will be successful is given by

$$\beta(v,K)$$

with

$$\beta_v \ge 0, \beta_K < 0, \tag{A.2}$$

where v is the amount of violence supplied by the landowner and K represents the position of the courts, with a higher K signifying a stand more favorable to the squatters.

The objective of both the landowner and the squatters in a conflict is to end up with the ownership of the land. Each side will supply violence so as to maximize the expected value of the land that they will receive. Table A.1 presents the value of the land to each party under each possible outcome of the conflict. In order to simplify, it is assumed that both the squatters and the farmer value owning the land at L.

If the squatters are evicted, the farmer keeps the land and they get nothing. Another possible outcome is for the farmer to be unable to evict the squatters but there be no expropriation. In this case the squatters remain on the land, but the farmer continues having a claim to it. Eventually this situation will have to be resolved, but it may remain in this state for a long time. The value of the land to the squatters in this case is πL and to the farmer it is δL, where $0 < \pi < 1$ and $0 < \delta < 1$. If INCRA does expropriate the farm from the farmer, it is given to the squatters and the farmer is compensated. Although the farmer is compensated at a "fair" price

TABLE A.1.   Farmers' and Squatters' Valuation of the Land

Outcome	Squatters' Valuation of Land	Farmer's Valuation of Land
I. Squatters evicted	0	L
II. No eviction—no expropriation	πL	δL
III. Land expropriated	L	γL

according to the Constitution, the payment is done with titles of the agrarian debt redeemable in 5 to 20 years, depending on the size of the farm. Therefore, being expropriated is generally valued by the farmer as being worse than keeping the land.[28] Therefore, it is assumed that $\gamma < \delta < 1$.

Squatters must determine how much violence to use to maximize their payoff in land value:

$$\text{Max}_s\ (1 - \beta(v,K))\ [(1 - \theta(s,P,G))\ \pi L + \theta(s,P,G)L] - C^S(s). \qquad (A.3)$$

The landowner must select the amount of violence that maximizes the expected value of the land:

$$\text{Max}_v\ \beta(v,K)L + (1 - \beta(v,K))$$
$$[(1 - \theta(s,P,G))\delta L + \theta(s,P,G)\gamma L] - C^F(v). \qquad (A.4)$$

Assume that the amount of violence by the squatters and the farmer belongs to the real line and that the land value functions for both parties are twice continuously differentiable in s and v. Assume also that the land function is strictly concave in each party's use of violence, so that the second-order conditions for maximization are satisfied and the first-order conditions are sufficient for a Nash equilibrium.

Functions (A.3) and (A.4) are simply a linear combination of the payoffs to each type for each possible outcome, weighted by the probability of that outcome, minus the cost of supplying violence, where $C^S(s)$ and $C^F(v)$ are the cost of supplying s and v units of violence respectively.

The first-order conditions for maximization are[29]

$$(1 - \beta)\ \theta_s(1 - \pi)L = C^S_s \qquad (A.5)$$

$$\beta_v(1 - \delta)L + \beta_v\theta(\delta - \gamma)L = C^F_v. \qquad (A.6)$$

The left-hand side in (A.5) is the expected marginal benefit for the squatters of supplying an additional unit of violence. Doing so increases the probability that INCRA will expropriate the farm in their favor, which moves the squatters from outcome II to outcome III in table A.1, weighted by $(1 - \beta)$ the probability that the squatters are not evicted. At the optimum this marginal benefit must equal the cost of the marginal unit of s.

Analogously, the left-hand side in (A.6) is the expected marginal benefit to the farmer of an additional unit of violence. By adding an additional unit of v the farmer increases the probability of eviction by β_v. This moves the farmer from outcome II to outcome I, thus avoiding a loss of $(1 - \delta)L$, and, were it the case that an expropriation would occur if the eviction were not successful, moves the landowner from outcome III to outcome II, thus avoiding a further loss of $(\delta - \gamma)L$. The right-hand side in (A.6) is the marginal cost of the farmer's violence.

Given that each side is acting strategically, understands the rules of the game, and possesses all the information regarding the probability functions and valuations, it is reasonable to expect that they will end up in a Nash equilibrium, which is the joint solution to the optimization problem. In such an equilibrium the farmers choose v^* and the squatters choose s^* such that equations (A.5) and (A.6) hold simultaneously. For any given level of P, G, and K the probability of expropriation is $\theta(s^*,v^*,P,G)$ and the probability of an eviction is $\beta(v^*,K)$.

In order to visualize the interaction between the landowner and the squatters, it is useful to derive the reaction curves for each party. Let λ^S be the objective function of the squatters and λ^F that of the landowner. That is,[30]

$$\lambda^S(s,v) = (1 - \beta(v))[(1 - \theta(s,v))\pi L + \theta(s)L] - C^S(s) \tag{A.7}$$

and

$$\lambda^F(s,v) = \beta(v)L + (1 - \beta(v))$$
$$[1 - \theta(s)\delta L + \theta(s)\gamma L] - C^F(v). \tag{A.8}$$

Let

$$\lambda^S_s(s,v) = \frac{\partial \lambda^S(s,v)}{\partial s} \tag{A.9}$$

and

$$\lambda^F_v(s,v) = \frac{\partial \lambda^F(s,v)}{\partial v}. \tag{A.10}$$

To find the slopes of the reaction curves, define $R^S(v)$ to be the best action that the squatters can take given that the landowner chooses v, and $R^F(s)$ to be the best action that the landowner can take given that the squatters choose s. The first-order condition for the squatter is therefore $\lambda^S_s = (R^S(v),v) = 0$, and for the landowner $\lambda^F_v = (s,R^F(s)) = 0$. In a Nash equilibrium the squatters will be playing $s^* = R^S(v^*)$ and the landowner will be playing $v^* = R^F(s^*)$.

The slope of each reaction curve can be obtained by differentiating

$\lambda_s^S = 0$ with respect to v and $\lambda_v^F = 0$ with respect to s. For λ_s^S this yields $\lambda_{sv}^S + \lambda_{ss}^S \dfrac{\partial R^S}{\partial v} = 0$, and for λ_v^F it yields $\lambda_{vs}^F + \lambda_{vv}^F \dfrac{\partial R^F}{\partial s} = 0$. Rearranging,

expressions for the slopes of the reaction curves are obtained:

$$\frac{\partial R^S}{\partial v} = -\frac{\lambda_{sv}^S}{\lambda_{ss}^S} \qquad (A.11)$$

and

$$\frac{\partial R^F}{\partial s} = -\frac{\lambda_{vs}^F}{\lambda_{vv}^F} \ . \qquad (A.12)$$

Because the denominator of these expressions is negative, from the second-order condition for maximization, the sign of the reaction curves depends on the signs of λ_{sv}^S and λ_{vs}^F, which are[31]

$$\lambda_{sv}^S = -\beta_v \theta_s (1 - \pi) L \leq 0 \qquad (A.13)$$

and

$$\lambda_{vs}^F = \beta_v \theta_s (\delta - \gamma) L \geq 0. \qquad (A.14)$$

Therefore, the squatters' reaction curve is negatively inclined and landowners' positively inclined. This means that violence is a strategic substitute for the squatters but a strategic complement for the landowner.[32] That is, the squatters react to more violence from the landowner by offering less violence, and the landowner reacts to more violence from the squatters by offering more.[33]

Figure A.1 shows the reaction curves for the squatters and the farmer. At the intersection of both curves each side is taking the best response to what the other side is doing, so neither wants to change their action, and that point is a Nash equilibrium.[34]

To simplify the derivation of testable hypotheses, a few assumptions are made.[35] We assume that $\pi = 0$, $\delta = 1$, and $\gamma = 0$; that is, the squatters' valuation of the land, if there is neither eviction nor expropriation, is zero and the farmer values the land at its full value, L; additionally, there is no compensation to the farmer if the land is expropriated. These simplifications allow us to focus on the effects of changes in squatter and farmer

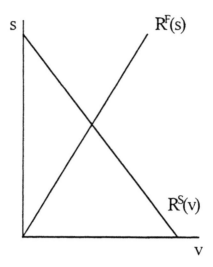

Fig. A.1.   Farmers' and squatters' reaction curves

violence, s and v, on the probabilities of expropriation and eviction. With these simplifications equations (A.5) and (A.7), the squatters' and farmer's first-order conditions, respectively become:

$$(1 - \beta(v,K))\theta_s(s,P,G)L - C_s^S(s) = 0 \qquad\qquad (A.15)$$

$$\beta_v(v,K)\theta(s,P,G)L - C_v^F(v) = 0. \qquad\qquad (A.16)$$

In a Nash equilibrium equations (A.15) and (A.16) hold simultaneously, allowing us to differentiate both equations with respect to an exogenous variable or a parameter and to solve the resulting system to determine the impact on squatter and farmer violence. Accordingly, we analyze the impact of (*a*) changes in the level of property rights security, P; (*b*) changes in land value, L; (*c*) changes in the cost functions, C^S and C^F; and (*d*) changes in the position of the courts, K. Differentiating equations (A.8) and (A.9) with respect to P and rearranging yields a set of simultaneous equations that we solve to obtain the expressions for the effect of a change in the level of property rights security on the amount of violence offered by the squatters and by the farmer.[36]

$$\begin{bmatrix} (1-\beta)\theta_{ss}L - C^{S}_{ss} & -\beta_{v}\theta_{s}L \\ \beta_{v}\theta_{s}L & \beta_{vv}\theta L - C^{F}_{vv} \end{bmatrix} \begin{bmatrix} \dfrac{\partial s}{\partial P} \\ \dfrac{\partial v}{\partial P} \end{bmatrix} = \begin{bmatrix} -(1-\beta)\theta_{sP}L \\ -\beta_{v}\theta_{P}L \end{bmatrix}. \qquad \begin{matrix} \text{(A.17)} \\ \text{(A.18)} \end{matrix}$$

In order to interpret the comparative statics results it is necessary to determine the signs of each term in the above equations. It will be assumed that β_{vv} and θ_{ss}, the second derivatives of the probability functions, are all negative. This assumption seems reasonable since probabilities are bounded between zero and one, so that it should be expected that as violence increases the functions would tend asymptotically to one. Additionally, the second derivatives of the cost functions, C^{S}_{ss} and C^{F}_{vv}, are reasonably assumed to be positive. The term $|\det|$ is the determinant of the first matrix above. Given that β_{vv} and θ_{ss} are assumed negative, and that the terms on the main diagonal are negative due to the second-order condition to maximization, $|\det|$ is seen to be positive.

Solving (A.17) and (A.18) the following expressions are obtained:

$$\frac{\partial v}{\partial P} = \frac{[(1-\beta)\theta_{ss}L - C^{S}_{ss}][-\beta_{v}\theta_{P}L] - [\beta_{v}\theta_{s}L][-(1-\beta)\theta_{sP}L]}{|\det|} \qquad \text{(A.19)}$$

$$\frac{\partial s}{\partial P} = \frac{[-(1-\beta)\theta_{sP}L][\beta_{vv}\theta L - C^{F}_{vv}] - [-\beta_{v}\theta_{P}L][-\beta_{v}\theta_{s}L]}{|\det|}. \qquad \text{(A.20)}$$

By definition $\theta_{P} \leq 0$ and $\theta_{sP} \leq 0$; an increase in the level of the farmer's property rights security decreases the probability of INCRA intervening in the conflict. The term θ_{P} is the direct effect of the more secure tenure on INCRA's probability of expropriating, and the term θ_{sP} is the indirect effect of INCRA becoming less sensitive to squatter violence when tenure is more secure. Given these considerations, $\partial v/\partial P$ can be shown to be unambiguously nonincreasing. To understand the logic behind this result it is necessary to look at the farmer's first-order condition (A.16). The term $\beta_{v}\theta L$ is the marginal benefit to the farmer from an additional unit of v. That is, by increasing v the probability of an eviction is increased by β_{v}, and thus the potential loss θL, which would result from an expropriation, will occur with a smaller probability. If the farmer's tenure security is increased, then θ will be smaller and the potential loss will be reduced. This means that an eviction by the farmer would be avoiding a smaller loss and the marginal benefit from a higher v is reduced. The farmer will thus supply less violence.

The sign of $\partial s/\partial P$ does not have an unambiguous sign. It depends on two effects that can be seen in the squatter's first-order condition (15). The term $(1 - \beta)\, \theta_s\, L$ is the marginal benefit to the squatter of offering an additional unit of violence. Because the farmer will offer less violence given an increase in P, the term $(1 - \beta)$ will be larger, implying a larger marginal benefit, which leads the squatters to choose a higher level of s. On the other hand, the term θ_s will be smaller due to the increase in P, since θ_{sP} is negative. This reduces the marginal benefit, and the squatters will prefer to offer less violence. The first of these effects is the softening of the farmer due to improved tenure security, and the second is the desensitizing of INCRA to squatters' violence. The sign of $\partial s/\partial P$ will therefore depend on which of these effects dominates.

Figure A.2 shows the effect on the farmer's reaction curve of an increase in P, that is, in a strengthening of the farmer's property rights to land. The comparative statics have shown that this change should lead to a decrease of the amount of v. In the graph this is represented by an upward shift in the farmer's reaction curve as P goes from P_0 to P_1. For a given value of s the farmer now prefers to offer less violence $v_1 < v_0$.

The change in P also affects the squatter's reaction curve. According to the comparative static results, the change in P has two effects on the amount of violence offered by the squatter. The first effect is the direct one of making an expropriation less probable, which makes the squatters offer less violence. In figure A.3 this is depicted as a downward shift of the squatters' reaction curve, so that for any given value of v, the squatters will offer a smaller amount of violence, $s_d < s_0$ (where the subscript d refers to the direct effect). The second effect comes from the reduced amount of v that occurs due to the increase in P. In the graph this indirect effect is represented by an upward shift of the squatters' reaction curve, so that for any given v the squatters will offer a higher s, $s_1 > s_0$. Depending on which effect is stronger, the final result of the increase in P will be a lower or a higher s, or no change if both effects cancel out.

In order to determine the effect of an increase in the price of land on the amount of violence, equations (A.15) and (A.16) are differentiated with respect to L and the following expressions are obtained:

$$\frac{\partial v}{\partial L} = \frac{[(1 - \beta)\theta_{ss} L - C^S_{ss}][-\beta_v \theta] - [\beta_v \theta_s L][-(1 - \beta)\theta_s]}{|\det|} \tag{A.21}$$

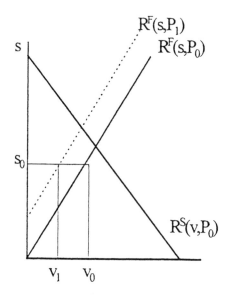

Fig. A.2. Effect of a change in *P* on the farmer's reaction curve

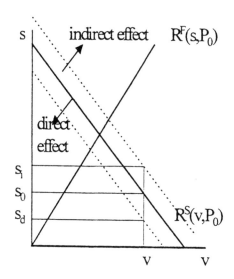

Fig. A.3. Effect of a change in *P* on the squatter's reaction curve

$$\frac{\partial s}{\partial L} = \frac{[-(1-\beta)\theta_s][\beta_{vv}\theta L - C_{vv}^F]-[-\beta_v\theta][-\beta_v\theta_s L]}{|det|} . \tag{A.22}$$

In equation (A.21) the first term in brackets is negative, from the second-order condition to maximization, the second term in brackets is also negative, the third term is positive, and the fourth term is negative. Thus an increase in the value of land unambiguously leads to an increase in the amount of violence offered by the farmer. This is easily seen in the farmer's first-order condition (A.16), since an increase in L increases the benefit of offering an additional unit of v.

The sign of (A.22), as in the previous case, depends on two different effects. The increase in L increases the marginal benefit in the squatters' first-order condition, $(1-\beta)\theta_s L$, leading the squatters to offer more violence. However, the increase in land value also leads to a higher value of v and thus a lower value for $(1-\beta)$, which decreases the marginal benefit and prompts a lower value of s. If the positive direct effect of the increase in land value is stronger than the negative effect of a more aggressive farmer, then the increase in land value will lead to a higher supply of violence by the squatters.[37]

A third issue of interest is to determine how a parametric shift in the squatters' and farmer's cost functions will affect the amount of violence supplied by each. In order to do this it is assumed that their cost functions contain parameters X and Y, respectively, which shifts them up and down. These parameters can represent anything that makes it more or less costly for the parties to offer violence. The cost functions are thus $C^S(s, X)$ for the squatters and $C^F(v, Y)$ for the farmers, such that $C_X^S \geq 0$, $C_{sX}^S \geq 0$, $C_Y^F \geq 0$, and $C_{vY}^F \geq 0$. The effects of a change in X can be shown to be

$$\frac{\partial s}{\partial X} = \frac{[C_{sX}^S][\beta_{vv}\theta L - C_{vv}^F]}{|det|} \tag{A.23}$$

$$\frac{\partial v}{\partial X} = \frac{-[\beta_v\theta_s L][C_{sX}^S]}{|det|} . \tag{A.24}$$

As can easily be seen, both of these expressions are nonincreasing. When it becomes more expensive for squatters to supply violence, they will supply less. Given that squatters are putting in less violence, the farmer's marginal benefit in (15), $\beta_v\theta L$, is smaller and she will choose to supply less v.

The effects of a change in Y can be shown to be

$$\frac{\partial s}{\partial Y} = \frac{-[C_{vY}^F][-\beta_v \theta_s L]}{|det|} \tag{A.25}$$

$$\frac{\partial v}{\partial Y} = \frac{[(1-\beta)\theta_{ss}L - C_{ss}^S][C_{vY}^F]}{|det|}. \tag{A.26}$$

Expression (A.26) is nonincreasing, since as violence becomes more expensive for the farmer, he supplies less of it. Expression (A.25), on the contrary, is nondecreasing. Because an increase in Y reduces the level of v, the squatter's marginal benefit in (A.15), $(1-\beta)\theta_s L$, becomes higher and the squatter chooses a higher s.

The final comparative static result examined is the effect of a change of the position of the courts K on the levels of s and v. These effects can be obtained following the same procedure as above.

$$\frac{\partial s}{\partial K} = \frac{[\beta_K \theta_s L][\beta_{vv}\theta L - C_{vv}^F] - [-\beta_{vK}\theta L][-\beta_v \theta_s L]}{|det|} \tag{A.27}$$

$$\frac{\partial v}{\partial K} = \frac{[(1-\beta)\theta_{ss}L - C_{ss}^S][-\beta_{vK}\theta L] - [\beta_v \theta_s L][\beta_K \theta_s L]}{|det|}. \tag{A.28}$$

The expression in equation (A.27) is nondecreasing, which shows that as the courts become more favorable to the squatters, they will offer more violence. This happens because $\beta_K \le 0$, so the increase in K increases the squatters' marginal benefit in their first order condition (A.15), by making it less likely that they will get evicted by the farmer. The effect of the change by the courts on the farmer's supply of violence is not unambiguous. The sign of expression (A.28) is affected in different directions by the change in K and the change in s. As can be seen in the farmer's first-order condition (A.16), an increase in K decreases the farmer's marginal benefit, since $\beta_v K \le 0$, but the accompanying decrease in s increases the marginal benefit through θ. The final sign of $\partial v/\partial K$ will depend on which effect dominates. It is interesting, therefore, that according to the model a change that makes the courts more responsive to land reform and squatters' rights will not only increase the amount of violence from the squatters, but may also lead to more violence from the farmers, leading to an overall increase

TABLE A.2. Determinants of Violence

Parameter	Effect on Violence by the Farmer	Effect on Violence by the Squatter
Property rights; P	–	+ or –
Land value; L	+	+ or –
Squatter's cost; X	–	–
Farmer's cost; Y	–	+
Court's position; K	+ or –	+

in violence, a result opposite to that which was intended by the policy change.

NOTES

1. This chapter draws from Alston, Libecap, and Mueller 1998a.

2. The formal equations corresponding to the following discussions are contained in the appendix, equations 19–28.

3. The responses to the actions of others are known in game theory as the reaction functions. A discussion and graphs of the reaction functions can be found in the appendix.

4. This theoretical ambiguity may explain why invasions occur on land that has varying degrees of property rights security.

5. INCRA homepage, <http://www.incra.gov.br/qdfa.htm>. In the first six months of 1996 the government expropriated 676,901 hectares, denoting a further increase in the rate of land expropriations.

6. The data on violence for 1996 and 1997 is not yet available, but it is certain that the number will have increased compared to 1995.

7. The correlation coefficient is not particularly large because the number of projects in most states increased in 1992 with no upsurge in violence that year. Nevertheless, the correlation suggests that there is a link between settlement projects and conflicts. The correlation coefficient between conflicts and settlement projects is 0.28, which, with 216 observations, is statistically different from zero at a 1 percent confidence level.

8. Harvey 1991, 303–5. More precisely, causality from x to y is inferred to exist when lagged values of x_t have explanatory power in a regression of y_t on lagged values of y_t and x_t.

9. Because the data consists of a panel of 27 states for nine years, we estimated the coefficients using a pooling technique that takes into consideration the possibly cross-sectionally heteroskedastic and timewise autoregressive nature of the data. The estimation method used was the Pool command of SHAZAM version 7.0 econometric software, which uses the pooling technique described in Kmenta 1986, sec. 12.2, 616–25. In essence, the method performs a double transformation

of the variables in order to correct first for autoregression, and then for heteroskedasticity.

10. One important issue in a causality test is how to decide the number of lags to use. We performed the tests with one lag (columns 1 and 2) and with two lags (columns 3 and 4). Because with every additional lag we lose an observation, and because we only have nine time-series observations for each state, adding more lags would reduce the power of the test significantly. The value of the Schwartz criterion, frequently used to select the number of lags, is presented in table 25. The specification that minimized the Schwartz criterion in both cases was the use of two lags. The results were robust to the use of one or two lags. Given the small length of the time-series, we could not use unit-root tests to determine if the series are stationary; however, performing the test on first-differenced data did not alter the results of the hypothesis test.

11. In May 1997 the government assembled a committee of land policy specialists from various sectors of society to develop new guidelines for land reform.

12. This number is not the same as that shown in table 23 because the Pastoral Land Commission files of município-level data that we used do not have a description of all conflicts. Hence, we did not include some entries, even though those conflicts are counted in the overall state total.

13. A new census was done in 1996; however it was not available at the time of writing.

14. The dependent variable is (cumulative deaths/1980 rural population) times 1,000. The analysis in this section draws from Alston, Libecap, and Mueller 1998a.

15. Cleared farm area is calculated from the census by dividing the number of hectares of cleared agricultural land by the total amount of agricultural land in the município. The area cleared was defined as the sum of the land in permanent crops, annual crops, planted pasture, natural pasture, planted forest, and unused but usable land, as defined by the census.

16. Our price data for 1975 and 1985 are in 1985 cruzados. Land values generally are from the *Censo Agropecuário,* published by IBGE as noted earlier. The value of land in 1985 in Pará was not provided in the census. It was estimated by taking the ratio of land value to the value of farms (which included the value of investments, machinery, and animals) for 1970, 1975, and 1980. The growth rates of this ratio were obtained and an average growth rate calculated. The 1980 ratio was then multiplied by this average growth rate to give the 1985 ratio, which in turn was multiplied times the 1985 agricultural farm value as provided in the census.

17. Municípios are considered under INCRA's jurisdiction if the capital of the município is within 100 km of a federal highway. Under Brazilian law such lands in the Amazon were placed under federal, rather than state, control.

18. Because of this condition, we avoid simultaneity between conflict and expropriation and settlement indicated in our Granger causality tests.

19. After 1985 a number of municípios were subdivided, creating 22 new municípios, but we use the municípios that existed in 1985 for our analysis. Additionally, in our statistical analysis we dropped the municípios of Belém, Ananindeua, and

Benevides because they primarily were urban. Viseu was dropped because its census (cumulative) investment data were impossibly listed as negative.

20. The land value variable, of course, may be affected by land conflicts as well, by limiting the demand for land and site-specific investment. At the same time, increases in land values potentially increase violent conflicts. To address possible simultaneity we also estimated equation (1) within a simultaneous equations model of land value, investment, and titling as developed in chapter 6. From this simultaneous model we used two-stage least squares to construct an instrument for the Increase in Land Values variable. With this approach, the coefficient on the Change in Value variable becomes significant at approximately the 95 percent level. We report this estimation in the section that follows.

21. Equation (2) is identical to equation (1), estimated earlier except that we used two-stage least squares to construct an instrument for the variable Increase in Land Values. The motivation for this construction is described in chapter 6.

22. The substantive difference between this equation and the land value equation estimated in chapter 7 is that, rather than a dummy variable measuring land conflict, we now measure land conflict with a continuous measure, deaths due to land conflict in 1985.

23. The only difference between this equation and the title equation in chapter 7 is that we do not include our land conflict measure. Recall that in chapter 7 the coefficient on violence in the title equation was not statistically significant.

24. In this equation we added a variable measuring credit availability: the percentage of farm establishments receiving credit.

25. We performed a test proposed by Davidson and Mackinnon (1981) to decide between a linear and log-linear specification for the value of land and investment equations. We performed the test outlined by Breusch and Pagan (1979) for heteroskedasticity and corrected for it as necessary. Where heteroskedasticity is found, the estimation is corrected by using White's (1980) consistent estimator of the covariance matrix.

26. We calculated the expected value of land with mean variable values and the estimated coefficients in table 28, setting 1985 deaths equal to zero and using the expected value of investment when cumulative deaths were equal to zero. We compared the resulting land value to one calculated with the expected value of 1985 deaths and with investment estimated with the expected value of cumulative deaths.

27. Speech at the Universidade de Brasília, July 11, 1996.

28. Occasionally landowners are able to secure compensation above the market price of the land, either through corruption involving INCRA officials or through the court. Such cases, however, are exceptions.

29. The arguments of the probability functions will be omitted in the first-order conditions. Derivatives are denoted by a subscript, e.g., $\partial\beta(v, K)/\partial v = \beta_v$.

30. To simplify notation, only s and v are included as arguments.

31. It is assumed that θ_{sv} is negative given that $\theta(.)$ is a probability function that must be less than or equal to one.

32. This classification comes originally from Bulow, Geanakopolos and Klemperer 1985. See also Tirole 1992.

33. Note that the reaction curves are only an expositional device since in fact it is a one-shot game and both parties move simultaneously.

34. The curves have been drawn with slopes that guarantee that the process converges to the equilibrium allocation from the initial position. The condition for this is $\lambda_{ss}^S \lambda_{vv}^F > \lambda_{sv}^S \lambda_{vs}^F$.

35. None of these simplifications alter the basic results obtained below.

36. From here on we drop the arguments of β and θ to simplify the presentation.

37. The effects of the change in L and other variables examined below have an analogous effect on the reaction curves to that caused by a change in P. These effects will not be shown graphically here.

CHAPTER 9

Equity and Efficiency: The Political Provision of Property Rights and Their Distribution on the Frontier

Commerce and manufactures can seldom flourish long in any state which does not enjoy a regular administration of justice, in which the people do not feel themselves secure in the possession of their property, in which the faith of contracts is not supported by law, and in which the authority of the state is not supposed to be regularly employed in enforcing the payment of debts from all those who are able to pay. Commerce and manufactures, in short, can seldom flourish in any state in which there is not a certain degree of confidence in the justice of government. (Smith 1937, 862)

However:

Wherever there is great property, there is great inequality. For one very rich man, there must be at least five hundred poor, and the affluence of the few supposes the indigence of the many. The affluence of the rich excites the indignation of the poor, who are often both driven by want, and prompted by envy, to invade his possessions. It is only under the shelter of the civil magistrate that the owner of the valuable property, which is acquired by the labor of many years, or perhaps of many successive generations, can sleep a single night in security. . . . The acquisition of valuable and extensive property, therefore, necessarily requires the establishment of civil government. (Smith 1937, 669)

The quotations from Adam Smith in *The Wealth of Nations* summarize the problems of providing tenure to land on the frontier. As settlement occurs, secure property rights promote expansion of the market, lower enforcement costs, and provide the confidence and collateral for land-specific investment. These activities in turn raise land values. Since land is the principal asset for frontier settlers, the provision and enforcement of formal property rights contributes to the growth of wealth and well-being among the population.

At the same time, however, the assignment of property rights to land necessarily outlines the distribution of wealth and political power in the community. If the accompanying distribution is very unequal, so as to be considered as unjust and as limiting opportunities for nonowners, then social pressures will emerge for redistribution. Unfortunately, these demands for redistribution or "land reform" weaken the security of property rights and their attending aggregate economic benefits. Accordingly, there is a trade-off between equity and efficiency that must be considered in the assignment of property rights, their enforcement, and their redistribution.

Adam Smith emphasized the role of the "civil magistrate" in defending property rights. But civil magistrates are political offices and hence subject to political pressures from many competing constituencies in assigning, enforcing, or reallocating property rights. Indeed, property rights to land are political institutions that are molded by legal precedents, competing demands for land, and the relative political influence of competing constituencies.

As we have demonstrated, Brazil has had a very skewed distribution of land for a long period of time. There also are large numbers of poor, landless peasants who migrate to urban areas and often are unemployed. The economic and social problems that result present formidable problems for the country. Land reform, or redistribution, has long been seen as a solution. Land reform also has been bitterly resisted by those who would lose land and be undercompensated for their losses. Land reform typically has not included full compensation for transfers because to do so dramatically increases the budgeted costs of redistribution and, hence, the ability of politicians and bureaucrats to directly respond to redistribution demands. Moreover, large landowners who are the targets of most redistribution efforts have been among the most politically influential constituents in the country. They have been able over time to block or mitigate land reform.

The Amazon frontier illustrates the conflicting tensions between the timely assignment of clear and enforced property rights that facilitate market extension and economic development and land reform policies to redistribute land to the landless. The region is the new frontier, with large tracts of unoccupied land that potentially provide opportunities for settlement and economic advancement. As such, the Amazon has attracted both large and small land claimants.

Title is well understood throughout Brazil as necessary for signifying government recognition of ownership and for accessing capital markets. All settlers, large and small claimants alike, desire title, especially as land values rise with improvements in transportation. Accordingly, the demand for title follows the movement of the economic frontier across the Amazon.

At the same time, however, Brazil has a highly skewed distribution of landholdings, and large, titled farms contribute to that skewed distribution. As an offset, the Brazilian Constitution requires that land be placed in beneficial use. That is, large holdings are not to be left idle in the face of large numbers of land claimants. The beneficial-use criteria vary according to region and are vague. In the Amazon, the failure to clear forest on large farms can be interpreted as a failure to place the land in beneficial use. Hence, large holdings that are heavily forested are vulnerable to invasion by squatters and expropriation by INCRA for redistribution to smallholders.

The invasion of privately owned farms can involve disputes between landowners (and their agents, the courts and police) and squatters. For squatters to successfully mount an invasion, they must be well organized. As we have shown, agrarian unions, such as the MST, provide discipline and organization to direct invasions and to pressure the government (particularly INCRA) to intervene on behalf of squatters. INCRA intervention can bring expropriation of the farm and its reallocation to the invaders. Ostensibly INCRA will, at some point, provide title to those individuals it has settled on the expropriated farm. The fact that this appears not generally to be the case is an issue we address below. Invasions, evictions, and expropriations provide the environment for violent conflicts and regional turmoil that weaken property rights and the economic advantages they provide. Our empirical results indicate that violent conflict reduces the expected returns from investment, which in turn reduces land values on the frontier.

Herein is the dilemma faced by Brazil and other developing countries—the need to provide secure property rights as a foundation for economic growth and the often competing requirement for a reallocation of land as part of land reform. As we have documented, these twin objectives have complicated the provision of secure property rights to land on the frontier.

How the goals of the timely supply and enforcement of titles and land redistribution are met has important practical consequences in the Amazon both for the welfare of its people and for the protection and wise use of its resources. The development of the region is still in its infancy. Recent estimates indicate that only about 6 percent of the Amazon rain forest has been settled and deforested.[1] Major migration to the area began in the late 1960s, accelerated in the early 1970s, and then waned in the 1980s with a slump in the overall Brazilian economy. More significant movement to the Amazon began to occur once again in the late 1990s. This record of settlement means that much of the Amazon rain forest and other natural resources remain relatively untouched. It also means that there will be many new frontiers in the Amazon as migration intensifies. Hence, the problems of devising institutions for the allocation and distribution of frontier lands are both immediate and long term.

Most of the land that is open to private settlement and claiming is in the hands of the state and federal governments. Hence, government policies play a central role in how the development of the Amazon proceeds. How smoothly and completely governments provide property rights institutions is key in determining whether the potential wealth of the Amazon is captured by the settlers or dissipated in competition for control of the land. Property rights institutions also determine whether frontier settlement occurs with a minimum of environmental damage and whether important parts of the rain forest endowment can be preserved.

The literature that we cited in chapter 1 provides a mixed score card for the Brazilian government in the management of the frontier. The history of land policy described in chapters 2 and 3 also presents a sobering array of failed programs elsewhere in Brazil that provide precedents for future policies that will be difficult to overcome in the Amazon. Further, conflicting government and bureaucratic jurisdictions have confused the provision of definitive property rights to land. Finally, inconsistencies between civil law and its protection of title, and populist constitutional law and its emphasis on land redistribution, have set the stage for violent confrontation between owners and squatters, with the accompanying dissipation of land rents.

Even so, with much of the Amazon yet relatively untouched, the opportunity exists for new institutional design. Such institutional change must be based on an understanding of the objectives of the competing interests for Amazon land, the behavior of the government agencies involved in settlement and land reform, the incentives created by current land reform policies and the associated economic costs of violent conflict, and the potential contributions of clear title for raising land values and protecting the unique natural resources of the region. The analysis of this book provides a framework for understanding and predicting whether and in what ways government policies toward tenuring and land reform might be modified as settlement of the Amazon proceeds.

A Summary of Major Points

Our study of the private demand for and political supply of property rights illustrates how complex is the process of institutional change, even when the economic benefits of such change are quite clear. This case study of the development of property rights for land on the Amazon frontier illustrates the point made by Douglass North (1981, 1990) that institutions do not necessarily emerge and evolve in a manner that promotes economic growth and development.[2]

Property rights institutions for land in Brazil often have been associated with serious rent dissipation. There is a path dependency in the way in which property rights have been allocated to land in Brazil historically and the difficulty of satisfactorily addressing land reform demands today. Government land was granted to large claimants, who became among the most politically influential groups in the country. Over time, through past distributions and consolidation due to economies of scale in modern agricultural production, landownership became and remained highly skewed. Since the 1960s, this skewed distribution has fostered serious demands for government intervention for land reform. Political tensions between those who have land and those who do not have made it difficult to devise land redistribution schemes that minimize the negative impact on property rights while at the same time achieving land allocation goals. Most of the redistribution schemes either have not been implemented or have failed to have much impact on landownership patterns. The political process has not successfully devised the side payments necessary to reduce the opposition of large landowners. Further, the failure to satisfactorily address land reform demands has resulted in a climate of distrust and conflict between landowners and squatters. This conflict is both economically and socially damaging, and it has persisted for a long time.

A strict neoclassical economics framework alone is insufficient for understanding frontier land settlement, titling, and land reform in the Amazon. Accordingly, we have emphasized the muddled politics and bureaucratic objectives that underlie current institutions and policies. The analysis of earlier frontiers in Paraná between 1940 and 1970, relative to those in Pará between 1970 and 1985, indicates that tenuring and distributional policies are less successful on Amazon frontiers. Whereas in Paraná settlement and titling appear to have been quite routine, much like the pattern observed in nineteenth-century North America, in Pará titling has been less complete as land values have increased. Indeed, the Amazon region has had chronically higher levels of farms and farmland occupied by squatters (farmers without title) than have other regions of Brazil since 1940. The state of Pará also has the largest number of deaths due to land conflicts between squatters and landowners. Since the Amazon is the newest frontier in Brazil, this pattern of comparatively limited titling and higher levels of violent conflict over land indicates that current policies are leading to serious rent dissipation and missed economic opportunities.

As an example of contemporary conditions, the slow and incomplete provision of title on the Amazon frontier that we document in Tucumã and the apparent failure of INCRA to follow expropriations with the granting of titles to squatters elsewhere in Pará are likely to have significant wealth consequences. Our study of frontier settlement in the state of Pará revealed that settlers considered the payoff to having title high; in some cases interviewed farmers claimed that it raised land values by 50 percent or more. Hence, they were willing to expend considerable resources in lobbying the land agency, INCRA, to provide title. Further, having title significantly raised investment, and investment and title were the two most important variables in boosting land values.

Even so, our statistical and qualitative evidence suggests that INCRA seriously undertitles. An agency under siege, it devotes scarce budgets and staffing to expropriation and settlement in response to violence. We argue that this reaction only encourages further invasions and land violence. Invasions and conflict reduce the security of ownership, lower time horizons, and, hence, dampen the incentive to invest. Our evidence indicates that violent conflict has reduced estimated investment in the survey region by approximately 19 percent. Lower investment in turn lowered estimated land values by nearly 8 percent.

In an effort to firm up their property rights to land and, hence, to avoid invasion and expropriation, large landowners have an incentive to rapidly and extensively cut rain forest to prove "beneficial" use. We do not have systematic evidence at this time of the significance of this practice in terms of overall deforestation in the Amazon. If not checked, it may be an important contributor to the loss of forest, which is of worldwide concern. Defensive deforestation is an example of rent dissipation encouraged by a weak property rights framework.

We have emphasized two models of institutional development in this volume and used them to guide our analysis. The first model relates distance to the net present value of land. This model outlines why the demand for more precise property rights institutions for land rise as land values increase. The model provides a framework for following institutional change as the economic frontier moves with improvements in transportation infrastructure.

With this framework we see that on the economic frontier there is little demand for formal property rights. Those individuals who occupy the frontier will have low opportunity costs and be young, with limited education and capital. As transportation costs fall (or alternatively, the closer one is to the market center), the range and value of potential land uses expand, and competition for control increases. Eventually this demand will give rise to informal institutions (local agreements) that will successfully deal with competition for the resource for some time. But with continued migration and competition for control, eventually these informal institutions will break down. Several forms of rent dissipation may occur—increased time of patrolling claims, forgone land sales, missed investment opportunities. Avoiding this dissipation and capturing the increased land value made possible by title encourages settlers to organize and lobby land agencies and politicians to provide title. Empirically, we see that these activities are time consuming and often unsuccessful in the Amazon.

As the demand for formal property rights from the government arises, it may not be met at the optimal time (may be too early or may be too late), and the particular form of the property rights may not necessarily be that which most effectively minimizes rent dissipation and raises land values. This imperfect outcome occurs because the supply of title is through the political process. Politicians respond to many constituencies in crafting tenure policies, and in the case of Brazil, tenuring policies are compromised by land reform demands that siphon resources from the primary land agency, INCRA. Bureaucrats who administer land policies must be responsive to different political constituencies and at the same time allocate scarce budgets and staffs to meet those constituent demands. These conditions help to explain why there appears to be more violence and more accompanying rent dissipation in the Amazon than occurred on earlier frontiers in Brazil. This outcome emphasizes the importance of understanding the political and bureaucratic processes by which demands for formal property rights are met.

The second model we have developed is one for rural conflicts over land. Through a game-theoretic framework, we have identified the parties involved and described their incentives within an environment of conflicting civil and constitutional laws and competing political and bureaucratic objectives for titling and land reform. The model explicitly includes INCRA, the courts, the president, landowners, and squatters. It predicts how the two antagonists (landowners and squatters) will respond to shifts in land value, in the position of the courts, in the costs of resorting to violence, government policies toward land reform, and in the security of property rights to land. By taking into account how each of these factors influence the payoffs to the parties involved, the model allows us to see how institutional arrangements create incentives for landowners and squatters to engage in violence. In this way we can outline how land reform policies and their cycle of violence, expropriations, and settlement can have the unanticipated effect of encouraging even more violence, rather than mitigating the sources of conflict.

In this book we have demonstrated that titles promote investment and, through investment, increase land values. Yet, this raises a puzzle: if titles are so valuable, why are they not more prevalent, especially in the Amazon region, where land use by squatters without title has been greater than elsewhere in Brazil? Although our conjectures focus on the Brazilian Amazon, the absence of titles is prevalent in many developing countries, and the reasons may be similar.[3]

Our survey of smallholders in Pará indicates that claimants want titles. The most frequent reason given was that titles would allow claimants to access capital markets. This rationale is consistent with our empirical finding that titles are positively associated with investment. Further, it is important to point out that our measure of investment covers only longer-term, site-specific investments, such as fencing and permanent crops. Yet farmers seek credit (when available) for non-site-specific assets such as plows and chainsaws and for annual expenditures on seeds and fertilizers. Having title provides collateral to obtain credit for such purchases.[4]

Although land claimants view titles as increasingly desirable as land values rise, this acknowledgment does not necessarily translate into effective political demand for titles. Small claimants without title in the Amazon face classic free-rider problems and are neither numerous enough nor wealthy enough to directly influence the actions of politicians or the bureaucracy.

To overcome these problems, both large and small land claimants have organized into lobby groups. Since 1984, small claimants have been organized through the MST, or landless peasants' union. The MST not only provides effective organization for lobbying the Brazilian Congress and president and the federal land agency INCRA, but searches for farms that are likely candidates for invasion and expropriation. Additionally, the MST has developed broader-based political support from the media and general public. The MST, however, appears to demand land for the landless while placing less emphasis on securing titles for landholders. This observation reflects the mixed political benefits to INCRA and the MST of titling settlers and the high costs of providing title that would divert budgets and staff from land reform. We turn to these issues in the following section.

The Apparent Neglect of Titling

Both census data and our survey of smallholders in Pará indicate a relative lack of titling in the Amazon. In our statistical work regarding the incidence of title among smallholders, we overpredicted title, considering land values and the characteristics of individual settlers, compared to our empirical observations. We predicted title for 144 settlers, but in fact only 125 had title. Further, as shown in table 3, the absence of title in the Amazon region is chronic. These results are consistent with the impression that neither INCRA nor the MST desires to focus resources on titling. Both organizations state their land reform goals in terms of the number of landless to be settled.

We believe that this focus on settlement, rather than on titling the settled, is more than a semantic issue. Budgets and staffing are limited. Titling is costly. During the rapid migration of the mid-1970s INCRA recognized the difficulties of providing formal property rights to land on the frontier (INCRA 1984). Cadastres in the Amazon were then, and remain, very incomplete and incorrect. Additionally, most properties are not demarcated. Determining actual boundaries involves both surveys and resolving competing claims. Resolving disputes is difficult because of poor documentation of when settlers arrived (to establish priority of claim), claim limits, and from whom the settler purchased or received the land. Past fraud and competing government jurisdictions (INCRA and ITERPA— the Pará land agency) with associated contending land grants have added to the problem. Hence, the provision of clear title to settlers diverts resources from expropriations and new settlement efforts.

Both INCRA and the MST are reluctant to devote resources in that manner. INCRA and sponsoring politicians can respond to immediate political demands to address the problem of the landless by concentrating attention on expropriations and settlement projects. Investments in titling recently settled farmers will likely provide fewer short-term political benefits, and if significant resources were involved in slowing land reform, a political backlash might develop. Moreover, there is a dependency relationship with smallholders that may benefit INCRA and MST if titles are not provided. Absent title and potential access to capital markets, small settlers remain dependent on INCRA for credit, on other settlement subsidies for housing, food, and planting, and on the MST as an advocate for their interests. In return, settlers donate 2 to 5 percent of the funds they receive from INCRA to the MST.[5] The MST organizes settlers to pressure INCRA to pay the promised settlement subsidies. Once their farms are titled, settlers no longer would have the same claim on INCRA funds. Hence, while land values remain low, settlers too may prefer not to have title at that time. These same settlers provide an entrenched political constituency for INCRA in protecting its budgets and mandates and for MST in maintaining its political influence.

In addition, both INCRA and the MST may prefer not to provide titles to settlers as a means of limiting mobility and on the margin, slowing the growth of the number of landless claimants. As we discussed in chapter 4, titles raise land values in part by broadening the market. With a title it is easier to sell one's claim. If a settler sells his plot, he may (temporarily) return to the pool of landless. Given the political concern with the number of landless, the rationale for settling, but not titling, is clear to politicians, bureaucrats, and advocacy groups. The theme would be this: Settle people, but do not make it easy for them to sell their land. For all of these reasons, perhaps fewer than 10 percent of the settlement projects following expropriations in the Amazon have had titles issued.

As land values rise, however, and the benefits of titling become more apparent, demand may shift. If settlers had security of title to their land claims, they would be less dependent upon MST and INCRA and potentially have access to alternative sources of funds. As these conditions emerge, politicians have an incentive to provide title. As evidence of this incentive, prior to state elections ITERPA has been particularly aggressive in providing titles to land. Politicians see granting titles as a means of currying favor among settlers, and in this way they are able to capture part of the political benefits resulting from any increased economic growth due to more secure property rights to land.

Violence: Is There a Solution?

In chapter 8 we argued that violence has both costs to the participants and external costs to the community at large. Violence results in deaths, lowers investment and land values, and contributes to local deforestation.[6] Given the costs of violence, why does it persist?

The origins of violent conflict over land lie in the conflicts between civil and constitutional law in Brazil over property rights to land. The former guarantees property rights, the latter conditions those guarantees with a beneficial-use mandate. "Unused" properties can be expropriated as a means of land reform. Violence typically occurs as squatters invade perceived unused lands and as landowners, either directly or through the courts and local police, attempt to evict them. Squatters rely upon INCRA intervention to support their claims to the invaded farm. Violence occurs in part due to uncertainty among landowners and squatters as to whether INCRA will intervene. Violence also is used as a tool by MST and other squatters' organizations to embarrass politicians and INCRA, and thereby force the agency to expropriate land and redistribute it to the invaders.

To break this cycle we examine policy options that might encourage greater voluntary land redistribution and reduce the incidence of violence that weakens the property rights structure. We consider (1) raising the costs of holding idle land; (2) improving rental markets; and (3) facilitating voluntary transfers.

Raising the Costs of Holding Idle Land

Because of a history of inflation, holding land in Brazil has been a common hedge against price increases. Further, there have been tax credits and other subsidies to landowners to promote development in the Amazon that could be transferred to other, nonagricultural uses. As a result of these incentives, large plots were often privately owned but not put into production. Hence, they have not fulfilled the beneficial-use requirement of the Constitution. Where these tracts were remote, neither owners nor squatters have shown much interest in them. As roads have been constructed, however, squatters have moved on site and owners have sought eviction.

Accordingly, the existence of privately owned, but idle tracts of land has been a contributing factor in land violence. Some of the underlying forces, however, have diminished recently. Inflation has declined sharply, reducing the benefits from holding idle land as a hedge. Further, tax credits for development in the Amazon have been eliminated or reduced. Additionally, the government has passed a new rural land tax on unproductive land. The law, as written, will tax unproductive land at 20 percent of the value of land. If enforced, this law has potential to raise the costs of holding idle land and thereby encourage the owners of large holdings (latifundia) either to place them into production or to subdivide and sell their holdings. Although there is little record of effective tax collection in rural areas, the enactment of the tax legislation signal that other tax legislation or statutes that raise the costs of holding unused land may be on the horizon.

These actions may encourage subdivision and land use and thereby help to alleviate social tensions over landownership. At the same time, this may not be good news for those who would like to see large tracts of land held in forest. So long as forested land is viewed as unused and thereby subject to expropriation, the populist provisions of the Constitution and the desires to promote natural forest holdings will conflict.

Improving Rental Markets

An alternative to sale is subdivision of large holdings and rental of farmlands. The renting of farmlands through a variety of arrangements can be a means of promoting small farms and developing a more egalitarian wealth distribution. What is remarkable in Brazil is how little rental markets are developed. In 1985 only 18 percent of all farms were rented or sharecropped, and only 4 percent of the total area in farms was rented or sharecropped. Interestingly, these figures are almost identical to the percentage of farms occupied by squatters and percentage of farm area held by squatters in 1985—18 percent and 5 percent, respectively (IBGE 1985).

An important reason why rental markets and sharecropping have not developed significantly in Brazil is the insecurity of property rights. That is, large landowners are wary of contracting with tenants for the agricultural use of their lands, lest this provide the basis for subsequent reallocation of the land to those who actually use the soil. Indeed in 1985 during debate over the PNRA (the National Program for Land Reform discussed in chapter 2), the transfer of lands to sharecroppers and tenant farmers was discussed as a means of land reform. Although not enacted, alarmed landowners apparently evicted sharecroppers and tenants as a precaution against such provisions (Gomes da Silva 1987, 88).

A solution, then, would be to legislatively reaffirm property rights to land that is rented. Matching renters with landowners through either fixed cash or share rentals would enable each to contribute to production according to their resource endowments. Typically, landlords will have better access to capital markets and the latest in agricultural technology. These strengths can be shared with tenants who, if partial residual claimants, will have strong incentives to work hard with relatively little supervision. If the government would guarantee landowners that they would not lose their land if they engaged in renting, the practice might increase and thereby provide opportunities for small farmers.

Promoting Credit Markets and Voluntary Transfers

Currently, there is little private credit available for either small or large holdings. The absence of formal, secure property rights to land is a contributing factor. The impact is greatest on smallholders, who are less likely to have title for the reasons we have described. Absent title, farmers lack recognized collateral to obtain loans for investment and short-term production financing. Even for large holders, credit is limited because it is often difficult for creditors to foreclose if borrowers are delinquent.[7] The bulk of credit available is for short-term expenditures in seeds, fertilizers, and machinery. If it were recognized that strengthening the rights of creditors would contribute to private credit for large and small farmers and hence, a more equal land distribution, there might be some chance of reforming the mortgage laws.

In recognition of the lack of a mortgage market the World Bank has financed a pilot program in cooperation with INCRA that will supply credit for the landless to purchase land. Prospective land purchasers with the assistance of INCRA will negotiate a price with a landowner, and the World Bank will supply the funding. Given that the new landowners have an obligation to repay, they have an incentive to negotiate a low price with the previous owner. It is unclear how costly or extensive such programs will be, but because they promote the voluntary exchange of land, they can defuse the tensions that lead to violence and weaken property rights to land.

The Future of the Amazon

In closing, the research reported in this book reaffirms the importance of definitive property rights to land on the frontier as a means of promoting the extension of markets and investment and of reducing private enforcement costs. Settlers, large and smallholders alike, understand the role of title. Yet the political arena and bureaucratic agencies have not supplied or enforced title in a smooth, routine manner in the Amazon. Conflicting political objectives, most notably land reform goals, have complicated the process, as we have demonstrated. The efficiency gains of well-defined and well-enforced property rights to valuable land are clear. At the same time, distributional concerns in the face of a very skewed landownership allocation threaten those economic benefits. Land reform, then, is a legitimate political and economic concern. But land reform must be implemented in a manner that differs from current policies that promote violence and rent dissipation.

We do not suggest that new land reform measures that rely on voluntary transactions and the development of rental and credit markets will be easy to devise and implement. The political debate is intense, and there is a long history of thwarted attempts at land redistribution in Brazil. Hayami (1997, 174) comments on the prospects for land reform in developing countries. He notes that land redistribution was quite successful in Japan, Korea, and Taiwan in resulting in a highly egalitarian, agrarian structure. Although it is not clear if land reform increased agricultural productivity, it did lead to increased social and political stability. Hayami, however, points out the conditions for land redistribution in these three countries were quite different than are found in most developing countries today. Land reform was implemented at a time when landowners were politically weak and unable to block legislation—immediate postwar conditions in Japan, Korea, and Taiwan. Equally important were the existence of a relatively well-disciplined bureaucracy, a body of accurate data on landownership and tenure relations, and well-organized tenant farmers.

None of these conditions exist in Brazil, or in many other developing countries today, where the competing demands of secure property rights and land reform remain formidable challenges. Even so, the potential economic gains at stake through secure property rights and the benefits of a more egalitarian land distribution in reducing social and political tensions provide motivation for effective institutional change. The results will determine the future of the Amazon.

NOTES

1. The estimates of deforestation vary dramatically. See Anderson et al. 1996, 36–39, where 6 percent is above most of the estimates given for the late 1980s.

2. The problems encountered in negotiating institutional changes are described in other empirical contexts by Libecap 1989 and in Alston, Eggertsson, and North 1996.

3. Under many land reforms, curiously, settlement and not titling is the objective. For example, in the land reforms in Bolivia and Peru, settlers received use rights that could be passed on to heirs, but they could not sell the land. Similarly, the recent agricultural land reform in China provided limited use rights but not more complete property rights to land.

4. We recognize that credit markets in the Amazon are very underdeveloped and that credit is often not available. It is not clear what is the causal mechanism. The Amazon is a frontier, and, as we have shown in chapter 2, over a third of the farms in the region lack title. In many areas, the proportion without title is probably greater. The absence of clear property rights to land certainly inhibits the development of private credit markets. Further, elsewhere in Brazil credit markets are more developed, and migrants to the Amazon understand the benefits of title and credit. Accordingly, the desire for credit fuels the derived demand for title even where and when credit is very limited.

5. These payments form a large share of the MST budget. The newspaper *Folha de São Paulo* stated that the largest source of revenue for the MST (approximately U.S.$4 million) came from these payments by settled families. Another U.S.$1 million came from 61 cooperatives that were created on settlement projects organized by the MST. Squatters waiting to be settled also contribute funds to the MST (see Sá 1997).

6. We are currently investigating the impact of violence on deforestation. It appears that both squatters and title holders can strengthen their property rights by deforesting.

7. In the United States, in response to state-imposed moratoria on farm foreclosures in the 1930s, creditors reduced the number of mortgage loans. See Alston 1984.

References

Abramovay, Ricardo. 1985a. Reforma Agrária, Desenvolvimento Capitalista e Democracia. In *Reforma Agrária da Nova República: Contradições e Alternativas,* ed. Laécio Leal. São Paulo: Editora Cortez.

―――. 1985b. Nova forma de luta pela terra: Acampar. *Reforma Agrária* (Campinas), May–July, 55–60.

Alston, Lee J. 1984. Farm Foreclosure Moratorium Legislation: A Lesson from the Past. *American Economic Review* 74:445–57.

Alston, Lee J., Thrainn Eggertsson, and Douglass C. North. 1996. *Empirical Studies in Institutional Change.* New York: Cambridge University Press.

Alston, Lee J., Gary D. Libecap, and Bernardo Mueller. 1997. The Development of Property Rights to Land: When Is Violence Part of Institutional Change? In *Frontiers of the New Institutional Economics,* ed. John Drobak and John Nye. San Diego: Academic Press.

―――. 1998a. Property Rights to Land and Land Reform: Legal Inconsistencies and The Sources of Violent Conflict in the Brazilian Amazon. Working paper, Karl Eller Center, University of Arizona, Tucson.

Alston, Lee J., Gary D. Libecap, and Bernardo Mueller. 1998b. Property Rights and Land Conflict: A Comparison of Settlement of the U.S. Western and Brazilian Amazon Frontiers. In *Latin America and the World Economy since 1800,* ed. John Coatsworth and Alan Taylor. Cambridge: Harvard University Press.

Alston, Lee J., Gary D. Libecap, and Robert Schneider. 1995a. Property Rights and the Preconditions for Markets: The Case of the Amazon Frontier. *Journal of Institutional and Theoretical Economics* 151:89–107.

―――. 1995b. The Demand and Supply of Property Rights on the Frontier: The Cases of North America and Brazil. In *The Privatization Process: A Worldwide Perspective,* ed. Terry L. Anderson and Peter J. Hill. Lanham, Md.: Rowman and Littlefield.

―――. 1996a. Violence and the Assignment of Property Rights on Two Brazilian Frontiers. In *The Political Economy of Rent Seeking and Conflict,* ed. Michelle R. Garfinkel and Stergios Skaperdas. New York: Cambridge University Press.

―――. 1996b. The Determinants and Impact of Property Rights: Land Titles on the Brazilian Frontier. *Journal of Law, Economics, and Organization* 12:25–61.

Anderson, Lykke E., Clive W. J. Granger, Ling-Ling Huang, Eustáquio J. Reis, and Diana Weinhold. 1996. Report on Amazon Deforestation. Working paper, University of California, San Diego.

Anderson, Terry L., and Peter J. Hill. 1975. The Evolution of Property Rights: A Study of the American West. *Journal of Law and Economics* 18:163–79.

———. 1990. The Race for Property Rights. *Journal of Law and Economics* 33:177–97.

Bakx, Keith. 1990. "The Shanty Town, Final Stage of Rural Development? The Case of Acre." In *The Future of Amazônia: Destruction or Sustainable Development?* ed. David Goodman and Anthony Hall. London: Macmillan.

Bardhan, Pranab. 1989. The New Institutional Economics and Development Theory: A Brief Critical Assessment. *World Development* 17:1389–95.

Barro, Robert J. 1991. Economic Growth in a Cross Section of Countries. *Quarterly Journal of Economics* 106 (2): 407–44.

Barzel, Yoram. 1989. *Economic Analysis of Property Rights.* New York: Cambridge University Press.

Becker, Gary S. 1983. A Theory of Competition among Pressure Groups for Political Influence. *Quarterly Journal of Economics* 68 (3): 371–400.

Besley, Timothy. 1995. Property Rights and Investment Incentives: Theory and Evidence from Ghana. *Journal of Political Economy* 103:903–37.

Binswanger, Hans P. 1989. Brazilian Policies That Encourage Deforestation in the Amazon. Environment Department Working Paper No. 16, World Bank, Washington, D.C.

Binswanger, Hans P., and Klaus Deininger. 1993. South African Land Policy: The Legacy of History and Current Options. *World Development* 21:1451–73.

Binswanger, Hans P., Klaus Deininger, and Gershon Feder. 1995. Power, Distortions, Revolt, and Reform in Agricultural Land Relations. In *Handbook of Development Economics,* ed. J. Behrman and T. N. Srinivasan, vol. 3. Amsterdam: North Holland.

Bogue, Allan. 1963. *From Prairie to Corn Belt.* Chicago: University of Chicago Press.

Brandão, Antônio Salazar. 1992. Mercado de Terra e Estrutura Fundiária. In *Os Principais Problemas da Agricultura Brasileira: Análise e Sugesttes,* ed. A. S. Brandno. Rio de Janeiro: Serie PNPE.

Breusch, T., and A. Pagan. 1979. A Simple Test for Heteroskedasticity and Random Coefficient Variation. *Econometrica* 47:1287–94.

———. 1980. The LM Test and Its Applications to Model Specification in Econometrics. *Review of Economic Studies* 47:239–54.

Bulow, J., J. Geanankopolos, and P. Klemperer. 1985. Multimarket Oligopoly: Strategies, Substitutes, and Complements. *Journal of Political Economy* 93:488–511.

Bunker, Steven G. 1985a. *Underdeveloping the Amazon: Extraction, Unequal Exchange, and the Failure of the Modern State.* Chicago: University of Chicago Press.

———. 1985b. Misdirected Expertise in an Unknown Environment: Standard Bureaucratic Procedures as Inappropriate Technologies on the Brazilian

"Planned Frontier." In *The Frontier after a Decade of Colonization,* ed. John Hemming. Manchester: Manchester University Press.

Butler, John R. 1985. Land, Gold, and Farmers: Agricultural Colonization and Frontier Expansion in the Brazilian Amazon. Ph.D. diss., University of Florida, Gainesville.

Carlson, Gerald A., David Zilberman, and John A. Miranowski. 1993. *Agricultural and Environmental Resource Economics.* New York: Oxford University Press.

Centro Ecumenico de Documentação e Informação (CEDI). 1986. *Quem Tem Medo da Reforma Agrária: Dossiê das Reações ao 1º PNRA.* São Paulo: Princeps Gráfica Editora.

Cheung, Steven N. S. 1970. The Structure of a Contract and the Theory of a Non-Exclusive Resource. *Journal of Law and Economics* 13:49–70.

Coase, Ronald H. 1960. The Problem of Social Cost. *Journal of Law and Economics* 3:1–44.

———. 1992. "The Institutional Structure of Production." *American Economic Review* 82:713–19.

Comissão Pastoral da Terra. 1987–95. *Conflitos no Campo.* Goiania: CPT.

Conley, Timothy, and David W. Galenson. 1998. Nativity and Wealth in Mid–Nineteenth Century Cities. *Journal of Economic History* 58, no. 2: 468–93.

Cornia, Giovanni Andrea. 1985. Farm Size, Land Yields, and the Agricultural Production Function: An Analysis for Fifteen Developing Countries. *World Development* 13:513–34.

Cowell, Adrian. 1990. *The Decade of Destruction: The Crusade to Save the Amazon Rain Forest.* New York: Henry Holt.

Curti, Merle. 1959. *The Making of an American Community.* Stanford: Stanford University Press.

Danhof, Clarence H. 1936. The Homestead Act and Labor Surplus. *American Historical Review* 41 (4): 637–51.

———. 1941. Farm-Making Costs and "The Safety Valve," 1850–60. *Journal of Political Economy* 49:317–59.

Dasgupta, P. S., and G. M. Heal. 1979. *Economic Theory and Exhaustible Resources.* New York: Cambridge University Press.

Davidson, J., and J. Mackinnon. 1981. Several Tests for Model Specification in the Presence of Alternative Hypotheses. *Econometrica* 49:781–95.

Davis, Lance, and Douglass C. North. 1971. *Institutional Change and American Economic Growth.* Cambridge: Cambridge University Press.

Dawes, R. M. 1975. Formal Models of Dilemmas in Social Decision Making. In *Human Judgement and Decision Processes: Formal and Mathematical Approaches,* ed. M. F. Kaplan and S. Schwartz. New York: Academic Press.

Deacon, Robert T. 1994. Deforestation and the Rule of Law in a Cross Section of Countries. *Land Economics* 70:414–30.

———. 1995. Assessing the Relationship between Government Policy and Deforestation. *Journal of Environmental Economics and Management* 28:1–18.

Dean, Warren. 1971. Latifundia and Land Policy in Nineteenth-Century Brazil. *Hispanic-American History Review,* November, 606–25.

Demsetz, Harold. 1967. Towards a Theory of Property Rights. *American Economic Review* 57:347–59.

———. 1972. When Does the Rule of Liability Matter? *Journal of Legal Studies* 1:13–28.

Dinar, Ariel, and Andrew Keck. 1997. Private Irrigation Investment in Columbia: Effects of Violence, Macroeconomic Policy, and Environmental Conditions. *Agricultural Economics* 16 (1): 1–16.

Dutra, Domingos. 1992. Poder Judiciário e a Violência no Campo. *Reforma Agrária* (Campinas), April, 132–39.

Eder, James F. 1990. Deforestation and Detribalization in the Philippines: The Palawan Case. *Population and Environment* 12:99–116.

Editora Turistica e Estatistica. 1988. *Republica Federativa do Brasil, Estado do Pará, Rodoviario, Politico e Estatistico.* 3d ed. Goiania.

Eggertsson, Thrainn. 1990. *Economic Behavior and Institutions.* New York: Cambridge University Press.

Éleres, Paraguassú. 1996. Números da Intervenção Territorial Federal no Pará. *Pará Desenvolvimento.* No. 29, edição especial, 85–89.

Ellickson, Robert C. 1991. *Order without Law: How Neighbors Settle Disputes.* Cambridge: Harvard University Press.

Ensminger, Jean. 1995. Changing Property Rights: Reconciling Formal and Informal Rights to Land in Africa. Working paper, Department of Anthropology, Washington University, St. Louis.

Fachin, Luiz E. 1991. A Justiça dos Conflitos no Brasil. *Reforma Agrária* (Campinas), April, 87–94.

Food and Agriculture Organization/Ministério da Agricultura e Reforma Agrária (FAO/UNDP/MARA). 1992. *Principais Indicadores Sócio-Econômicos dos Assentamentos de Reforma Agrária.* Brasília: MinistJrio da Agricultura e Reforma Agrária.

Fearnside, Philip M. 1985. Environmental Change and Deforestation in the Brazilian Amazon. In *Change in the Amazon Basin,* ed. John Hemming. Vol. 1, *Man's Impact on Forests and Rivers.* Manchester: Manchester University Press.

———. 1986. *Human Carrying Capacity of the Brazilian Rain Forest.* New York: Columbia University Press.

Feder, Gershon, and David Feeny. 1991. Land Tenure and Property Rights: Theory and Implications for Development Policy. *World Bank Economic Review* 3:135–53.

Feder, Gershon, and Tongroj Onchan. 1987. Land Ownership Security and Farm Investment in Thailand. *American Journal of Agricultural Economics* 69:311–20.

Feder, Gershon, Tongroj Onchan, Yongyuth Chalamwong, and Chira Hongladrarom. 1988. *Land Policies and Farm Productivity in Thailand.* Baltimore: Johns Hopkins University Press.

Ferrie, Joseph P. 1997. Migration to the Frontier in Mid–Nineteenth Century America: A Re-Examination of Turner's "Safety Valve." Working paper, Department of Economics, Northwestern University.

Foweraker, Joseph. 1981. *The Struggle for Land: A Political Economy of the Pioneer Frontier in Brazil, 1930 to Present.* New York: Cambridge University Press.

Friedman, Lawrence. 1985. *A History of American Law.* 2d. ed. New York: Simon and Schuster.

Fundação Getúlio Vargas (FGV). 1997. Preço de Terra: uma Queda Esperada, *Agroanalysis* (Rio de Janeiro), January, 18–22.

Fundação Instituto Brasileiro de Geographia e Estatístico (FIBGE). 1940, 1950, 1960a, 1970a, 1975a, 1980a. *Censo Agropecuario—Paraná.* Rio de Janeiro: FIBGE.

———. 1960b, 1970b, 1975b, 1980b, 1985. *Censo Agropecuario—Pará.* Rio de Janeiro: FIBGE.

———. 1965, 1990a, 1991a. *Anuário Estatístico do Brasil.* Rio de Janeiro: FIBGE.

———. 1990b. *Estatísticas Históricas do Brasil.* Rio de Janeiro: FIBGE.

———. 1990c. *Geografia do Brasil—Região Sul.* Vol. 2. Rio de Janeiro: FIBGE.

———. 1991b. *Geografia do Brasil—Região Norte.* Vol. 3. Rio de Janeiro: FIBGE.

Furtado, Celso. 1961. *Formação Econômica do Brasil.* 4th ed. Rio de Janeiro: Editora Fundo de Cultura.

Furubotn, Eirik G., and Rudolf Richter. 1993. The New Institutional Economics: Recent Progress, Expanding Frontiers. *Journal of Institutional and Theoretical Economics* 149:1–10.

Garfinkel, Michelle, and Stergios Skaperdas, eds. 1996. *The Political Economy of Conflict and Appropriation.* New York: Cambridge University Press.

Gasques, José C., and Clando Yokomizo. 1986. Resultado de Vinte Anos de Incentivos Fiscais na Agropecuária da Amazônia. In *XIV Encontro Nacional de Economia, ANPEC,* Brasília, December, vol. 2.

Gates, Paul W. 1968. *History of Public Land Law Development.* Washington, D.C.: Government Printing Office.

Gillis, Malcolm, and Robert Repetto. 1988. *Deforestation and Government Policy.* New York: Cambridge University Press.

———. 1989. *Public Policy and the Misuse of Forest Resources.* New York: Cambridge University Press.

Gomes da Silva, José. 1987. *Caindo Por Terra: Crises da Reforma Agrária na Nova República.* São Paulo: Busca Vida.

———. 1989. *Buraco Negro: A Reforma Agrária na Constituinte de 1987/88.* Rio de Janeiro: Paz e Terra.

Gondim, Abnor, and Marta Salomon. 1997. Jungamnn Cobra Estados por Impunidade no Campo. *Folha de São Paulo,* February 3, p. 6.

Goodland, Robert. 1985. Brazil's Environmental Progress in Amazonian Development. In *Change in the Amazon Basin,* ed. John Hemming. Vol. 1, *Man's Impact on Forests and Rivers.* Manchester: Manchester University Press.

Gordon, H. Scott. 1954. The Economic Theory of a Common Property Resource: The Fishery. *Journal of Political Economy* 2:124–42.

Graziano, Fransisco. 1991. *A Tragédia da Terra: O Fracasso da Reforma Agrária no Brasil.* São Paulo: IGLU/FUNEP/UESP.

Graziano da Silva, José. 1985. *Para Entender o Plano Nacional de Reforma Agrária.* São Paulo: Editora Brasiliense.

Greene, William H. 1992. *LIMDEP: User's Manual and Reference Guide.* Bellport, N.Y.: Econometric Software.

———. 1993. *Econometric Analysis.* 2d ed. New York: Macmillan.

Grossman, James R. 1994. *The Frontier in American Culture: Essays by Richard White and Patricia Nelson Limerick.* Berkeley and Los Angeles: University of California Press.

Halcrow, Harold. 1980. *Economics of Agriculture.* New York: McGraw-Hill.

Hale, William Harlan. 1950. *Horace Greeley, Voice of the People.* New York: Harper.

Hardin, Garrett. 1968. The Tragedy of the Commons. *Science.* 162:1243–48.

Harvey, A. 1991. *The Econometric Analysis of Time Series.* 2d ed. Cambridge: MIT Press.

Hayami, Yujiro. 1997. *Development Economics: From the Poverty to the Wealth of Nations.* New York: Oxford University Press.

Hess, Charlotte. 1996. *Common Pool Resources and Collective Action: A Bibliography.* Vol. 3. Workshop in Political Theory and Policy Analysis, Indiana University, Bloomington.

Hoff, Karla, Avishay Braverman, and Joseph E. Stiglitz, eds. 1993. *The Economics of Rural Organization: Theory, Practice, and Policy.* New York: Oxford University Press.

Hoffman, Roldolfo. 1982. Evolução da Distribuição da Posse da Terra no Brasil no Período 1960–80. *Reforma Agrária* (Campinas), November–December, 17–34.

Hughes, Jonathan R. T. 1977. *The Government Habit: Economic Controls from Colonial Times to the Present.* New York: Basic Books.

Human Rights Watch. 1991. *Rural Violence in Brazil.* New York: Human Rights Watch.

Hurst, James W. 1956. *Law and the Conditions of Freedom in the Nineteenth Century United States.* Madison: University of Wisconsin Press.

Ianni, Octavio. 1979. *Colonização e Contra-Reforma Agrária na Amazônia.* Petrópolis: Editora Vozes.

International Bank for Reconstruction and Development/International Development Association (IBRD/IDA). 1997. *Brazil: Land Reform and Poverty Alleviation Pilot Project.* Project Appraisal Report, Latin America and the Caribbean Regional Office, Brasília.

Instituto do Desenvolvimento Econômico-Social do Pará (IDESP). 1986. Tímido Desempenho no Período. *Pará Agrário* (Belém), 1:1–9.

———. 1990. *Pará Agrário—Conflitos Argários* (Belém). Edição Especial.

———. 1992. *Pará Agrário* (Belém), 8:6–8.

Instituto Nacional de Colonização e Reforma Agrária (INCRA). 1984. *Simpósio Internacional de Experiência Fundiária.* Brasília: INCRA.

———. 1992, 1993. *Relatório Anual de Atividades.* Brasília.

———. 1996. *Relatório sobre Projetos de Assentamento.* Brasília, INCRA, Department of Settlements, OF/INCRA/DP/No 104/96.

James, William, and James Roumasset. 1984. Migration and the Evolution of Tenure Contracts in Newly Settled Regions. *Journal of Development Economics* 14:147–62.

Johnson, Ronald N., and Gary D. Libecap 1980. Agency Costs and the Assignment of Property Rights: The Case of Southwestern Indian Reservations. *Southern Economic Journal* 47:332–46.

———. 1982. Contracting Problems and Regulation: The Case of the Fishery. *American Economic Review* 72:1005–22.

———. 1994. *The Federal Civil Service System and the Problem of Bureaucracy: The Economics and Politics of Institutional Change.* Chicago: University of Chicago Press.

Johnston, J. 1984. *Econometric Methods.* 3d ed. New York: McGraw-Hill.

Judge, George G., et al. 1988. *Introduction to the Theory and Practice of Econometrics.* New York: John Wiley and Sons.

Junqueira, Messias. 1976. *O Instituto Brasileiro das Terras Devolutas.* São Paulo: Edições Lael.

Kanazawa, Mark T. 1996. Possession Is Nine Points of the Law: The Political Economy of Early Public Land Disposal. *Explorations in Economic History* 33:227–49.

Kawagoe, Toshihiko, Yujiro Hayami, and Vernon Ruttan. 1985. Intercountry Agricultural Production Function and Productivity Differences among Countries. *Journal of Development Economics* 19:113–32.

Kelejian, Harry H., and Wallace E. Oates. 1981. *Introduction to Econometrics.* 2d ed. New York: Harper and Row.

Kennedy, Peter. 1989. *A Guide to Econometrics.* 2d ed. Cambridge: MIT Press.

Keohane, Robert O., and Elinor Ostrom. 1995. *Local Commons and Global Interdependence: Heterogeneity and Cooperation in Two Domains.* London: Sage Publications.

Kmenta, Jan. 1986. *Elements of Econometrics.* 2d ed. New York: Macmillan.

Leal, Laécio, ed. 1985. *Reforma Agrária da Nova República: Contradições e Alternativas.* São Paulo: Editora Cortez.

Levy, Brian, and Pablo Spiller. 1994. The Institutional Foundations of Regulatory Commitment: A Comparative Analysis of Telecommunications Regulation. *Journal of Law, Economics, and Organization* 10:201–46.

Libecap, Gary D. 1978. Economic Variables and the Development of the Law: The Case of Western Mineral Rights. *Journal of Economic History* 38:338–62.

———. 1979. Government Support of Private Claims to Public Minerals: Western Mineral Rights. *Business History Review* 53:364–85.

———. 1989. *Contracting for Property Rights.* New York: Cambridge University Press.

Libecap, Gary D., and Ronald N. Johnson. 1980. Legislating Commons: The Navajo Tribal Council and the Navajo Range. *Economic Inquiry* 18:69–86.

Libecap, Gary D., and Steven N. Wiggins. 1985. The Influence of Private Contractual Failure on Regulation: The Case of Oil Field Unitization. *Journal of Political Economy* 93:690–714.

Lima, Ruy C. 1954. *Pequena História Territorial do Brasil: Sesmarias e Terras Devolutas.* Porto Alegre: Edições Sulina.

Lovell, S. Jarvis. 1986. *Livestock Development in Latin America.* Washington, D.C.: World Bank.

Lueck, Dean. 1995. The Rule of First Possession and the Design of the Law. *Journal of Law and Economics* 38:393–436.

Maddala, G. S. 1983. *Limited-Dependent and Qualitative Variables in Econometrics.* New York: Cambridge University Press.

Maddala, G. S., and L. F. Lee. 1976. Recursive Models with Qualitative Endogenous Variables. *Annals of Economic and Social Measurement* 5 (4): 525–45.

Mahar, Dennis J. 1989. *Government Policies and Deforestation in Brazil's Amazon Region.* Washington, D.C.: World Bank.

Mandim, Antônio M. 1995. Advogado dos Latifundiários. *Folha de São Paulo,* November 27, 9.

Mattos, Marla Maria, and Christopher Uhl. 1994. Economic and Ecological Perspectives on Ranching in the Eastern Amazon. *World Development* 22:145–58.

McDonald, John, and Robert Moffit. 1980. The Uses of TOBIT Analysis. *Review of Economics and Statistics* 62:318–20.

Migot-Adholla, Shem, Peter Hazell, Benoît Blarel, and Frank Place. 1991. Indigenous Land Rights Systems in Sub-Saharan Africa: A Constraint on Productivity? *World Bank Economic Review* 5:155–75.

Monteiro, Benedito. 1980. *Agrarian Law.* Rio de Janeiro: PLG Comunicação.

Monteiro, Maria José C. 1995. O Crédito Rural nos Anos 90. *Agroanalysis* (São Paulo), April, 14–15.

Monteiro, Maria José C., and Adib Jamil Amin. 1994. APreço da Terra: 25 anos de Observação. *Agroanalysis* (São Paulo), December, 42–44.

Moog, Viannna. 1955. *Bandeirantes e Pioneiros: Paralelo Entre Duas Culturas.* Rio de Janeiro: Editora Globo.

Moran, Emilio F. 1975. Pioneer Farmers of the TransAmazon Highway: Adaptation and Agricultural Production in the Lowland Tropics. Ph.D. diss., University of Florida.

———. 1981. *Developing the Amazon.* Bloomington: Indiana University Press.

———. 1984. Colonization in the TransAmazon and Rondonia. In *Frontier Expansion in Amazonia,* ed. Marianne Schmink and Charles H. Wood. Gainesville: University of Florida Press.

———. 1987. Socio-economic Considerations in Acid Tropical Soils Research. In *Management of Acid Tropical Soils for Sustainable Agriculture,* ed. P. Sanchez, E. Pushparajah, and Eric Stoner. Bangkok: International Board for Soil Research and Management.

———. 1989a. Adaptation and Maladaptation in Newly Settled Areas. In *The*

Human Ecology of Tropical Land Settlement in Latin America, ed. Debra A. Schumann and William L. Partridge. Boulder, Colo.: Westview Press.

————. 1989b. Government-Directed Settlement in the 1970s: An Assessment of Transamazon Highway Colonization. In *The Human Ecology of Tropical Land Settlement in Latin America*, ed. Debra A. Schumann and William L. Partridge. Boulder, Colo.: Westview Press.

————. 1993. Deforestation and Land Use in the Brazilian Amazon. *Human Ecology* 21:1–21.

Mueller, Bernardo. 1994. The Political Economy of Agrarian Reform in Brazil. Ph.D. diss., Department of Economics, University of Illinois.

Mueller, Bernardo, Lee J. Alston, Gary D. Libecap, and Robert Schneider. 1994. Land, Property Rights, and Privatization in Brazil. *Quarterly Review of Economics and Finance.* Special issue.

Mueller, Charles. 1980. Frontier Based Agricultural Expansion: The Case of Rondonia. In *Land, People, and Planning in Contemporary Amazonia*, ed. Francoise Barbira-Scazzocchio. Center of Latin American Studies, Occasional Publication No. 3. Cambridge: Cambridge University.

————. 1987. Censos Agropecuários. *Agroanalysis* (Rio de Janeiro), June, 21–23.

————. 1992. Colonization Policies, Land Occupation, and Deforestation in the Amazon Countries. Working Paper No. 15, Department of Economics, University of Brasília.

Nicholls, William N., and Ruy Miller Paiva. 1969. *Ninety-nine Fazendas: The Structure and Productivity of Brazilian Agriculture.* Nashville: Vanderbilt University, Graduate Center for Latin American Studies.

North, Douglass C. 1981. *Structure and Change in Economic History.* New York: Norton.

————. 1990. *Institutions, Institutional Change, and Economic Performance.* New York: Cambridge University Press.

O'Grady, Mary Anastasia. 1995. Muddled Policies Spark Brazilian Land Wars. *Wall Street Journal*, October 20, A15.

Oliveira, Élcio V. 1995. *Bancada Ruralista na Câmara dos Deputados, Brasília.* INESC, October, Year III, no. 27, 3–30.

Oliveira, Lea L. C., and Fransisco C. Silva. 1986. Questno Fundiária e Tensno Social no Meio Rural Paraense. *Pará Desenvolvimento* (Belém), no. 18.

Oliveira, R. F. 1991. A Propriedade e os Sem-Terra. *Folha de São Paulo*, April 28, 4–6.

Olson, Mancur. 1965. *The Logic of Collective Action.* Cambridge: Harvard University Press.

Olson, Sherry. 1961. *The Depletion Myth: The History of Railroad Use of Timber.* Cambridge: Harvard University Press.

Onis, Juan de. 1992. *The Green Cathedral: Sustainable Development in the Amazon.* London: Oxford University Press.

Ostrom, Elinor. 1990. *Governing the Commons: The Evolution of Institutions for Collective Action.* New York: Cambridge University Press.

Ostrom, Elinor, Roy Gardner, and James Walker. 1994. *Rules, Games, and Common-Pool Resources.* Ann Arbor: University of Michigan Press.

Ozório de Almeida, Anna Luiza. 1992. *The Colonization of the Amazon.* Austin: University of Texas Press.

Pará Pastoral Land Commission. 1989. *People Killed in Land Conflicts.* Belém.

Peltzman, S. 1976. Toward a More General Theory of Regulation. *Journal of Law and Economics* 19:211–40.

Pinheiro, Jonas. 1992. Comisãno Parlamentar de Inquérito Destinada a Apurar as Origens, Causas e Consequêcias da Violência no Campo Brasileiro. *Reforma Agrária* (Campinas), January–April, 98–118.

Pinto, Lúcio F. 1980. *Amazônia: No Rastro do Saque.* São Paulo: Hucitec.

Place, Frank, and Peter Hazell. 1993. Productivity Effects of Indigenous Land Tenure Systems in Sub-Saharan Africa. *American Journal of Agricultural Economics* 75:10–19.

Prado, Caio, Jr. 1979. *A Questão Agrária no Brasil.* São Paulo: Editora Brasiliense.

Repetto, Robert. 1988. *Economic Policy Reform for Natural Resource Conservation.* Environment Department Working Paper No. 4, World Bank, Washington, D.C.

Rezende, Gervásio C. 1982. Crédito Rural Subsidiado e Preço da Terra no Brasil. *Estudos Econômicos* (São Paulo) 12 (2): 117–38.

Ribeiro, Nelson F. 1987. *Caminhada da Esperança da Reforma Agrária: A Questão da Terra na Constituinte.* Rio de Janeiro: Paz e Terra.

Rossi, Clóvis. 1997. Terra, Itica e Economia. *Folha de São Paulo,* March 6, 2.

Rothenburg, Denise, Maria Lima, and Monica Gugliano. 1996. Briga Política Atrasa Reforma Agrária. *O Globo* (Rio de Janeiro), April 24, 3.

Rua, Maria G. 1992. Políticos e Burocratas no Processo de Policy-Making: A Política de Terras no Brasil, 1954–84. Ph.D. diss., Instituto Universitário de Pesquisas do Rio de Janeiro.

Rudel, Thomas K. 1993. *Tropical Deforestation: Small Farmers and Land Clearing in the Ecuadorian Amazon.* New York: Columbia University Press.

———. 1995. When Do Property Rights Matter? Open Access, Informal Social Controls, and Deforestation in the Ecuadorian Amazon. *Human Organization* 54:187–94.

Sá, Junia Nogueira. 1997. Anatomia das Invasões. *Folha de São Paulo,* March 9, 12.

Santos, Roberto. 1984. Law and Social Change: The Problem of Land in the Brazilian Amazon. In *Frontier Expansion in Amazonia,* ed. Marianne Schmink and Charles H. Wood. Gainesville: University of Florida Press.

Sawyer, Donald R. 1984. Frontier Expansion and Retraction in Brazil. In *Frontier Expansion in Amazonia,* ed. Marianne Schmink and Charles H. Wood. Gainesville: University of Florida Press.

Schaefer, Donald F. 1985. A Statistical Profile of Frontier and New South Migration: 1850–1860. *Agricultural History* 59:563–67.

———. 1987. A Model of Migration and Wealth Accumulation. *Explorations in Economic History* 29:130–57.

Scherr, Sara J. 1995. Economic Factors in Farmer Adoption of Agroforestry: Patterns Observed in Western Kenya. *World Development* 23:787–804.

Schmink, Marianne, and Charles H. Wood, eds. 1984. *Frontier Expansion in Amazonia.* Gainesville: University of Florida Press.

———. 1992. *Contested Frontiers in Amazonia.* New York: Columbia University Press.

Schneider, Robert R. 1994. *Government and the Economy on the Amazon Frontier.* Report No. 34, Latin America and the Caribbean Technical Department, Regional Studies Program. Washington, D.C.: World Bank.

Scott, Anthony A. 1955. The Fishery: The Objectives of Sole Ownership. *Journal of Political Economy* 63:116–24.

Serrão, Emmanuel Adilson S., Daniel Nepstad, and Robert Walker. 1996. Analysis: Upland Agricultural and Forestry Development in the Amazon: Sustainability, Criticality, and Resilience. *Ecological Economics* 18:3–13.

Shafer, Joseph. 1937. Was the West a Safety Valve for Labor? *Mississippi Valley Historical Review* 24 (3): 299–314.

SHAZAM. 1993. *User's Reference Manual Version 7.0.* New York: McGraw-Hill.

Silva, Fábio C. 1987. Poder Econômico e Política Fundiária no Pará. *Pará Agrário* (Belém), 2:3–11.

Simonsen, Roberto C. 1937. *História Econômica do Brasil: 1500–1820.* Vol. 1. São Paulo: Companhia Editora Nacional.

Skaperdas, Stergios. 1992. Cooperation, Conflict, and Power in the Absence of Property Rights. *American Economic Review* 82:720–39.

Smith, Adam. 1937. *An Inquiry into the Nature and Causes of the Wealth of Nations.* New York: Random House.

Smith, Lynn T. 1954. *Brazil: People and Institutions.* Baton Rouge: Louisiana State University Press.

Smith, Nigel J. H., Italo C. Falesi, Paulo de T. Alvim, and Emmanuel Adilson S. Serrão. 1996. Agroforestry Trajectories among Small Holders in the Brazilian Amazon: Innovation and Resilience in Pioneer and Older Settled Areas. *Ecological Economics* 18:15–27.

Smith, Roberto. 1990. *Propriedade da Terra e Transição.* São Paulo: Editora Brasiliense.

Southgate, Douglas, and M. Whitaker. 1992. Promoting Resource Degradation in Latin America: Tropical Deforestation, Soil Erosion, and Coastal Ecosystem Disturbance in Ecuador. *Economic Development and Cultural Change* 40:787–807.

Spears, John. 1988. Containing Tropical Deforestation: A Review of Priority Areas for Technological and Policy Research. Environment Department Working Paper No. 10, World Bank, Washington, D.C.

Stone, Steven W. 1996. Economic Trends in the Timber Industry of the Brazilian Amazon: Evidence from Paragominas. CREED Working Paper Series No. 6, International Institute for Environment and Development, Vrije Universiteit, Amsterdam.

Swerienga, Robert. 1970. Land Speculation and Frontier Tax Assessments. *Agricultural History* 44:253–66.

Tendrih, Leila. 1989. Incentivos Fiscais na Amazônia: Uma Política de Desenvolvimento. *Agroanalysis* (Rio de Janeiro), April, 6–12.

Tirole, J. 1992. *The Theory of Industrial Organization.* Part 2. Cambridge: MIT Press.

Tribunal de Contas da União. 1996. *Relatório e Parecer Prévio sobre as Contas do Governo da República.* Brasília.

Turner, Frederick Jackson. 1947. *The Frontier in American History.* New York: Holt, Rinehart, and Winston.

Umbeck, John. 1977. The California Gold Rush: A Study of Emerging Property Rights. *Explorations in Economic History* 14:197–226.

———. 1981. Might Makes Right: A Theory of the Foundation and Initial Distribution of Property Rights. *Economic Inquiry* 19:38–59.

U.S. Department of the Interior. Bureau of the Census. 1892. *Compendium of the Eleventh Census, 1890.* Part 1. Washington, D.C.: Government Printing Office.

Veiga, José Eli. 1990. *A Reforma Que Virou Suco: Uma Introdução ao Dilema Agrário do Brasil.* Petrópolis: Editora Vozes.

Violence Grows in Brazilian Land Battle. 1996. *New York Times,* April 2, 8.

Walker, Robert, and Alfredo Kingo Oyama Homma. 1996. Land Use and Land Cover Dynamics in the Brazilian Amazon: An Overview. *Ecological Economics* 18:67–80.

Westphalen, M. C., B. Pinheiro Machado, and A. P. Balhana. 1968. Preliminary Note to the Study of the Occupation of Land in Modern Paraná. *Boletim da Universidade Federal do Paraná* (Curitiba), no. 7.

White, H. 1980. A Heteroskedasticity Consistent Covariance Matrix and a Direct Test for Heteroskedasticity. *Econometrica* 48:817–38.

Wiggins, Steven N., and Gary D. Libecap. 1985. Oil Field Unitization: Contractual Failure in the Presence of Imperfect Information. *American Economic Review* 75:368–85.

Williamson, Oliver E., and Sidney G. Winter, eds. 1991. *The Nature of the Firm: Origins, Evolution, and Development.* New York: Oxford University Press.

Wittman, Donald. 1995. *The Myth of Democratic Failure: Why Political Institutions Are Efficient.* Chicago: University of Chicago Press.

Wood, Charles, and John Wilson. 1984. The Magnitude of Migration to the Brazilian Frontier. In *Frontier Expansion in Amazonia,* ed. Marianne Schmink and Charles H. Wood. Gainesville: University of Florida Press.

Yokota, Paulo. 1981. *Questão Fundiána Brasileira.* Brasília: INCRA.

Index